American Language Hub

LEVEL 3B
Student's Book

JEREMY DAY
GARETH REES

macmillan education

Contents

Irregular Verbs

Base form	Simple past	Past participle
be	was/were	been
become	became	become
begin	began	begun
break	broke	broken
bring	brought	brought
build	built	built
buy	bought	bought
can	could	been able to
catch	caught	caught
choose	chose	chosen
come	came	come
cost	cost	cost
cut	cut	cut
drink	drank	drunk
eat	ate	eaten
fall	fell	fallen
feel	felt	felt
find	found	found
forget	forgot	forgotten
get	got	got
give	gave	given
go	went	gone/been
grow	grew	grown
have	had	had
hear	heard	heard
hit	hit	hit
hold	held	held
hurt	hurt	hurt
keep	kept	kept
know	knew	known
leave	left	left
lend	lent	lent
let	let	let

Base form	Simple past	Past participle
lose	lost	lost
make	made	made
mean	meant	meant
meet	met	met
must	had to	had to
pay	paid	paid
put	put	put
read	read	read
ride	rode	ridden
run	ran	run
say	said	said
see	saw	seen
sell	sold	sold
send	sent	sent
set	set	set
shut	shut	shut
sing	sang	sung
sit	sat	sat
sleep	slept	slept
speak	spoke	spoken
spell	spelled	spelled
spend	spent	spent
stand	stood	stood
steal	stole	stolen
take	took	taken
teach	taught	taught
tell	told	told
think	thought	thought
throw	threw	thrown
understand	understood	understood
wear	wore	worn
win	won	won
write	wrote	written

PHONETIC SYMBOLS											
Single vowels			Diphthongs			Consonants					
/ɪ/	fish	/fɪʃ/	/uw/	news	/nuw/	/p/	pen	/pen/	/s/	snake	/sneɪk/
/iː/	bean	/biːn/	/eɪ/	face	/feɪs/	/b/	bag	/bæg/	/z/	zoo	/zuː/
/ʊ/	foot	/fʊt/	/ɔɪ/	boy	/bɔɪ/	/t/	tea	/tiː/	/ʃ/	shop	/ʃɒp/
/uː/	shoe	/ʃuː/	/oʊ/	nose	/noʊz/	/d/	dog	/dɒg/	/ʒ/	television	/'telɪvɪʒən/
/e/	egg	/eg/	/ju/	use	/juz/	/ʧ/	chip	/ʧɪp/	/m/	map	/mæp/
/ə/	mother	/'mʌðər/	/aɪ/	eye	/aɪ/	/ʤ/	jazz	/ʤæz/	/n/	name	/neɪm/
/ɜː/	word	/wɜːrd/	/aʊ/	mouth	/maʊθ/	/k/	cake	/keɪk/	/ŋ/	ring	/rɪŋ/
/ɔː/	talk	/tɔːk/				/g/	girl	/gɜːrl/	/h/	house	/haʊs/
/æ/	back	/bæk/				/f/	film	/fɪlm/	/l/	leg	/leg/
/ʌ/	bus	/bʌs/				/v/	verb	/vɜːrb/	/r/	road	/roʊd/
/ɑː/	arm	/ɑːrm/				/θ/	thing	/θɪŋ/	/w/	want	/wɒnt/
/ɒ/	top	/tɒp/				/ð/	these	/ðiːz/	/j/	yes	/jes/

6 SPORTS AND HOBBIES

You can discover more about a person in an hour of play than in a year of conversation.

Richard Lingard

A surfer rides the inside of a wave at End of the road Beach, Tahiti.

- describe a sport or game
- give a short, persuasive talk
- talk about hobbies and free time activities
- discuss trying new things
- express your opinion
- write an article for a magazine

Work with a partner. Discuss the questions.

1 Do you agree with the quote?

2 Look at the picture. Why do some people take part in sports like this?

3 How interested are you in these free time activities?

team sports | running | music | collecting

6.1 Take part!

- Describe a sport or game
- Give a short, persuasive talk

G modals of obligation **V** adjectives ending in *-ive*; sports **P** rhythm: pausing
S listening for main and supporting points

COMPETITIVE SNOWBALL FIGHTING HITS SCOTLAND!

If you think snowball fights are just for school kids, think again. **Competitive** snowball fighting (*Yukigassen*) is a sport for grown-ups that has just arrived in Scotland.

It began as an official sport in Japan in 1987 and since then it has spread to countries such as Canada, Australia, Norway and Sweden. And this weekend sees the first ever matches in Scotland.

Angus Campbell, the captain of the Glasgow Ice Warriors, says 'I think *Yukigassen* is going to be **massive** here. We have the snow and it's a fun and **inexpensive** sport that's **attractive** to everyone. Each match only lasts nine minutes, so you don't have to be super athletic to take part in a game.'

The snowball fights take place on a small court (40 m x 10 m) between two teams of seven players – each team must include male and female members. To win a game, a team has to capture the other team's flag or take out all their opponents with direct snowball hits. If a player is hit, he or she has to leave the game.

The rules are fairly simple, but Angus insists that having an **effective** strategy is the key to success. 'You must work together as a team, be **decisive** and keep calm when under pressure from your opponents. You shouldn't just run for the flag – you'll soon get hit and be out. You need to be more **creative** than that. Your team only has 90 snowballs, which the referee gives you before the game. You must not make any more during the game.'

Six teams are taking part in the event this weekend, and there will be trial sessions for anyone who wants to try it out. 'It looks a little **aggressive** at first, but you shouldn't feel nervous. It's only snow, and all players have to wear a helmet, which we'll provide. However, you should bring some warm gloves!'

If you're interested in trying something **active** on these cold winter days, you simply must go. The games are **impressive** to watch, and great to play. After all, what's more fun than playing in the snow?

The first game starts at 2 pm, on Saturday, in the city park. Entrance is free. Families are welcome.

READING

A SPEAK Write down the names of the different sports you know in pictures 1–4. Then check with another student. What do you know about these sports? Tell your partner.

B READ FOR GIST Read *Competitive snowball fighting hits Scotland!* Where do you think the article comes from? Why?

a a national newspaper
b a sports science academic journal
c a local news and information website
d a travel blog

C READ FOR DETAIL Put the sentences in the order the information appears in the article.

a New players do not need to bring any safety equipment. ___
b There are two ways to beat the other team. ___
c There are men and women on every team. ___
d Generally, people think children, not adults, have snowball fights. 1
e A good game plan is important. ___
f Several countries play competitive snowball fighting. ___

D SPEAK Work in pairs. What is your opinion of *Yukigassen*? Would you like to play it?

1

2

GRAMMAR

Modals of obligation

A WORK IT OUT Look at the sentences from *Competitive snowball fighting hits Scotland!* Write *nc* (you have no choice, this is 100 percent necessary) or *c* (you have a choice, this is not necessary) next to each sentence.

1 All players **have to** wear a protective helmet. ___
2 You **don't have to** be super athletic. ___
3 You **should** bring some warm gloves. ___
4 You **shouldn't** just run for the flag. ___
5 Each team **must** include male and female members. ___
6 You **must not** make any more during the game. ___
7 You **shouldn't** feel nervous. ___

B Match the beginnings of the rules (1–4) with the endings (a–d).

Modals of obligation

1	We use *must / have to / need to*	a	to talk about what is or is not a good idea.
2	We use *must not* when	b	for rules and situations that are necessary (strong obligation).
3	We use *don't have to* when	c	we describe things that are not necessary, but you may still do them.
4	We use *should / shouldn't*	d	we describe something that is not allowed.

C Go to the Grammar Hub on page VI.

D SPEAK Work in pairs. Compare the pairs of sports below. How are they similar and different? Think about their basic rules and the qualities of good players and successful teams.

baseball and cricket soccer and basketball
marathon running and running a 100 meter race tennis and racquetball

VOCABULARY

Adjectives ending in *-ive*

A Look at the adjectives in bold in *Competitive snowball fighting hits Scotland!* Then complete the definitions with the correct adjective.

1 A ________ person makes choices quickly and confidently.
2 A ________ sport involves two teams trying to beat each other.
3 If something is ________, it is very big or, in informal English, very popular.
4 An ________ suggestion or idea is one that people are interested in.
5 An ________ plan works well and produces the result that is wanted.
6 An ________ activity doesn't cost a lot of money to do.
7 Having an ________ lifestyle means you do not sit around all day.
8 ________ behavior includes being rude or angry in order to get what you want.
9 You admire an ________ performance because it is very good and shows a lot of skill.
10 A ________ person thinks of new or unusual ways to do things.

B SPEAK Complete the questions with adjectives from Exercise A. Then work in pairs and interview your partner. Take turns. Give reasons and examples to explain your answers.

1 What is the most ________ sport that you have played?
2 Are you a very ________ person? Why do you say that?
3 Which actors do you think are very ________?

SPEAKING

A You are going to write six sentences to describe a sport or game without naming it. Your classmates will try to guess what it is. Think about:

- reasons why you like it.
- the skills and qualities you need to play it well.
- how it is played and what you need to play it.

B Work in groups. Read your sentences to the group. Can your classmates guess the sport or game?

C Work in groups and discuss the questions.

1 Which of the sports and games described have you played? What do you think of them?
2 Which haven't you played? Would you like to try them?
3 Which is the most popular sport or game?

LISTENING

A SPEAK Work in pairs and discuss the questions. What are the pros and cons of playing video games?

6.1 **B LISTEN FOR GIST** Listen to a talk about eSports and choose the correct answers.

1 What is the best title for the talk?
- a Video gaming: is it good for you?
- b Video gaming: the professional sport of the future
- c Video gaming: nothing more than a free time activity
- d Video gaming: the next Olympic sport?

2 What is the purpose of the talk?
- a to give general information about eSports
- b to encourage people to watch and play eSports
- c to persuade people to agree with the speaker's opinion of eSports
- d to give a balanced analysis of eSports

6.1 **C LISTEN FOR DETAIL** Listen again to the introduction. What is the main idea of the talk? What are the supporting points? Use the strategies in the box to help you.

Listening for main and supporting points

When giving a talk, speakers usually give a main idea and then support it with detailed points, in the form of examples, statistics, names or dates.

Listen carefully to identify the main ideas and the supporting points that follow.

6.2 **D** Listen again to another part of the talk. What is the main idea? What are the supporting points?

6.1 **E LISTEN FOR DETAIL** Listen again to the whole talk and choose the correct answers.

1 The speaker thinks that many people in the audience …
- a play video games at home.
- b understand how popular eSports are.
- c don't realize that video gaming is played professionally.

2 She says playing video games is a sport because …
- a players practice a lot.
- b the games have clear rules.
- c there are winners and losers.

3 She says a great eSports player
- a has a strong mind and body.
- b plays other traditional sports.
- c spends all their time training.

4 She says eSports are different from traditional sports because …
- a they are growing in popularity.
- b young people like them.
- c people watch them online.

5 The Olympic Games wants to include sports that …
- a involve physical activity.
- b young people like.
- c have professional players.

F SPEAK Work in pairs and discuss the questions.

1 In your opinion, what is the difference between a sport and a game?

2 Do you agree with the speaker's arguments? Which of her points do you think are strong or weak?

3 Do you think eSports should be an Olympic sport? Why/Why not?

VOCABULARY

Sports

A Check (✓) the nouns that refer to people.

1	champion	☐	6	stadium	☐
2	coach	☐	7	fan	☐
3	final	☐	8	top player	☐
4	league	☐	9	tournament	☐
5	spectator	☐	10	trophy	☐

B Complete the sentences with the correct form of the nouns in Exercise A.

1 In the Olympic Games, the winners receive a gold medal, not a ________________.

2 Usain Bolt and Michael Phelps are two of the most famous Olympic ________________.

3 The FIFA World Cup is a soccer ________________ that is held every four years.

4 If you are a Manchester United ________________, you should wear something red to the game.

5 The Camp Nou, in Barcelona, is the largest soccer ________________ in Europe. It can hold nearly 100,000 ________________.

6 ________________ can earn a lot of money from advertising and sponsorship contracts.

7 If a team loses a lot of games, the ________________ usually loses his or her job.

8 Nothing in sport is certain – you don't always see the two best teams in a ________________.

9 There are 20 teams in the national ________________. Each team plays the others twice, so each team plays 38 games in a year.

C SPEAK Work in groups and discuss the questions.

1 What are the popular spectator sports and sports tournaments in your country?

2 Who are the top sportsmen and women in your country? What do you know about them?

PRONUNCIATION
Rhythm: pausing

Pausing

We use pauses to support the meaning of what we say, and to help the listener follow and understand.

- Use very short pauses to group words that go together in phrases or clauses. This is similar to using a comma in writing, but can be more frequent.
- Use short pauses at the end of sentences and paragraphs. This is similar to using a period in writing.
- Make the pauses a little longer to add emphasis or drama.

6.3 **A** Listen to the beginning of the talk about eSports. Mark where the speaker pauses. The first two pauses have been marked (/) to help you. Which pauses are longer to add emphasis or drama?

Soccer, / basketball, / golf, tennis – four of the world's most popular sports. They are played by millions and watched by millions more, and all four are in the greatest festival of sports, the Olympic Games.

6.4 **B** Where do you think the speaker pauses in the next part of the talk? Mark (/) each pause. Then listen and check your answer.

However, there is one sport that is just as popular as those, but it still hasn't been accepted in the Olympics, and indeed, many people say that it is not even a sport. What sport am I talking about? eSports. Yes, electronic sports, or competitive video gaming.

C SPEAK Work in pairs. Practice saying the extracts in Exercises A and B. Listen and check that your partner pauses in the correct places.

SPEAKING HUB

A You are going to give a short persuasive talk (1–3 minutes). Choose one of the titles and write notes for your talk.

- eSports are not sports and should not be part of the Olympic Games.
- Playing video games is a good activity for children.
- Video games are generally more negative than positive.
- Professional athletes earn too much money. Their pay should be limited.
- ________________ is the best sport to both play and watch.

B PLAN Look at your notes and use these tips on how to improve a persuasive talk.

- Have a good introduction and conclusion.
- Use confident language, e.g. *I strongly believe …; It's undoubtedly true that …*
- Use rhetorical questions, e.g. *Why should we do this?; I'm sure you agree, don't you?*
- Support your main points with good examples and arguments.
- Practice your pausing and rhythm when giving the talk.

C PRESENT Work in groups. Give your talks. Write down the main ideas and supporting points of the other talks.

D REFLECT Work in groups. Did you agree or disagree with the speakers? Which points do you think were strongest?

- Describe a sport or game
- Give a short, persuasive talk

6.2 Hobbies

- Talk about hobbies and free time activities
- Discuss trying new things

V – hobbies and free time activities
S – identifying tone
G – present perfect progressive; *had to* / *needed to*
P – *been*: unstressed

LISTENING

A SPEAK Work in pairs and discuss the questions.

1 Describe the pictures (a–e). What are the people doing?
2 Which free time activities are you most interested in? Why?

6.5 **B LISTEN FOR GIST** Listen to a radio show about hobbies and free time activities. Match the pictures (a–e) with the guest speakers (1–5).

1 ___ 2 ___ 3 ___ 4 ___ 5 ___

6.5 **C LISTEN FOR DETAIL** Listen again. Choose the best answers for each person.

1 Speaker 1
  a buys and sells new cars.
  b spends a lot of money on his hobby.
  c makes enough money from his hobby to pay for his vacations.
2 Speaker 2
  a finds his hobby stressful at times.
  b also works as a photographer.
  c is learning how to do something new.
3 Speaker 3
  a wants her husband to spend more time on his hobby.
  b says her husband spends a lot of time on his hobby.
  c shares her husband's hobby.
4 Speaker 4
  a shares her interest with her friends.
  b has her own social media site about her interest.
  c regularly stays at hotels in Boston.
5 Speaker 5
  a usually has a few hobbies at the same time.
  b finds it hard to get interested in things.
  c has had many different hobbies.

D SPEAK Work in groups and discuss the questions.

1 Are there any hobbies you would like to try? Which ones?
2 What are the benefits of having a hobby?

VOCABULARY

Hobbies and free time activities

A WORK IT OUT Look at the three sets of verb phrases from the radio show. Match the beginnings of the phrases with the endings (a–d).

1	join	a	interest in a hobby
	be	b	a hobby
	lose	c	a society
	take up	d	my thing
2	be	a	into something
	be	b	you in shape
	keep	c	of a singer
	be a fan	d	a member of a fan club
3	get	a	relaxing
	be	b	from daily stress
	collect	c	you out of the house
	escape	d	something, like stamps or art

B Complete the table with the verb phrases from Exercise A.

Show enthusiasm for a hobby	Something you may do as part of a hobby	Benefits of a hobby	Start a new hobby
be into something	___	___	___
___	___	___	
___	___	___	
___		___	
___			

C Go to the Vocabulary Hub on page XVI.

D SPEAK Rewrite these sentences so they are true for you. Then work in pairs and compare your answers. Give reasons and examples.

1 I'm a big fan of the singer Ed Sheeran.
2 I need to find a way to get myself out of the house more frequently.
3 I've collected a lot of different things during my life.
4 I don't do much to stay in shape. I should do more.
5 I've never been a member of a fan club nor joined a society.
6 Cooking isn't really my thing.
7 I've had a few hobbies that I've lost interest in.
8 This year, I've taken up a new hobby.

GRAMMAR
Present perfect progressive

A WORK IT OUT Look at the sentences from the radio show and choose the correct answers.

1 Which sentence describes a single action that continues up to now? Which sentences describe an action or activity that is frequently repeated up to now?
  - **a** He's been doing it since his teens.
  - **b** We've been waiting here all day.
  - **c** For the last six months, I've been going to pottery classes.

2 In each sentence, is the main verb a state or an action verb?
  - **a** He's been doing it since his teens.
  - **b** I've had this interest since I was a child.
  - **c** I've been a member of his fan club for a long time.

3 What are the recently completed actions in the sentences? Which sentence focuses on the fact that the action is completed? Which sentence focuses on the duration of the action?
  - **a** I've been working in the studio this afternoon – that's why my hands are so dirty.
  - **b** I've just bought an old Mini, so I'll start working on that tomorrow.

B Complete the rules (1–5) with the words in the box.

progressive long now past present repeated state

Present perfect progressive

1 We usually use the present perfect progressive to talk about an action that started in the ________ and is continuing ________. The emphasis is on the unfinished activity.

2 We also use it to talk about a past action that has just finished, but which has a ________ result.

3 We can use it to talk about ________ or frequently ________ actions.

4 We do not use the present perfect progressive with ________ verbs.

5 We use the present perfect progressive to talk about how ________ something has been happening.

C Go to the Grammar Hub on page VI.

D SPEAK Work in pairs. Student A – go to the Communication Hub on page XIX. Student B – go to the Communication Hub on page XXIII.

PRONUNCIATION
been: unstressed

6.6 **A** Listen to three sentences. What do you notice about the pronunciation of *been* in each sentence? Does it rhyme with *seen* or *thin*?

been

In the present perfect progressive, *been* is an auxiliary verb and it is normally unstressed and pronounced /bɪn/.

The stressed words are usually the main verbs and key information words, not the auxiliary verbs.

6.7 **B** Listen and repeat.

SPEAKING HUB

A Choose one of your hobbies or free time activities and prepare to talk about it. Answer the following questions.

1 When did you take it up and why?
2 How much time and money do you spend on it?
3 What do you like about it?
4 Is there anything you dislike about it?
5 What benefits does it bring to you and your life?
6 Why would someone else enjoy your hobby?

B SPEAK Go around the class and interview three or four of your classmates about their hobbies. Write notes.

C DISCUSS Work in groups. Tell each other about your interviews. Which hobbies were:

- the most unusual?
- the most interesting?
- the most dangerous?
- the most expensive?

READING

A SPEAK Work in pairs. When was the last time you:

- tried a new food or drink?
- listened to a new singer or group?
- visited a new place?

B READ FOR MAIN IDEA Read the first two paragraphs of *My six months of trying new things*. Then complete the summary with a word in the box.

interesting relaxing

Candie is not very active. She decided to spend the first six months of this year doing different activities because she wants to find a hobby that will make her free time more ________________.

My **six months** of trying new things

By Candie Carmichael

July 15

I've never been the kind of person who does lots of exciting things in their free time. Paragliding, swimming with dolphins, climbing Mount Everest – not me! My idea of danger is to sit on the couch and watch the latest crime series on TV. The closest I get to nature is when I 'like' my friends' cat pictures on social media. As for climbing Himalayan mountains – forget it! I'd rather climb the stairs to bed.

But at one point toward the end of last year, I started to feel that my life was becoming a little … well … boring. I needed to take up a hobby. But which one? There are so many things out there – how do you know what you will enjoy? So I decided to spend the first six months of this year trying out a new hobby each month. I was a complete beginner at every activity I tried.

Here's what happened:

January: Fly fishing

The first thing I learned was that no flies are harmed in fly fishing. You make a pretty, artificial 'fly' and attach it to a hook on a fishing line. [1]__ When a fish takes a bite you … oh, I don't know. I did NOT do well at this. One month: lots of badly made 'flies', and ZERO fish (apart from the ones I got at the fish and fries place on my way home).

February: Stamp collecting

Why does anyone do this? [2]__ After a whole four weeks of attaching little squares of paper from around the world into a big book with blank pages, I still have no idea.

March: Ping-Pong

This one really surprised me. I'm actually good at it! I joined a club, and I didn't need to spend a lot of time practicing before I started winning games. After only a month, I was already one of the best players in the group. I really can't believe it. [3]__

April: Beekeeping

Surely all I had to do was keep some flying insects in a box? [4]__ About a hundred bee stings later, I realized that a lot can go wrong and beekeeping is a serious (and sometimes painful) business. I think I'll just get my honey from the grocery store in future.

May: Playing the ukulele

The ukulele is like a very small guitar. It has four strings. It makes you look like a giant when you play it. [5]__ I didn't have to be in great shape. It wasn't dangerous and it wasn't painful. And at the end of the month, I could play *Rivers of Babylon* all the way through. If that isn't success, I don't know what is!

C READ FOR KEY WORDS Read the rest of the article. Match the activities (1–6) with Candie's experiences (a–f).

1 fly fishing
2 stamp collecting
3 yoga
4 beekeeping
5 playing the ukulele
6 Ping-Pong

a This hobby caused her pain.
b She wasn't successful at all.
c She was able to complete a whole song.
d She was surprised by how good she was at this activity.
e She learned that she is not able to do this kind of thing well because she isn't athletic.
f She didn't understand why this is a popular hobby.

D READ FOR DETAIL Read again. Fill in the blanks in the article (1–6) with the sentences (a–f).

a Is this really a hobby?
b What could possibly go wrong?
c Maybe there's a chance for me to get in shape after all.
d Then you throw the line on the water.
e I really enjoyed this.
f I am not very flexible.

Identifying tone

An essay or serious news article will usually have a formal or serious tone. Other kinds of text, like emails between friends or some web or magazine articles, may have an informal or humorous tone.

You can identify a text's tone from the way it is written and the author's choice of phrases, adverbs and adjectives, capital letters and punctuation.

E Look at the highlighted words and phrases. What do the capital letters, punctuation and word choice tell us about the article's tone?

F SPEAK Work in pairs. If you had to choose one of these activities to take up for a month, which would you choose? Why? Tell your partner.

June: Yoga

Ouch! I thought yoga was relaxing. I didn't realize I had to be super athletic and flexible. After one month of downward dogs and (falling over!) tree poses, I learned some very important things about me: I am not very athletic. 6___ I do not like yoga.

GRAMMAR
had to / needed to

A WORK IT OUT Look at the sentences from *My six months of trying new things*. Then choose the correct words to complete the rules.

I needed to take up a hobby.

All I had to do was keep some flying insects in a box.

I didn't have to be in great shape.

I didn't need to spend a lot of time practicing before I started winning games.

had to / needed to

1 We use ***had to*** and ***needed to*** when we talk about things that were necessary in the ***present / past***.

2 We use ***didn't have to*** and ***didn't need to*** when we talk about things that were ***not allowed / not necessary but possible*** in the past.

B Go to the Grammar Hub on page VI.

C SPEAK Work in pairs. Tell your partner:

- three things you *had to / needed to* do yesterday. Explain why.
- three things you *didn't have to / didn't need to* do yesterday. Explain why.

SPEAKING HUB

A Think of one or two new activities that you have tried. Use the list to help you or your own ideas.

get a pet
plant flowers or grow a plant
make a birthday present instead of buying one
try a new form of exercise
take language classes
make a photo album
learn a new board game

B PLAN Think about:

- how and why you did it.
- what was easy/difficult about it.
- the things you had to / needed to do.
- the things you didn't have to / didn't need to do.
- why you stopped/continued doing it.

C SPEAK Work in pairs. Tell your partner about the new activity you tried. Then listen to your partner and ask him/her questions about the activity.

Talk about hobbies and free time activities
Discuss trying new things

Café Hub

6.3 You got served

F– express your opinion   P– intonation for expressing opinions

COMPREHENSION

A Work in pairs. Tell your partner how you prepare for exercising or playing sports. What do you do before you start?

B ▶ 00:00–00:32 Watch the first part of the video. Are any of the things you discussed in Exercise A in the video? Who do you think will win the game?

C ▶ 00:33–03:15 Watch the second part of the video. Check (✓) *Gaby* or *Sam* or both.

Gaby	Sam	
		thinks it's unusual to put butter on toast.
		thinks British breakfast is more than buttered toast and milky tea.
		thinks Spanish food is better than English food.
		thinks tortilla is boring.
		changes their mind at the end.

FUNCTIONAL LANGUAGE

Expressing your opinion

A ▶ Complete the phrases in the table. Then watch the video again and check your answers.

Give an opinion	I [1]________ that's very strange. [2]________ you think that's horrible? I [3]________ British food is better than ever these days. In my [4]________, British food is still really bad. If you ask [5]________, it's your opinion that's really bad. Spanish food is so much better. Don't [6]________ agree? Do you know [7]________ I think? Tortilla is a bit boring.
Give examples to support an opinion	[8]________ instance, … To give you an example, …
Agree with an opinion	I agree. You are probably [9]________. Absolutely!
Disagree with an opinion	I disagree. I [10]________ don't think that's true. Nonsense. To be brutally [11]________, no!

B Work in groups. Decide which are the three countries with the best food in the world.

MILLY

SAM

NEENA

ZAC

GABY

USEFUL PHRASES

A Match the useful phrases (1–5) with the phrases that come before or after them (a–e). Then watch the video and check your answers.

1 Game, set and match – Sam!
2 Not hugely.
3 Wake up! Say something!
4 I didn't realize you were so passionate about food.
5 British food is average!

a So you don't like Spanish food?
b Sam, are you OK?
c I'm sorry! I got a bit angry.
d I was right!
e Nonsense!

B How do you say these useful phrases in your language?

PRONUNCIATION

Intonation for expressing opinions

6.8 **A** Listen and repeat the extracts from the video. Copy the stress and intonation.

A: In my opinion, British food is still really bad.
B: Well, if you ask me, it's your opinion that's really bad.
A: Spanish food is so much better – don't you agree?
B: To be brutally honest, no!
A: Do you want to know what I think? I think tortilla is a bit boring.
B: Boring!

B Work in pairs. Make similar conversations. Change the information.

SPEAKING

A Complete the statements with opinion phrases from Functional Language Exercise A.

… eat before exercising.
If you ask me, you shouldn't eat for one hour before exercising.

… do an hour of aerobic exercise every day.
____

… tennis is more exciting to watch than soccer.
____

… the gym is boring.
____

… female athletes should be paid the same as men.
____

… running is the best sport in the world.
____

… boxing is too violent.
____

… eSports are more exciting than real sports.
____

B DISCUSS Work in pairs. Take turns reading out your statements from Exercise A and agree or disagree with your partner's statements.

Express your opinion

➤ Turn to page XXIV to learn how to write an article for a magazine.

Unit 6 Review

GRAMMAR

A Complete the conversation between a soccer coach and some new players with the correct modals of obligation.

Coach: The rules say so. You ¹_______________ touch the ball with your hands. It isn't allowed.

Player 1: But what about the goalkeeper? He sometimes ²_______________ use his hand to stop a shot. I've seen it on TV.

Coach: OK, OK! Everyone except the goalkeeper ³_______________ follow that rule. And you all ⁴_______________ warm up before a game. I insist on that. If you don't warm up, you don't play.

Player 2: I can't get here until 6 pm.

Coach: That's a little late, the game starts at 6:15 pm. You ⁵_______________ start warming up at 5:45, by 6 pm at the latest. You bike here, don't you? If so, you ⁶_______________ do a big warm-up. But you ⁷_______________ be here by six, OK?

B Complete the TV interview with the present perfect or present progressive form of the verbs in parentheses.

Reporter: Hi, everyone. I'm with champion surfer Sally Gowen. Sally, ¹_____________ you _____________ (*surf*) here all day?

Surfer: Hi, Maisie. Yes, I sure have. The water ²_______________ _______________ (*be*) excellent all day. I love it here. I ³_______________ (*come*) here a lot recently.

Reporter: What ⁴_______________ you _______________ (*practice*) today? Some new moves?

Surfer: No, no. Nothing too special. OK, I'm going back on the surf now.

Reporter: Oh, I ⁵_______________ (*finish*) yet. Just one more … Sally? Sally! Oh, she ⁶_______________ (*go*).

C Complete the text with *had to*, *didn't have to*, *needed to* or *didn't need to*. Sometimes more than one answer is possible.

I remember my first year at college well. It was so different from being at high school. Finally, we ¹_______________ wear a uniform every day, and I ²_______________ tell my parents where I was all the time. I enjoyed that new freedom, and I ³_______________ grow up quickly, too. I ⁴_______________ take more responsibility for everyday things. I was lucky though because I lived in a student residence. I ⁵_______________ live there, but I chose to because I wanted to meet other people easily. It was a good decision. We ⁶_______________ follow a few rules, but having a housekeeper was great. I mean, we still ⁷_______________ wash the dishes and keep things clean, but a housekeeper every week was good.

VOCABULARY

A Choose the best adjectives to complete the sentences.

1 Don't delay any more. Make your mind up. It's time to be *decisive / aggressive*.

2 Stop yelling! You're being very ***effective / aggressive***.

3 He's very ***creative / competitive***. He hates losing.

4 eSports are already ***massive / expensive***. They'll definitely be in the Olympics soon.

5 You won 7–2? That's ***impressive / aggressive***!

6 Running with the ball is not very ***effective / competitive***. It's better to pass it quickly.

B Complete the text about sports with the missing words.

I loved my time as a soccer player. I only played for one club in the national ¹l_e_a_g_u_e, but what a club! I had great ²c_ _ _ _ _ _ who really improved my game, and our ³f_ _ _ were amazing, always singing and cheering us on. It was a great feeling walking into the ⁴s_ _ _ _ _ _, to hear that noise at the beginning of the game. And, of course, I played for the national team at three World Cup ⁵t_ _ _ _ _ _ _ _ _ _, and the 2018 one was the highlight of my career. How can anything be better than winning the ⁶f_ _ _ _ and lifting the ⁷t_ _ _ _ _, knowing you are the ⁸c_ _ _ _ _ _ _ _ of the world? I bet all the ⁹s_ _ _ _ _ _ _ _ _ watching in the stadium and on TV were jealous! I think I can safely say I was a ¹⁰t_ _ _ _ _ _ _ _ _. After all, I won the 'Player of the Year' award twice! I certainly miss those days. I don't get the same feeling from running a restaurant.

C Complete the radio vox-pop with the words in the box.

am been collect get joined lost took

Yes, I ¹_______________ stamps. I've ²_______________ into stamp collecting for a long time. I ³_______________ it up when I was just a kid. Some people think it is boring, but I have never ⁴_______________ interest in it, and I'm 45 now. Of course, I ⁵_______________ a member of my local stamp collecting society. I ⁶_______________ that ten years ago. The weekly meetings ⁷_______________ me out of the house.

FUNCTIONAL LANGUAGE

Complete the TV discussion with the correct phrases to express opinions.

Mario: Let's ask our panel of experts. You first, Tim, what do you think?

Tim: Well, in my ¹_______________, they should be banned.

Asif: If you ²_______________ me, we shouldn't ban them.

Ana: As far as I'm ³_______________, a ban is the answer.

Sue: I think we should do more research. Don't you ⁴_______________?

Tim: To be ⁵_______________, I disagree completely. We already know enough. To ⁶_______________ you an example, there were five different stories about them in the newspapers last week.

7 FOOD

So long as you have food in your mouth, you have solved all questions for the time being.

Franz Kafka

Lunch in Marrakesh: Rainbow salad bowl, falafel and mint tea.

OBJECTIVES

- talk about eating out
- make speculations and deductions about food
- compare different types of food
- compare a range of solutions and choose the best one
- make suggestions
- write a reply in an online discussion forum

Work with a partner. Discuss the questions.

1. Look at the photo. How many types of food can you name?
2. Read the quote. What do you think it means?
3. Do you think it is important to eat with your family or friends? Why/Why not?

7.1 Eating out

- Talk about eating out
- Make speculations and deductions about food

P – diphthongs; word stress with modals
G – modals of speculation and deduction
V – phrasal verbs; adjectives to describe food
S – hidden contrasts

READING

A SPEAK Work in groups and discuss the questions.

1 Do you usually eat out in a restaurant? Why/Why not?

2 Do you usually leave a tip to thank the waiter for good service?

B READ FOR MAIN IDEA Read *Super supper clubs*. What are supper clubs? Why do many customers prefer supper clubs to traditional restaurants?

C Complete the notes on the differences between supper clubs and traditional restaurants. Use the strategies in the box to help you.

Paragraph	Supper clubs	Traditional restaurants
Choosing a dish (2)	*the chef chooses*	*you choose from a menu*
Where customers sit (2)		
Choosing when to go (2)		
What to cook (4)		
The food (4)		
The experience (5)		

Hidden contrasts

In articles about new or unusual things, writers frequently use words like *instead*, *just* and *even* to show contrasts with more normal things. These contrasts are usually hidden, so it's difficult to notice them. But they help you to understand the points that the writer wants to make.

SUPER
SUPPER CLUBS

1 Anti-restaurants. Underground restaurants. Pop-up restaurants. Guestaurants. Whatever <u>you</u> call them, there's no <u>doubt</u> that supper clubs are one of the hottest trends in eating out today.

2 The idea is simple: instead of going to a traditional restaurant, you eat in the chef's home. Instead of choosing a dish from a menu, you eat what the chef gives you. And instead of sitting quietly at separate tables, all the customers eat together, talking and making friends. But if that sounds like your perfect evening, there's some bad <u>news</u> . You can't just show up when you're feeling hungry; you'll need to <u>join</u> a waiting list and then <u>wait</u> for an invitation from the chef.

3 The modern idea of supper clubs took off in Cuba in the 1990s. Cuba now has a huge amount of supper clubs, or *paladares*. Most of them started off as simply a room in the chef's <u>home</u>. They're popular with tourists, as well as people who want a simple home-cooked meal at a fair price. One of Cuba's best *paladares* is Castas y Tal, on the 11th floor of a large apartment building in central Havana. The main restaurant area has only eight seats, but there are wonderful views of the city below.

4 For chefs, supper clubs clearly seem like a great idea. They're fairly cheap and easy to set up because the chef can do everything at home. Instead of having to cook the same food again and again, supper clubs give chefs control over what to cook. Customers don't mind giving up some choice because they know they'll eat amazing food that they've never eaten before. They <u>might</u> not like it, but at least it won't be boring.

5 At the St. Jude Project in Mumbai, India, Chef Gresham Fernandes tries out ideas while he's cooking … and even while he's serving up the meal! He cooks in front of the guests, explaining what he's doing as he works.

6 So next time you're feeling adventurous, why not visit a supper club? It's sure to be an experience you won't forget!

PRONUNCIATION
Diphthongs

A Look at the underlined words in *Super supper clubs*. Match the words with their correct pronunciation (1–8). Then listen and check your answers.

7.1

1 weɪt ________
2 ju ________
3 dʒɔɪn ________
4 maɪt ________
5 hoʊm ________
6 daʊt ________
7 nuwz ________

B WORK IT OUT The words in Exercise A all contain diphthongs. Choose the best word or phrase to complete the rules.

Diphthongs

1 Diphthongs are long *vowel* / *consonant* sounds made from *two* / *three* short sounds.
2 We pronounce diphthongs by moving quickly from one sound to the next / saying the two sounds separately.
3 American English has *seven* / *ten* diphthongs: /eɪ/, /aɪ/, /oʊ/, /ɔɪ/, /aʊ/, /ju/, and /uw/.

C SPEAK Work in pairs. Make sentences using at least three of the words from Exercises A and B. Then practice saying your sentences.

VOCABULARY
Phrasal verbs

A Look at *Super supper clubs* again. Find sentences that have the same meaning as the ones below. Which words are used instead of the underlined words?

1 You can't just arrive without making a reservation when you're feeling hungry.
2 The modern idea of supper clubs really became popular in Cuba in the 1990s.
3 Most of them began their existence as simply a room in the chef's home.
4 They're fairly cheap and easy to get ready to start.
5 Customers don't mind losing some choice.
6 Chef Gresham Fernandes experiments with ideas while he's cooking … and even while he's putting the food on plates.

B WORK IT OUT Read the rules about phrasal verbs. Then complete the examples with phrasal verbs from Exercise A.

Phrasal verbs

1 Phrasal verbs are usually made of two parts: a verb (e.g. *work, try*) and a particle (e.g. *out, up*).
2 Sometimes it's possible to guess the meaning from the two words, but usually you just need to learn the meaning of the whole phrasal verb:
- *You can't just* [a] ________ ________ *at their house! Always call first to check it's OK.*

3 Some phrasal verbs can have an object. When the object is short (e.g. a pronoun or one or two words), it usually comes in the middle:
- *I have lots of ideas and I like to* [b] ________ *them* ________ *while I'm cooking.*

But when the object is a longer phrase, it usually comes at the end:
- *I like to* [c] ________ ________ *lots of new ideas while I'm cooking.*

C Go to the Vocabulary Hub on page XVI.

D SPEAK Complete the questions with the correct phrasal verbs. Then work in pairs and ask and answer the questions.

1 Do you think supper clubs will take ________ in your country?
2 Do you ever try ________ new meals while you're cooking or do you always plan carefully before you start?
3 Have your cooking skills ever let you ________? What went wrong?

SPEAKING

A Work in pairs. You are going to plan your own supper club. Write notes about:

- name
- location
- type of food
- cost
- number of guests
- what makes your supper club unique

B PRESENT Work in groups. Take turns presenting your supper club to the group.

C REFLECT Decide which supper club you would like to attend and why.

VOCABULARY

Adjectives to describe food

A Work in groups. Look at the pictures and discuss the questions.

1 Where do you think each dish is from?

2 What do you think it contains?

B Go to the **Vocabulary Hub** on **page XVII**.

C Many food adjectives end in *-y* (e.g. *spicy*). Complete the sentences with the missing adjectives. Use the words in bold to help you.

1 I didn't think this soup would **taste** very nice, but in fact it's really ___tasty___!

2 Honey is very ______________. It **sticks** to the bread like glue!

3 I really love ______________ pizza, so I always ask for extra **cheese** on the top.

4 This ______________ sauce is too rich for me. How much **cream** did you put into it?

D SPEAK Work in pairs. Think of some types of food and drinks that these adjectives might describe. Use the glossary to help you.

buttery chocolatey fatty fruity oily meaty milky nutty peppery runny salty watery

E SPEAK Work in pairs. Use adjectives to describe:

1 your favorite soft drink.

2 your favorite flavor of ice cream.

3 your perfect breakfast.

4 your least favorite types of food.

LISTENING

A SPEAK Work in pairs. If you are invited to eat dinner at somebody's house, do you bring:

- flowers
- a gift
- something to drink
- dessert
- nothing

B Complete the description with the words in the box.

course dessert ~~dinner party~~ dishes host appetizer surprise

A [1] ___dinner party___ is an event where one person (the [2] ______________) invites a group of friends to eat a meal at his or her house. At a traditional dinner party, the host cooks the food: an [3] ______________ and a main [4] ______________. But the guests usually bring something to drink, and perhaps also a [5] ______________. In a pot luck dinner party, everybody (the host and guests) prepares one or two [6] ______________. It's called pot luck because it's always a [7] ______________: nobody knows what the others will bring.

C 7.2 LISTEN FOR SPECIFIC INFORMATION Listen to a conversation at a pot luck dinner party. Match the people (1–5) with the dishes (a–e).

1 Vicky (the host)	a cheesy chicken pasta surprise
2 Charlie	b cream of chicken soup
3 Tina	c spicy buffalo wings
4 Felipe	d cheese and chilli salad
5 Markus	e chicken curry in a creamy sauce

Glossary

allergic (adj) affected by an allergy (a medical condition in which you become sick or your skin becomes covered with red marks as a reaction to something you eat, breathe or touch)

buffalo (n) a large African animal similar to a cow, with curved horns

dairy products (n) foods that are made from milk (e.g. cheese, butter, ice cream)

spicy (adj) food that has a strong hot flavor

7.2 **D** Listen again. Check (✓) the correct name(s).

	Vicky	Charlie	Felipe	Tina	Markus
1 Who arrived late?					
2 Whose dish needs to be heated up?					
3 Who is allergic to dairy products?					
4 Who doesn't like spicy food?					
5 Who doesn't like chicken?					

E SPEAK Work in groups and discuss the questions.

1 What went wrong with the pot luck dinner party?

2 Does it matter if some things go wrong at a party like this?

GRAMMAR

Modals of speculation and deduction

A WORK IT OUT Choose the correct meaning for the sentences from the conversation at the pot luck dinner party.

1 They **can't be** buffalo wings. Buffaloes don't have wings!
- a Maybe they aren't buffalo wings.
- b I'm sure they aren't buffalo wings.

2 They **could be** chicken or something like that.
- a It's possible that they're chicken.
- b It was possible that they were chicken.

3 You **must think** I'm so disorganized!
- a I'm sure you think this.
- b It's necessary for you to think this.

4 Well, they **might not be** chilies.
- a It isn't possible that they're chilies.
- b Maybe they aren't chilies.

5 Uh … you **may have** a problem there.
- a Maybe you have a problem.
- b I'm sure you have a problem.

B Look again at the sentences in Exercise A. Complete the rules (1–4) with the words in the box.

Modals of speculation and deduction

can't could may may not might might not must

1 We use ______ when we are sure something is true.

2 We use ______, ______ or ______ when we think something is possibly true, but we are not sure.

3 We use ______ or ______ when we think something possibly isn't true, but we are not sure.

4 We use ______ when we are sure something is not true.

C Go to the Grammar Hub on page VIII.

PRONUNCIATION

Word stress with modals

7.3 **A** Listen to the sentences (1–4) from the conversation at the pot luck dinner party. Then match the sentences with the rules (a–d).

1 Oh, that must be Felipe, right?

2 Hang on … that can't be right.

3 The name must come from the city, not the animal.

4 They might not be chilies.

a We usually place extra stress on the word *not* or a negative modal verb. ___, ___

b Modal verb + *be*: We usually stress the modal verb, not *be*. ___, ___

c Modal verb + main verb: We usually stress both verbs about the same. ___

d When we're speaking quickly, we usually don't pronounce the *t* in *must*. ___, ___

7.4 **B** Look at the highlighted words in the sentences below and underline the stressed words. Then listen and check your answers.

1 You're such a great host. You must have a lot of dinner parties!

2 'What's wrong with the oven?' 'I don't know. It might not be turned on.'

3 I made a lot of soup because some people may want two or three bowls.

4 Oh, no! Felipe can't be here already! The party doesn't start for another 20 minutes!

7.4 **C** Listen again and repeat the sentences. Then work in pairs and practice saying the sentences. Listen and check your partner's pronunciation.

D SPEAK Work in pairs. Make deductions and speculations about the people at the dinner party. Think about these questions.

1 How do they know each other?

2 What is the surprise in Tina's cheesy chicken pasta surprise?

SPEAKING HUB

A You have been invited to a pot luck dinner party. Write a short description of the dish you would like to bring.

B SPEAK Work in groups. Choose one person to be the host and give him/her your description. In your groups, decide:

- who brought which dish.
- which dishes you want to try.

C REFLECT Tell the class about your pot luck dinner party. Which dishes were the most popular?

- Talk about eating out
- Make speculations and deductions about food

7.2 Food fads

- Compare different types of food
- Compare a range of solutions and choose the best one

G comparatives and superlatives; *the …, the …* **P** vowel + *w* **V** waste **S** identifying people's opinions

READING

A SPEAK Read the definition of *fad*. Then work in pairs and discuss the questions.

> **fad** – definition and synonyms
> NOUN Pronunciation /fæd/
> 1 something that is popular or fashionable for only a short time

1 Can you think of any current food fads? Which foods are fashionable now?
2 Are there any food fads connected with different ways of cooking? Or different ways of eating?
3 Which older food fads have gone out of fashion?

B READ FOR GIST Read *Food fads* quickly. What is the writer's opinion about superfoods?

a They're just a fad – they aren't really very good for you.
b Expensive superfoods are much healthier than cheaper food.
c You don't need to spend a lot of money to buy some superfoods.
d Most superfoods are actually bad for your health.

FOOD FADS

Hi again! This week, I've decided to look at one of the biggest food fads of the 21st century: superfoods. Let's try to sort the facts from the fiction!

Quinoa has a long history as a superfood: it was known to the ancient Incas as 'the mother of all grains' because it was so healthy. Even today it's recommended by NASA as the perfect food for long space flights. Like all whole grains, it can help your body fight a variety of diseases, and it contains lots of vitamins, minerals and fiber. It's also one of the best sources of protein, so it's perfect for vegetarians and vegans, too. Amazing!

Goji berries are another great source of plant-based protein. These sweet berries have been used in China for centuries as a way to protect against illness. They contain less sugar than other fruits, so they're one of the healthiest snacks around. Unfortunately, they can be dangerous for some people, so always check with your doctor before eating them.

Açaí berries are perhaps the most successful superfoods of all: not long ago, they were unknown outside of Brazil. Now, açaí products are big business. Why are they so popular? Well, some people believe these berries will help them to grow old more slowly … or even to live longer. Like goji berries, they're full of chemicals which seem to protect our hearts and our brains. Sounds good, right?

Chia seeds are known as the healthiest food on the planet. The name 'chia' comes from the ancient Mayan word for 'strength'. Out of all the foods in the world, chia seeds contain some of the most nutrients for the fewest calories. They're also one of the best sources of fiber, which is great for your digestive system. Even better, they make you feel full … so you'll eat fewer snacks!

C READ FOR SPECIFIC INFORMATION Read again. Write *A* (açaí berries), *B* (broccoli), *C* (chia seeds), *G* (goji berries) or *Q* (quinoa).

According to the blog post, which superfood …

1 isn't only eaten on our planet? ___
2 is much cheaper than other superfoods? ___
3 might help you stay younger for longer? ___
4 can help you digest your food more effectively? ___
5 might not be safe for everybody? ___
6 has become popular very quickly? ___
7 helps you to eat less food between meals? ___

D SPEAK Work in groups and discuss the questions.

1 Do you think it's worth paying more money for superfoods? Why/Why not?
2 Do you think it is more important for you to eat healthy food or tasty food? Why?
3 What are some simple ways that we can eat more healthily?

But before you all rush out to buy superfoods from your local health food store, remember that superfoods are usually super expensive, too! And do you know what? Strawberries are probably just as good for you as goji berries and açaí berries. Similarly, quinoa and chia seeds are great because they're whole grains. But you can get all that fiber far more cheaply by eating plenty of brown bread, brown rice and whole grain pasta. And what's the best superfood of all? Broccoli! It's cheap, tasty and incredibly good for you. It isn't as exciting as quinoa, but it's a lot less expensive!

Glossary

fiber (n) the parts of fruit, vegetables and grains that your body cannot digest (= turn into substances it can use); it helps food to pass through your body

nutrient (n) a substance in food that plants, animals and people need to live and grow

protein (n) a substance in food, such as meat, eggs and milk, that people need in order to grow and be healthy

GRAMMAR

Comparatives and superlatives

A Cover the *Food fads* article. Complete the sentences with one word in each space. Then check your answers in the blog post.

1 This week, I've decided to look at one of ___*the*___ biggest food fads of the 21st century: superfoods.
2 They contain ________ sugar ________ other fruits, so they're one of ________ healthiest snacks around.
3 Chia seeds contain some of the ________ nutrients for the ________ calories.
4 Even better, they make you feel full … so you'll eat ________ snacks!
5 Some people believe these berries will help them to grow old ________ slowly … or even to live ________.
6 It isn't ________ exciting ________ quinoa, but it's a lot ________ expensive!

B Go to the **Grammar Hub** on **page VIII**.

C SPEAK Work in pairs. Compare each set of ideas.

1 quinoa vs white rice
2 broccoli vs ice cream
3 grocery stores vs health food stores
4 fast food vs superfoods
5 cooking vs eating out
6 eating alone vs eating in a large group

A: Quinoa is much tastier than white rice.
B: Yes, but it's a lot more expensive.

SPEAKING

Work in pairs. Use the superlative form of the words and phrases in the box to ask and answer questions.

bad · expensive · far (to travel for a meal) · few ingredients · little money (to spend on food) · much time (to spend preparing a meal) · spicy

A: What's the farthest you've ever traveled for a meal?
B: Not very far. I usually buy all my food in the local store. But once I spent an hour bike riding to the 'best ice cream store in town'. But it wasn't as good as I expected.

LISTENING

A Work in pairs. Take the **Reduce Your Waste** quiz. Then go to the Communication Hub on page XX to check your answers.

7.5 **B** You are going to listen to part of a radio show about a family who is trying to waste less food. Look at the pictures (1–6) and guess the answers to the questions. Then listen and check your answers.

REDUCE YOUR WASTE

1 How long can you store these things before they go bad?

a fresh milk in a fridge
b frozen vegetables in a freezer
c fresh bananas
d dry food (e.g. pasta)
e an opened bottle of apple juice in a fridge
f a plate of leftovers in a fridge

2 True or false?

a You can safely reheat food as many times as you like.
b Most food is still safe to eat after it has passed its best if used by date.
c You must eat rice within 24 hours of cooking it.

How much money does the average person lose from food waste every year?

Do ugly carrots taste as good as beautiful carrots?

What's the problem with growing lettuce in a greenhouse?

How many buckets of water does it take to make a loaf of bread?

What can you do with your leftovers if you don't want to waste them?

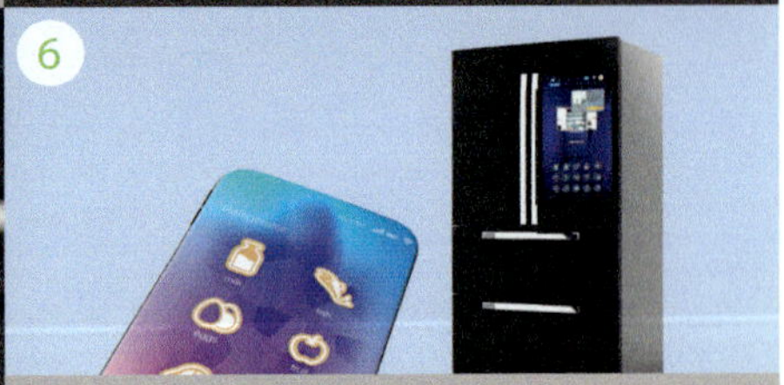

How can a cell phone app help us waste less food?

C Who expressed each of these opinions: *Mrs. Taylor*, *Mr. Taylor*, *Alison* or *Philip*? Use the strategies in the box to help you.

Identifying people's opinions

When you're listening, pay attention to whether people are just describing a situation or expressing an opinion about it.

Adjectives like *great* and *awful* usually show that the person is expressing an opinion.

1 Food doesn't need to be beautiful. ___Mrs. Taylor___
2 I like collecting and studying detailed information about our experiment. ______
3 Food waste is bad for our planet. ______
4 I didn't like eating the same food the next day. ______
5 I enjoy cooking meals to use up the food in the fridge. ______
6 Money isn't the most important reason for reducing waste. ______

D SPEAK Work in pairs. How much food do you think you waste in your family?

GRAMMAR

the …, the …

A WORK IT OUT Look at the sentences from the radio show. Match the beginnings of the sentences (1–5) with the endings (a–e).

1 The more I researched the topic,
2 The less food we throw away,
3 The less we cook,
4 The longer we do it,
5 The more carefully you count things,

a the more normal it feels.
b the better.
c the more I realized that we aren't just throwing away food.
d the more accurate your results will be.
e the less we waste.

B Read the rule and complete the example. Use the words in parentheses to help you.

the …, the …

To show that two changes are closely connected, we use *the* + comparative, *the* + comparative. As one thing changes, it makes the other thing change.

As far as I'm concerned, the ______ *(ugly), the* ______ *(good)!*

C Go to the Grammar Hub on page VIII.

PRONUNCIATION
Vowel + *w*

7.6 **A** How do you pronounce these words? Use the strategies in the box to help you. Then listen and repeat the words.

chew cow own raw stew

Vowel + *w*

Three vowels, ***a***, ***e*** and ***o***, when combined with ***w***, make a new sound. There are two possible sounds for ***e*** + ***w*** and ***o*** + ***w***.

a + *w* **/ɔː/** for, draw, awful, ________, ________

e + *w* **/juː/** you, few, view, ________

e + *w* **/uː/** too, jewelry, threw, ________, ________

o + *w* **/oʊ/** go, low, owe, ________, ________, ________, ________, ________

o + *w* **/aʊ/** out, how, wow, ________, ________, ________

7.7 **B** Look at the bold words in these sentences. Write them in the correct place in the box in Exercise A. Then listen and check your answers.

1 'Have you ever **flown** in a helicopter?' 'Yes, I **flew** in one a **few** weeks ago. It was **awesome**.'
2 You aren't **allowed** to **throw** away your trash here! Don't you **know** it's against the **law**!
3 The **flowers grew** fairly **slowly** at first, but **now** they're fully **grown**.

C SPEAK Work in pairs. Practice saying the sentences in Exercise B. Listen and check your partner's pronunciation.

VOCABULARY
Waste

A Match the definitions (1–8) with the words and phrases in the box.

garbage can cut down get rid of recycle reduce reuse garbage throw away use up ~~waste~~

1 to not use something that you could use ____waste____
2 a container for putting garbage in ________
3 things that you throw away because they are no longer useful ________
4 to use all of something, so there's no waste ________
5 to change waste materials such as newspapers and bottles so that they can be used again ________
6 to use something again ________
7 to use less of something ________, ________
8 to get rid of something that you no longer want ________, ________

B SPEAK Complete the questions with one word in each space. Then work in pairs and discuss the questions.

1 Do you ________ plastic and glass containers so they can be turned into new products, or do you just get ________ of them?
2 Do you ________ plastic bags again and again, or throw them in the ________?
3 How could restaurants cut ________ the amount of ________ they throw ________ each week?

SPEAKING HUB

A Work in pairs. How could you reduce food waste in your home by fifty percent? Write notes about:

- shopping habits (how often? how much?)
- meal planning (weekly menus)
- leftovers
- food storage (fridge? cupboard? special containers?)
- apps and gadgets

B PRESENT Use your notes to prepare a short presentation on how you can help people reduce their food waste. Present your ideas to the class.

C DISCUSS Work in groups. Use these questions to compare your ideas from Exercise B. Then choose the best two or three ideas.

- Which ideas will be easiest for people to understand and follow?
- Which ideas will make the biggest difference?
- Which ideas might cost people more money? Which ideas might save them money?

D REFLECT Work in groups and discuss the questions.

1 Are you going to try to reduce your own food waste? How?
2 Will you try to persuade others to cut their food waste? How?

- Compare different types of food
- Compare a range of solutions and choose the best one

7.3 Comfort eating

F– make suggestions P– suggestions

COMPREHENSION

A Work in pairs and discuss the questions.

What do you do when you're feeling upset or worried?

Do you cook, go for a run, call a friend, watch a good movie or something else?

B ▶ 00:00–01:30 Watch the first part of the video and answer the questions.

1 What is Gaby's big news?
2 What does Milly think about her news?
3 What is Gaby upset about?

C ▶ 00:56–01:21 Find and correct five mistakes in the story that Gaby told Milly. What advice do you think Milly will give? Watch to check your answers.

It was about a week ago. Last Wednesday, Sam had to leave work early and so he asked me to look after the café. I had decided to tell him how I felt, and so before I locked up, I wrote a poem expressing my true feelings for him. … And I left it on the doormat for him to find. He can't have seen it.

FUNCTIONAL LANGUAGE

Making suggestions

A Match the two halves of the extracts from the video.

Making a suggestion

1 Have you tried
2 What about
3 The best thing might be
4 If I were you, I'd
5 Why don't we
6 We could

a cook something delicious.
b take some time to think about it.
c talking to him about it?
d put on some whipped cream and sprinkles?
e sending a text or an email or something?
f to just ask him if he got the letter.

B Complete the phrases in the table.

Saying no to a suggestion	Saying yes to a suggestion
No, I ______________. I don't know what to say.	That's a good ______________.
No, that wouldn't ______________. To say what?	It's worth a ______________.
That's a ______________ idea. I'm already really embarrassed.	Good ______________.

C ▶ 01:21–04:13 Watch the second part of the video and check your answers to Exercises A and B.

MILLY

SAM

NEENA

ZAC

GABY

USEFUL PHRASES

A Match the useful phrases (1–4) with the screenshots (a–d).

1 What's up? ___
2 Great timing! ___
3 It'll help take your mind off Sam. ___
4 He's been acting like nothing happened! ___

a

b

c

d

B How do you say these useful phrases in your language?

PRONUNCIATION
Suggestions

7.8 **A** Listen to the extracts from the video and underline the stressed/key words. Does the intonation rise or fall at the end of each phrase?

Milly: Have you tried talking to him about it?
Gaby: No, I can't. I don't know what to say.
Milly: Or, what about sending him a text or an email or something?
Gaby: No, that wouldn't work. To say what?
Milly: I don't know exactly. The best thing might be to just ask him if he got the letter?
Gaby: No, no, no, no, no, no, no, no! That's a terrible idea. I'm already really embarrassed.
Milly: If I were you, I'd take some time to think about it.

B In pairs, practice the conversation. Copy the stress and intonation.

SPEAKING

A Work in pairs. Think about possible solutions to the problems below.

1 I'm having a dinner party, but I hate cooking.
2 I want to eat more healthily, but superfoods are too expensive.
3 I want to save some money, but I love going out to restaurants!
4 I frequently have leftover food, but I don't want to waste it.
5 I want to grow vegetables, but I live in an apartment.

B DISCUSS Take turns reading out a problem and make suggestions using the phrases in Functional Language Exercise A.

A: I'm having a dinner party, but I hate cooking.
B: What about getting takeout?

Make suggestions

➤ Turn to page XXV to learn how to write a reply in an online discussion forum.

Unit 7 Review

GRAMMAR

A Choose the best words to complete the conversation.

A: Do you want some of this pot luck stew? I made it from all of last week's leftovers: fish curry, cheesy chicken pasta, spicy vegetables …

B: Yuck! That [1]*can't / might not / must* taste disgusting!

A: Well, no, it actually tastes very good. Try it – you [2]*can / might / must* like it.

B: Really? OK. I guess it [3]*couldn't / might not / must not* be so bad. But don't forget I'm allergic to peanuts.

A: Don't worry, it [4]*can't / may not / might* contain any peanuts. I never cook with them. But it [5] *couldn't / may / must* contain some other types of nuts – I'm not sure. Is that OK?

B: Yes, that's fine. Hmm … this [6]*can't / could / must* be a big mistake, but … OK, I'll try it.

B Complete the sentences with the correct form of the words in parentheses.

1 I want to cook the most food for the ______________ (*little*) money. Any ideas?

2 Açaí berries are really good for you – they're much ______________ (*healthy*) than I thought.

3 If you want to lose weight, you need to eat ______________ (*few*) candy.

4 You should come to the restaurant on a Tuesday at lunchtime – that's the ______________ (*crowded*) time.

5 You baked this cake too quickly! Next time, try baking it ______________ (*slowly*).

6 Cooking for ten people is far ______________ (*stressful*) than cooking for one!

7 There's too much cream in this sauce. Can you make it a little ______________ (*creamy*) next time?

C Match the beginnings of the sentences (1–6) with the endings (a–f).

1 Bring all your friends to our dinner party – the more people who come,

2 The earlier you arrive at the restaurant,

3 The older I get,

4 The more sugar you add,

5 Natural food is much better for you; the fewer chemicals it contains,

6 Don't boil vegetables for too long; the longer you cook them,

a the more I prefer to stay in and cook at home.

b the less flavor they'll have.

c the more fun we'll have.

d the more likely you are to get a table.

e the sweeter it will be.

f the healthier it is.

VOCABULARY

A Complete the sentences with the correct form of the phrasal verbs in the box.

keep on clean up end up put off figure out

1 I can't ______________ how to turn on the microwave. Can you help me?

2 Sorry to interrupt your meal, but I need to go out for a minute. Please ______________ eating while I'm away.

3 I'm happy to cook dinner, but could you ______________ the dirty plates afterward?

4 If you want to learn to cook, don't ______________ it ______________! Join our cooking classes today!

5 I was planning to cook a big meal, but then the oven broke so I ______________ buying takeout pizzas for everybody.

B Choose the best adjectives to complete the sentences.

1 I think we need to cook this meat a little longer – it's still *delicious / mild / raw* in the middle.

2 I don't really like sweet snacks. Do you have anything *bitter / rich / savory*, like a sandwich?

3 Don't worry. This soup is very *buttery / mild / spicy* – there are no chilies or strong flavors in it.

4 The food was great, but it wasn't very *chewy / filling / spicy*. We were still hungry at the end of the meal!

5 I don't like dark chocolate – it's too *fatty / bitter / creamy* for me. I prefer something sweeter.

6 If you want a cheap and *disgusting / sour / tasty* lunch, Kate's café is the best place to go.

C Complete the advice about food waste with words in the box. There is one extra word.

garbage cans get recycle reduce reuse throw use

Try these tips:

- Don't [1]__________ rid of yesterday's bread just because it isn't fresh. Make toast to [2]__________ up the last few pieces.
- Don't [3]__________ old plastic away. You can [4]__________ the same shopping bags again and again.
- Use two (or more) [5]__________: one for food waste and one for containers that you can [6]__________.

FUNCTIONAL LANGUAGE

Find and correct the mistakes in the sentences.

1 I don't feel like cooking tonight. Why ~~we~~ don't ^we eat out tonight?

2 Yes, why not? What about go to The Food Zone?

____

3 Again? We went there last week. Could we going to that new supper club, The Spicy Kitchen, instead?

____

4 Good idea! The best thing might be call them. They might have a free table tonight.

____

5 Yes, that's worth to try. Can you call them and ask?

____

8 INNOVATION

To invent, you need a good imagination and a pile of junk.

Thomas Edison

A helicopter mechanic double checks some wiring, Germany.

OBJECTIVES

- explain how an invention works
- suggest and evaluate creative ideas
- use positive language to promote a new product
- give a friend advice about choosing a gadget
- give and follow instructions
- write a biography

Work with a partner. Discuss the questions.

1. Look at the picture. What characteristics would be helpful to have as a mechanic?
2. Look at the quote. Do you think you have to be imaginative to be an inventor?
3. Talk about a situation where you have been imaginative or innovative in your life.

8.1 Making a difference

- Explain how an invention works
- Suggest and evaluate creative ideas

V – word families; creative thinking G – adjective clauses P – adjective clauses
S – listening for problems and solutions

Eden Full Goh:

the inventor who is making a big difference

Eden Full Goh is perhaps not a name that you immediately recognize, but she is one of the most exciting and creative inventors of the 21st century.

Eden, who was born in Calgary, Canada, started to show talent at the age of nine, when she built a solar-powered toy car. That is where her interest in solar power began but certainly not where it stopped. She had not yet graduated from college when she came up with a very simple, but highly efficient, solar panel system that produces energy at low cost.

Eden's invention, which has won many prizes, is now used in 19 countries, where it makes a real difference to thousands of people's lives. Here is how to use it.

1. The SunSaluter is like a table. The top of the table is a solar panel, which can face in different directions.
2. Get up early in the morning when it's still dark. Fill one plastic bottle with sand and two more bottles with dirty water.
3. Attach the water bottles to the filter. At the bottom of the filter is a tube that takes clean water to a large container. At the top there's a hook that attaches the filter to the SunSaluter.
4. Hang the filter on one end of the SunSaluter, which will then go down. Hang the bottle that you filled with sand on the other end of the solar panel. Make sure the solar panel is facing the east, where the sun will rise.
5. At sunrise, when the sun comes up, the solar panel will start catching sunlight from the east.
6. During the day, the water will flow very slowly through the filter to the container, where it is stored. As the water bottles become lighter, the heavy sand bottle slowly pulls the other end of the SunSaluter down. At noon, when the sun is high in the sky, the solar panel will face upwards.
7. In the evening, when the water bottles are empty, the solar panel will face west. You can now drink the clean water that you collected during the day.

Glossary

solar panel (n) a piece of equipment that uses energy from the sun to create power

READING

A SPEAK Work in pairs and discuss the questions.

1. What famous inventors do you know? What did they invent?
2. What skills do inventors need?

B READ FOR GIST Read *Eden Full Goh: the inventor who is making a big difference*. What is special about Eden and her invention?

C READ FOR DETAIL Read again. Match the explanations (1–7) in the text with the pictures (a–g).

D SPEAK Make a list of your own life goals. Use the ideas in the box to help you. Then work in pairs and compare your lists.

awards and prizes   career   experiences   family   helping other people   certifications

VOCABULARY

Word families

A Read the box. Then complete the word families. Use *Eden Full Goh: the inventor who is making a big difference* to help you.

Word families

Word families can help you learn many words together, not just one at a time. Here's an example:

innovation (n) = a new idea or product

innovator (n) = someone who thinks of new ideas or products

innovate (v) = to invent or begin using new ideas or products

innovative (adj) = an adjective to describe an innovator or an innovation

Noun (thing/idea)	Noun (person)	Verb	Adjective
a success	a success	to succeed (in something)	1 successful
an 2 ______	an 3 ______	to invent something	inventive
a design	a designer	to 4 ______ something	–
a product	a producer	to 5 ______ something	productive
6 ______	a scientist	–	scientific
engineering	an 7 ______	to engineer something	–

B Complete the sentences with words from the same family as the words in bold.

1 You don't need to be **successful** every time. You just need to ___*succeed*___ in the most important things.

2 I could never **invent** something – I'm not a very ________________ person.

3 You can only call yourself an ________________ after studying **engineering** in college.

4 A ________________ should concentrate on **designing** things that work well. That's more important than making them look beautiful.

5 I always think like a **scientist**. Being ________________ means checking the facts before making a decision, and not focusing on opinions and feelings.

C SPEAK Work in pairs. Which sentences in Exercise B do you agree or disagree with? Tell your partner. Then make the sentences true for you.

GRAMMAR

Adjective clauses

A WORK IT OUT Look at *Eden Full Goh: the inventor who is making a big difference*. What do the highlighted words in the article refer to?

1 who = ___*Eden*___
2 when = ________________
3 where = ________________
4 which = ________________
5 that = ________________

B Read the rules and complete the examples with adjective clauses from the article.

Adjective clauses

Essential adjective clauses tell us which person, thing, place or time we are talking about. Without the adjective clause, the sentence isn't complete.

Eden Full Goh: the inventor [1] ________________________________.

Non-essential adjective clauses give extra information about a person, thing, place or time. We can cut the adjective clause and the sentence is still complete. We use commas to separate the adjective clause from the rest of the sentence.

Eden's invention, [2] ________________________, is now used in 19 countries.

C Go to the Grammar Hub on page X.

PRONUNCIATION

Adjective clauses

8.1 **A** Listen to the two sentences. What do you notice about the pronunciation of essential adjective clauses and non-essential adjective clauses?

1 The person who invented the SunSaluter has made a big difference to people's lives.

2 Eden Full Goh, who invented the SunSaluter, has made a big difference to people's lives.

8.2 **B** Listen and repeat the sentences.

1 Solar panels, which turn sunlight into electricity, are becoming cheaper all the time.

2 I've hidden my plans in a place where they'll be safe.

3 My favorite inventor is Mária Telkes, who created the first 100 percent solar-powered house in 1947.

C SPEAK Work in pairs. Practice saying the sentences in Exercise B. Listen and check your partner's pronunciation.

SPEAKING

A Work in pairs. Write down three sentences using adjective clauses. They should describe:

- a famous person
- a place
- an object

B Join another pair and take turns reading out your sentences, saying 'Beep' in place of the subject. The other pair must guess who, where or what you are talking about.

A: Beep, who is American, invented the light bulb.
B: Is it Thomas Edison?

Thinking outside THE BOX

Thinking outside the box means looking at a problem in a new way. It means forgetting about 'the way we normally do things', taking away unimportant rules and experimenting with new ideas. So for example, in the 'nine dots' problem, we see 'rules' that don't actually exist. Who said your lines have to stay inside the red box? In fact, do the lines even need to go through the middle of each dot?

It's the same with the light bulb problem. We can't stop ourselves from thinking of a light bulb as something that we see with our eyes, as something that can only be in two states, off or on. But what if we think of it as something we can touch with our hands? Are there still only two states?

Thinking outside the box also helps with brainstorming tasks, like the 'uses for old tickets' exercise. The key to successful brainstorming is to break it into two stages: generating ideas in the first place, and then evaluating those ideas to see if they're useful or not. We need to keep those stages separate; if we try to do both at the same time, we only generate boring, sensible ideas. But sometimes it's the silly ideas that help us to find excellent ideas. For example, a single bus ticket wouldn't make a great poster for your wall, but what about a poster made from 100 bus tickets from around the world?

READING

A SPEAK Work in pairs. How creative are you? Follow the instructions to find out.

1 Take an object from your pocket/bag (e.g. a used bus ticket). Try to think of as many different uses as possible for this object. Your ideas can be sensible or silly. What's your best idea?

A: We could cut it up to make a tiny jigsaw puzzle.
B: Why don't we write a short shopping list on the back?

2 Draw four straight lines to connect all the dots without taking your pen off the page. Now try again with only three straight lines.

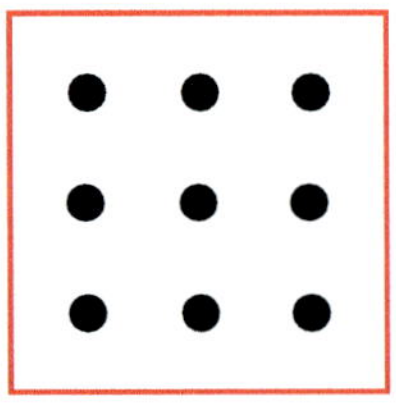

3 You're inside a room with three light switches on the wall. One of these switches turns on a light in a room on the other side of the house, but you don't know which switch. How can you find out? You can go to the other room to check only once.

B READ FOR GIST Read *Thinking outside the box*. How does it help with the questions in Exercise A?

C READ FOR DETAIL Choose *Do* or *Don't* for each piece of advice.

1 *Do / Don't* look at a problem in a new way.
2 *Do / Don't* do things the way you normally do them.
3 *Do / Don't* experiment with new ideas.
4 *Do / Don't* guess the rules and follow those rules.
5 *Do / Don't* evaluate ideas while you're generating them.

D SPEAK Work in groups. When do you need to brainstorm ideas? How could brainstorming silly ideas help you to think of useful ideas?

LISTENING

A SPEAK Work in pairs. The pictures show some techniques for becoming more creative. What do you think the techniques are?

8.3 **B LISTEN FOR GIST** Listen to a conversation between two friends, Caroline and Toby, to check your answers to Exercise A. Number the pictures in the order they are mentioned.

Glossary

wander (v) if your mind or thoughts wander, you stop concentrating and start thinking about other things

C Listen again. What was the solution to each problem? Use the strategies in the box to help you.

8.3

Listening for problems and solutions

When you're listening, it's useful to organize information into a set of problems and solutions. This usually makes it easier to understand a lot of information and to remember it better later.

Listen carefully when you hear people talking about problems because they'll probably present a solution next.

1 You don't learn how to be creative at school.
   - a Write stories and design clothes.
   - b Go to creativity classes.
   - c Read books about creativity.

2 You're too busy to stop working.
   - a Take a break to make yourself more productive.
   - b Work in the evenings so you can have a break during the day.
   - c Relax – your work isn't as important as you think.

3 Your brain is filled with too much information.
   - a Get some physical exercise.
   - b Watch TV and play games on your phone.
   - c Turn off your computer.

4 You need to think outside the box.
   - a Go to the library to get some ideas.
   - b Look at blue things.
   - c Listen to some music.

5 You have no ideas at all.
   - a Discuss your ideas with a group of friends.
   - b Close your eyes for a few minutes.
   - c Use letters of the alphabet to generate ideas.

D SPEAK Work in pairs. Which of Caroline's techniques have you used? Which might you use in the future? Tell your partner.

VOCABULARY
Creative thinking

A Match the beginnings of the sentences (1–10) with the endings (a–j).

1 I'm terrible at **coming up**
2 You can actually learn to **use your**
3 A break actually **boosted my**
4 You need to **unplug**
5 You need to **let your mind**
6 They're all good for **generating**
7 Whenever I need to **think outside**
8 You're letting your emotions **block**
9 You should **look at a problem**
10 **My mind's**

a **the box**, I go to the beach.
b **wander freely**.
c **imagination** better.
d **your creativity**.
e **gone blank**.
f **creativity**.
g **with new ideas**.
h **from the outside**.
i **completely**.
j **new ideas**.

B Look at the sentences in Exercise A. What do the phrases in bold mean?

C SPEAK Choose the best words to complete the questions. Then work in groups and ask and answer the questions.

1 Does your mind ever *boost* / *generate* / *wander* during boring activities? Think of some examples.
2 Is it possible to *come up* / *unplug* / *block* completely from the things that make you stressed? How can you do it?
3 What can you do when your *mind* / *creativity* / *imagination* goes blank in a stressful situation (e.g. when you're in an exam, giving a presentation or speaking English)?

SPEAKING HUB

A Work in groups. You have decided to create a website that will make a big difference to people's lives. Use the alphabet technique to generate some ideas – silly or serious!

Write down three letters of the alphabet.

- 1st letter: Who is your website for?
- 2nd letter: What problem do those people have?
- 3rd letter: How will you solve that problem?

B PLAN Think of five ideas for each of the questions below. Remember to think outside the box!

1 What will you call your website?
2 How can you make money from your website?
3 How will you tell the world about your website?

C ORGANIZE Look at your ideas from Exercise B. Turn your silly ideas into excellent ideas. Choose your best idea.

D PRESENT Present your idea to the class. Which teams' websites would you visit?

- Explain how an invention works
- Suggest and evaluate creative ideas

8.2 Must-have gadgets

- Use positive language to promote a new product
- Give a friend advice about choosing a gadget

V – positive adjectives
P – *'ll* and *won't*
G – zero and first conditionals; conditionals with modals and imperatives
S – topic sentences

LISTENING

A SPEAK Work in pairs. Look at the pictures of inventions (a–d) and discuss the questions.

1 What do you think the gadgets in the pictures do?
2 How useful are they?
3 Do you like gadgets? What gadgets do you own?

8.4 **B** LISTEN FOR MAIN IDEA Listen to a podcast about new gadgets and answer the questions.

1 Which gadgets from the pictures do the people discuss?
2 What is special about them?

8.4 **C** Listen again. Which gadgets do these sentences describe? Write *O* (Oombrella), *C* (CleverPet) or *B* (both).

1 It looks beautiful. ___
2 It's connected to the internet. ___
3 It sends messages to your phone. ___
4 It's useful for many years. ___
5 It gets more difficult to use over time. ___
6 It can lead to a longer life. ___

D SPEAK Work in groups and discuss the questions.

1 What is good about the two gadgets? Which one is more useful?
2 Who do you think will buy the gadgets? Why?

VOCABULARY
Positive adjectives

Using positive adjectives

As your English improves, try to avoid using words like *good* or *nice* too frequently. There are many other positive words that you can use like *amazing*, *excellent* and *wonderful*.

A Match the positive adjectives (1–10) with the meanings (a–j).

1 gorgeous
2 sensible
3 practical
4 unforgettable
5 impressive
6 unique
7 sophisticated
8 incredible
9 suitable
10 fascinating

a you admire it because it is very good, large or shows great skill
b making you very interested or attracted
c right for a particular purpose, person or situation
d not the same as anything or anyone else
e reasonable and practical
f will be remembered for a very long time
g surprising, or difficult to believe
h very beautiful
i complicated and advanced in design
j intended to be useful

B Go to the Vocabulary Hub on page XVII.

C SPEAK Work in pairs. Write down the names of your favorite three possessions. Use positive adjectives to tell your partner why you like each one. Ask questions about your partner's possessions.

a

b

GRAMMAR

Zero and first conditionals

8.5 **A** **Look at the extracts from the podcast about new gadgets. Match the beginnings of the sentences (1–4) with the endings (a–d). Then listen and check your answers.**

1 I never go for a walk
2 Will it keep me dry
3 If this Oombrella lasts for years,
4 Pets stay healthier and they live longer

a if there's a storm tomorrow morning?
b if they keep busy.
c I'll be very happy.
d unless the sun's shining.

B WORK IT OUT **Choose the correct words to complete the rules.**

Zero and first conditional

1 Conditional sentences usually have ***two* / *four*** clauses: the *if*-clause and the result clause.
2 When the *if*-clause comes first, we ***always* / *never*** need a comma between the clauses.
3 We can use ***unless*** instead of *if*. It means ***if not* / *because***.
4 We use the zero conditional to talk about things that are always true. We use ***past* / *present*** tenses in both clauses.
5 We use the first conditional to talk about possible situations in the ***future* / *past***. We usually use ***will*** in the result clause.

C **Go to the** Grammar Hub on page X.

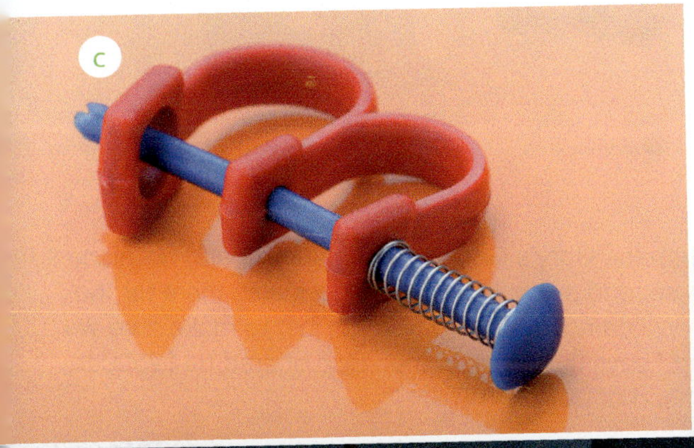
c

d

PRONUNCIATION

'll and *won't*

'll* and *won't

It's sometimes hard to hear the difference between words such as *you* and *you'll*, or *I* and *I'll*. It's also sometimes hard to hear the difference between *won't* and *want*. The rules for conditionals will help you figure out what you hear.

8.6 **A** **Listen and circle the words you hear.**

1 If you ***want to go* / *won't go*** to the grocery store, ***you* / *you'll*** need to bring a bag.
2 ***I lend* / *I'll lend*** you my raincoat if you ***want to borrow* / *won't borrow*** it.
3 If ***you* / *you'll*** like gadgets, ***you* / *you'll*** love this.
4 ***You learn* / *You'll earn*** a lot more if ***you* / *you'll*** listen carefully.

8.6 **B** **Listen again and repeat the sentences.**

C SPEAK **Work in pairs. Imagine you are going to lend your partner a gadget tonight. Follow the instructions.**

1 If you have a gadget with you (e.g. a phone, a smartwatch), show your partner what to do. Ask questions about your partner's gadget.
2 If you don't have a gadget, use an everyday object (e.g. a pen, your car keys) and pretend it's a gadget. Invent some cool functions for it.

SPEAKING

A **You are going to invent a new gadget and then promote it to the class. Use the ideas below and your own ideas to invent a gadget.**

What is it?	What's innovative about it?
a book, a chair, a food bowl, a hat, swimming goggles, a mirror, a light bulb, a plastic bottle, a puzzle, shoes, a toy, a TV, an umbrella	It can fly/talk/move by itself. It's connected to the internet. It contains a GPS device / a camera. It's for pets/birds/fish. It's very big/small.

B PLAN **Work in groups. Choose the best idea for your group's gadget and answer the questions:**

- What is special about your gadget?
- What problem does it solve?
- What else can you use to help you promote your gadget (e.g. pictures, stories)?
- What questions might people ask about your gadget?

C PRESENT **Promote your gadget to the class. At the end of each presentation, ask questions about other groups' gadgets.**

D REFLECT **Take a class vote to find out the most popular gadget. Would you like to buy the other groups' gadgets? Why/Why not? Do you think your gadgets could become real products?**

READING

A SPEAK Work in pairs. Look at the picture and answer the questions.

1 What do you think the people are doing? Why?
2 Have you ever done something similar? Why/Why not?

B PREDICT Work in pairs. Before you read *If you really can't wait …*, look at the five topic sentences (a–e) and discuss the questions. Use the strategies in the box to help you.

> **Topic sentences**
>
> The topic sentence is usually the first or second sentence in a paragraph. It tells you what the whole paragraph will be about.
>
> You can usually understand a lot about a text just by reading and thinking about the topic sentences.
>
> You can also use them to make predictions before reading the whole text to check.

a Marketers have a name for people who buy new gadgets before everyone else: innovators.
Why do you think marketers have a special name for these people? Why are marketers interested in them?

b A little further back in the line, I meet some fans who aren't just there to buy a phone.
Why do you think these fans are in the line?

c Near the back of the line, some people are feeling less positive.
Why do you think they're feeling less positive?

d It's five o'clock in the morning, and there are already over 200 people in the line outside the phone store.
Why do you think they're there so early in the morning?

e I decided to speak to some people in the line outside the phone store to find out … and I got a few surprises.
What surprises do you think the writer got?

If you really can't wait …

1 ___ It's cold and dark, but the people seem happy. In a few hours, the doors will open and they'll finally get their hands on the gadget of their dreams: a gorgeous new cell phone. Of course, if you don't want to stand in line all night, you can come to the store this afternoon when the lines will be gone. Even better, if you can wait six months or so, the same phone will cost half the price. But if you really need that phone right now, come and join the back of the line.

2 ___ I've always thought that was a terrible name – innovation normally means doing something extremely smart, like inventing a new machine. But what's innovative about buying expensive gadgets just because they're new? Of course, marketers love 'innovators' for two reasons: innovators are happy to spend a lot of money and they persuade the rest of us to buy those gadgets a few months later.

So why do they do it? 3 ___ The biggest surprise was that the people at the front of the line were actually being paid to be there. 'I work for a gadget store, Gary's Gadgets. My boss, Gary, is paying me,' said Bob, who is right at the front of the line. 'It's good for business because when the doors open, I'll be on TV around the world – wearing a T-shirt with the Gary's Gadgets logo.' Janice and Damian, who are second and third in the line, are also there for the money. 'We came here ten days ago, just to make sure we were first,' says Janice. 'But then Bob offered us $2500 to move ahead of us.'

4 ___ 'For me, it's a social event,' says a man named Mo. 'It's a great way to meet people who share my love of gadgets. I've had some amazing conversations in this line. Many of us come every year, so it feels like meeting old friends.' A woman named Ruby agrees, 'It's like going to a pop concert or a live sports game. I love the feeling of being at an important place at an important time.'

5 ___ 'I'm only here because of the special offer: 25 percent off for the first 200 customers,' explains a stressed-looking young woman named Lucy, 'so I'll be really annoyed if I'm number 201!' Her best friend, Fiona, looks annoyed already. 'I'm only here to keep Lucy company,' she says. 'I actually think it's a waste of time and money. I've been here all night and I'm really cold. I mean, this new phone looks exactly the same as last year's!' But Lucy looks shocked. 'There's only one difference that counts: the difference between the best … and second best.'

C **READ FOR GIST** Read the article. Match the topic sentences (a–e) with the paragraphs (1–5).

D **READ FOR DETAIL** Read again. Write *B* (Bob), *J* (Janice), *M* (Mo), *R* (Ruby), *L* (Lucy) or *F* (Fiona).

Which person …

1 has met people from the line at events like this before? M
2 paid to be at the front of the line? ___
3 doesn't want to buy a phone at all? ___
4 compares the experience to other exciting events? ___
5 arrived before anyone else? ___
6 enjoys talking to other people about gadgets? ___
7 is hoping to save some money? ___

E **SPEAK** Work in groups. Do you think it is right to call people who buy the latest gadgets *innovators*? Why/Why not?

Glossary

gadget (n) a small tool or piece of equipment that does something useful or impressive, sometimes using new technology
innovative (adj) new, original and advanced
innovator (n) a person who invents or begins using new ideas, methods, equipment, etc.

GRAMMAR

Conditionals with modals and imperatives

A **WORK IT OUT** Read the rules. Then look at paragraph 1 of *If you really can't wait …* again and complete the examples.

Conditionals with modals and imperatives

Zero conditionals and first conditionals are very common. They can be very varied. Many patterns are possible.

For example, we can use imperatives in the result clause:

If you really need that phone right now, ¹__________ *the back of the line.*

We can use modal verbs (e.g. *should, might, can, must*) in the *if*-clause or the result clause:

If you don't want to stand in line all night, you ²__________ *to the store this afternoon.*

If you ³__________ *six months or so, the same phone will cost half the price.*

B Go to the Grammar Hub on page X.

C **SPEAK** Work in pairs. Write five pieces of advice for people who are thinking of standing in line for the latest cell phone. Use these ideas and your own ideas:

- If you want to be at the front of the line, you should …
- If you can't afford a new phone right now, …
- If somebody offers you $2500 for your place in the line, …

SPEAKING HUB

A Work in pairs. Choose a gadget you both know well (e.g. phone, camera, laptop, webcam). You are going to give some advice to a friend who wants to buy one of these gadgets. Write notes on:

- price (simple version / best version?)
- features (what must/should it have?)
- risks (what might go wrong with it?)

B **SPEAK** Work in new pairs. Take turns role-playing the conversation. Student A is the friend who needs advice. Student B gives advice.

A: I don't know anything about photography. Do you have any recommendations for a new camera?

B: Well, it does really depend on how much you want to spend …

C **DISCUSS** What was the best advice you received? Would you buy the gadget your partner recommended?

Use positive language to promote a new product

Give a friend advice about choosing a gadget

8.3 Flat-packed

F – give and follow instructions   P – sentence stress

COMPREHENSION

A Work in pairs and discuss the questions.

- Have you ever tried to build a piece of furniture or put up a shelf?
- How would you describe the experience – successful, frustrating, etc?
- Are you good at giving and following instructions?

B Match the words in the box with the tools in the pictures (a–d). Which tools do you think Sam and Zac will need to build a shelf?

allen key   drill   hammer   helmet
pliers   screwdriver   spanner   tape measure

a

b

c

d

C ▶ 00:00–02:53 Watch the first part of the video. How many tools do they use?

D ▶ 00:00–02:53 Put the instructions in the correct order (1–5). Watch the first part again and check your answers.

___ Lay out all the pieces in a row.
___ Insert the screws on both sides.
___ Put the screws into the correct holes.
___ Take the packet of screws.
___ Organize all of the pieces into the correct order.

E ▶ 02:54–04:13 How is Sam feeling and why? Watch the second part of the video to check your ideas.

FUNCTIONAL LANGUAGE

Giving and following instructions

A ▶ 02:54–04:13 Complete the phrases with the words in the box. Then watch the second part of the video again to check your answers.

after   again   correct   do   how   let   sure   that   thing

Sequencing

1 The first ____________ to do is …
2 When you've done ____________ …
3 ____________ that, you …

Explaining

4 Make ____________ you …
5 ____________ me show you …
6 This is how you ____________ it.

Checking

7 Sorry, can you say that ____________.
8 Is this ____________ you do it?
9 Are you sure this is ____________?

Glossary

allen key **(n) (British)** = allen wrench **(n) (American)**
flat-packed **(adj.) (British)** = ready-to-assemble **(adj.) (American)**
spanner **(n) (British)** = wrench **(n) (American)**

MILLY SAM NEENA ZAC GABY

B Work in pairs. Cover the functional language in Exercise A, and add sequencing phrases to the instructions in Comprehension Exercise D.

1 *The first thing to do is to organize all of the pieces into the correct order.*
2 ______
3 ______
4 ______
5 ______

USEFUL PHRASES

A Who says it? *Sam*, *Zac* or *Gaby*?

1 I know when something's wrong with you. ______
2 It's complicated. ______
3 She's been acting strangely around me. ______
4 A bit cold and unfriendly. ______
5 Whatever! ______

B How would you describe how each person feels in Exercise A? Choose the most appropriate adjective for each phrase.

concerned confused puzzled uninterested upset

C How do you say these useful phrases in your language?

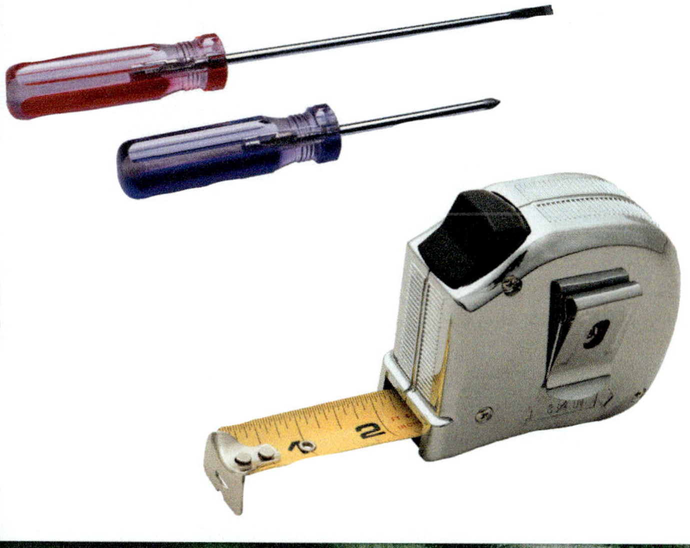

PRONUNCIATION
Sentence stress

8.7 **A** Underline the stressed words in the sentences (1–7). Then listen and check.

1 The first thing to do is to organize all of the pieces into the correct order.
2 Sorry, can you say that again?
3 What did you say?
4 When you've done that, take the packet of screws.
5 After that, you put the screws into the correct holes.
6 Is this how you do it?
7 Are you sure this is correct?

B Work in pairs. Practice saying the instructions in Exercise A, paying attention to the sentence stress.

SPEAKING

Work in pairs. Student A – go to the Communication Hub on page XX. Student B – go to the Communication Hub on page XXII. Follow the instructions.

Give and follow instructions

➤ Turn to page XXVI to learn how to write a biography.

GRAMMAR

A Complete the dialogue with the adjective clauses in the box.

when which who

A: Hey, I like your watch. Is it new?

B: Yeah, I bought it last week [1]________________ I was in Boston. It has a built-in phone and a button [2]________________ you press to connect to the internet.

A: Cool. So what's the time?

B: Uh … I don't know. It worked for the man [3]________________ sold it to me, but when I took it home, it didn't work at all.

B Choose the correct words to complete the article.

The liter of light

If [1]***you want / you'll want*** to make a difference in people's lives, a good, simple idea is best.
Brazilian engineer Alfredo Moser noticed that many people in his country live in houses with no electricity. Of course, if [2]***there'll be / there's*** no electricity, the houses are usually very dark.
It's hard for people to read or study at home [3]***if / unless*** they have enough light.
Alfredo's solution? Cut a hole in your roof and put a plastic water bottle through the hole. If [4]***you do / you'll do*** it properly, the light will fill your house.

C Match the beginnings of the sentences (1–5) with the endings (a–e).

1 If you can't think of any good ideas,
2 If you must have the new phone today,
3 If you wear your smartwatch in the bathtub,
4 You shouldn't watch TV all the time
5 Don't worry

a if you're late – I'll wait for you.
b it might stop working properly.
c if you want to be more creative.
d join the line outside the store.
e go for a long walk.

VOCABULARY

A Complete the sentences with the correct form of the words in parentheses.

1 My old website looked horrible, so I asked my sister to ________________ (*designer*) a new one for me.
2 A great ________________ (*produce*) is one that makes a difference.
3 This machine's broken again! Can you call an ________________ (*engineering*) to come and fix it?
4 We've tried really hard, but we haven't had much ________________ (*succeed*) yet.
5 You just copied all my ideas! That isn't very ________________ (*innovate*), is it?

B Complete the advice with one word in each space.

Do you find it hard to come up [1]________________ new ideas? Try these techniques to boost your creativity!

- If your mind goes [2]________________, you probably need to take a break.
- Too much TV can block your creativity. Try to [3]________________ completely.
- Try to relax and [4]________________ your mind wander freely.
- Don't follow rules that don't exist! Learn to think outside the [5]________________!
- Talk to a friend. This will help you to look at your problems [6]________________ the outside.

C Complete the sentences with the best adjectives from the box.

gorgeous impressive sensible sophisticated suitable unique

1 Each user has a ________________ username and password – it can't be the same as anybody else's.
2 **A:** 'I built a laptop computer in my garage when I was ten years old.'
B: 'Wow! That's ________________!'
3 This camera isn't really ________________ for taking underwater pictures. If water gets into the electronics, it might break.
4 The best thing about my watch is that it looks ________________. Isn't it beautiful!
5 You can buy a simple microphone in the grocery store, but if you need something more ________________, with lots more options, you need to go to a specialist store.
6 It's fine to use another person's computer, but you need to be ________________. For example, don't use it to check your bank account.

FUNCTIONAL LANGUAGE

Correct the mistake in each part of the dialogue.

1 **A:** OK, here are the instructions for the table. Let's build this! The first thing do is take everything out of the box.
2 **B:** After that, put the legs on. Careful don't to lose the screws.
3 **A:** This is how you do it?
4 **B:** No, no, no! Those are the wrong screws. Let show you how to do it.
5 **A:** Are you sure this correct is? It looks wrong! Give me the instructions.

9 THE ARTS

> Art is unquestionably one of the purest and highest elements in human happiness.
>
> John Lubbock

A young man comes face to face with nature in a London gallery.

OBJECTIVES

- suggest improvements to a proposal
- plan an arts event
- report a conversation
- create a collaborative story
- talk about movies and books
- write a review

Work with a partner. Discuss the questions.

1 Look at the picture. Do you think this is art?

2 Look at the quote. Do you agree? Why/ Why not?

3 Which of the arts do you like? What do you not like? Why? Are the arts important? Why/Why not?

9.1 Art for everybody

- Suggest improvements to a proposal
- Plan an arts event

V – the arts; verbal idioms G – second conditional P – /ʧ/, /ʃ/ and /k/
S – using linking words to understand the writer's opinion

A NEW ARTS VENUE FOR THE CITY CENTER

After the recent closure of a furniture factory in the city center, the city council has become the owner of a large warehouse. Council members voted last week to turn the warehouse into a major public arts venue. There will be a competition to choose the best use of the space. Please visit the council website for information on how to submit a proposal.
The warehouse consists of a large empty hall (120 m x 150 m), with offices upstairs.

LISTENING

A Look at the picture and read the article above. What would you like to use the warehouse for?

9.1 **B LISTEN FOR GIST** Listen to the three finalists from the competition speaking at a council meeting. Match the finalists (1–3) with the pictures (a–c).

1 Leon MacGregor ___
2 Violet Spring ___
3 Florian Quirk ___

9.1 **C LISTEN FOR DETAIL** Listen again. Choose the correct answers.

1 Who does Leon mostly want to help?
  - a people who don't work now
  - b professional musicians
  - c people who go out frequently

2 What exactly is Leon's dream?
  - a to teach people to play musical instruments
  - b to bring people together to learn new skills
  - c to make money by selling tickets to concerts

3 Why do people travel to other cities to visit the theater?
  - a because they are open every day
  - b because there's no theater in their own city
  - c because they don't want to spend their money at the Grand Theater

4 What is special about immersive theater?
  - a The audience is on the stage with the actors.
  - b Tickets are a lot more expensive than for other plays.
  - c The audience doesn't just watch the play.

5 Why does Florian think art is important?
  - a It makes money that can be spent on roads and schools.
  - b It helps you to understand new ideas.
  - c It helps you to relax when you're stressed.

6 How will Florian's idea help the people of the city?
  - a It will give them a place to perform.
  - b It will help the city's artists to sell their paintings.
  - c It will make them think in a different way.

D SPEAK Work in pairs. Which proposal sounds the most interesting? Explain why.

a

b

c

VOCABULARY
The arts

A Complete the table with the words in the box. Some words can go in more than one place.

~~an audience~~ a choir a display an exhibit a gallery an instrument a live concert a musician an orchestra to perform live a performance a recording studio a rehearsal room to rehearse a scene a spectator a stage

Theater	Art (e.g. paintings)	Music
an audience		an audience

B What other words can you add to each group? Think about people and places connected with each topic.

C SPEAK Work in pairs and ask and answer the questions.

1 Do you ever rehearse what you are going to say before you say it? Think of examples.

2 Do you prefer to be a performer on a stage or a member of the audience? Why?

3 Can you play any musical instruments? Would you like to?

GRAMMAR
Second conditional

A WORK IT OUT Work in pairs. Look at the sentences (a–d) from the council meeting and discuss the questions (1–3).

a If we open a community music center, it will change thousands of people's lives.

b If we turned the warehouse into a theater, it would make a lot of money.

c If we had a good, modern theater in this city, it would be extremely popular.

d If the city council had three warehouses, maybe we could do all of those wonderful things.

1 Sentences **a** and **b** are both about the future. Which speaker is more certain that their plans will really happen?

2 In sentence **c**, does the city have a theater right now?

3 In sentence **d**, does the city council have three warehouses? Can they do all three things?

B Complete the rules with the words in the box.

could base past unreal were

Second conditional

1 Conditional sentences usually have two clauses: the *if*-clause and the result clause. To make second conditional sentences, we use *If* + simple ______________ and *would* + ______________ form of the verb.

2 With the verb *be*, we use ______________ instead of *was*.

If I were you, I'd vote for the first proposal.

3 We use the second conditional to talk about ______________ or impossible situations in the present or future.

4 If we are not sure of the result, we can use *might* or ______________ instead of *would* in the result clause.

C Go to the Grammar Hub on page XII.

D SPEAK Work in pairs and discuss the questions.

1 How would you feel if somebody asked you to sing in public?

2 If you were a successful musician, what sort of music would you play?

SPEAKING

A Work in pairs. Student A – read the box below. Student B – go to the Communication Hub on page XXI. Student C – go to the Communication Hub on page XXII. Read about one of the proposals for the Warehouse Project. Write about the advantages and disadvantages.

Proposal 1: Community music center

Costs (= money going out)		Income (= money coming in)
Building work: $450,000	Employees: $50,000/year	None – everything will be free for community groups
Equipment: $350,000	Other costs (e.g. electricity): $100,000/ year	

- The community music center will save money by only opening for a few hours each day.
- Rehearsals/Workshops: Mondays, Wednesdays and Fridays, 10 am to 3 pm
- Concerts: Tuesdays and Thursdays, 12 pm to 2 pm
- Evenings and weekends: closed

B Tell your partner about your proposal. Then discuss what you like about each one. Suggest some improvements.

C Decide which proposal should win the competition. Why? Then share your ideas with the class.

READING

A SPEAK Work in pairs. Imagine you are watching a traditional play. What would you do if a character on the stage spoke to you? Would you be happy or would you feel uncomfortable?

B READ FOR MAIN IDEA Read the first paragraph of *The best (and the worst) of immersive theater*. Why has the writer written the article?

C READ FOR GIST Read the rest of the article. Match the recommendations (a–g) with the sections (1–6). There is one extra recommendation.

a Keep it simple.
b Tell a story.
c Make the audience feel special.
d Make it an experience for all the senses.
e Keep ticket prices as low as possible.
f Keep the rest of the audience out of sight.
g Make good use of the space.

The best (and the worst) of **immersive theater**

For most people, going to the theater is a chance to relax and let the actors do all the work. But in recent years, a new type of theater has appeared where the audience takes part in the play! When it works well, immersive theater can be breathtaking. But when it goes wrong, it can be awful. Here are my six recommendations based on my favorite (and least favorite!) immersive plays.

1 ___

Sometimes the building itself is part of the experience. A good example is *Hotel Impossible*, which took place in a real hotel building. Similarly, *The Dark Tunnels* took place inside real tunnels, which created a very scary atmosphere. However, a great location isn't everything. *Dangerous Heart* was in a beautiful palace, but the play didn't really take advantage of the space.

2 ___

In *Step by Step*, the audience was limited to 15, so we could interact one-on-one with the characters. During the play, the audience had to solve a crime, so we really had to pay attention to what we saw and heard. By the end, I was terrified and exhausted, but it was an unforgettable experience.

3 ___

Some immersive plays feel far too complicated, with too many characters and storylines. For example, *Yellow and Blue* had amazing special effects, but I couldn't keep track of who was who. In *The Quiet Visitors*, however, there were only six characters in a large empty room. We had to use our imaginations, and the effect was incredibly powerful.

4 ___

The worst thing about immersive theater? Other members of the audience! The play *Life with the Lions* got rid of this problem by making the audience wear animal costumes. I felt silly in my zebra costume, but at least we couldn't tell the difference between actors and spectators. In *The Dark Tunnels*, we all wore black clothes and masks so the members of the audience were almost invisible to each other.

5 ___

Without a strong story, immersive theater can easily fall flat – it feels like something's missing. In *Hotel Impossible*, for example, lots of interesting things happened, but the whole play didn't really go anywhere. In *The Quiet Visitors*, however, there was a clear beginning, a middle ... and a shocking surprise at the end.

6 ___

It isn't just about what the audience sees and hears. The best immersive plays make use of the senses of taste, smell and touch, too. In *Dangerous Heart*, we enjoyed a delicious meal as part of the experience. Similarly, in *The Dark Tunnels*, the unpleasant underground smell added to the sense of danger. And in *The Quiet Visitors*, when the room suddenly went as cold as ice, the effect was terrifying.

D Look at the highlighted words in the article. What is the writer's opinion? Use the strategies in the box to help you. Choose + (positive) or – (negative).

Using linking words to understand the writer's opinion

When you're trying to figure out the writer's opinion, don't just look for positive words (e.g. *amazing*, *interesting*) and negative words (e.g. *unpleasant*, *terrifying*).

Writers regularly use words like *for example*, *similarly* and *however* to link their opinions to earlier sentences.

1. the location for *The Dark Tunnels* + / –
2. the characters and story in *Yellow and Blue* + / –
3. the characters and story in *The Quiet Visitors* + / –
4. the story in *Hotel Impossible* + / –
5. the experience for the senses in *The Dark Tunnels* + / –
6. the experience for the senses in *The Quiet Visitors* + / –

E SPEAK Work in pairs. Which of the plays from the article would you most like to see? Which would you least like to see? Why? Tell your partner.

VOCABULARY

Verbal idioms

Verbal idioms

Verbal idioms are fixed phrases that work as verbs with a single meaning.

A Go to the Vocabulary Hub on page XVIII.

B SPEAK Complete the sentences so they are true for you. Then work in pairs and tell your partner what happened.

1. I had an opportunity to … but I didn't take advantage of it, because …
2. Everything went wrong when I …
3. I'm planning to get rid of …
4. I once tried to (tell a joke/story, etc.), but it fell flat, because …

PRONUNCIATION

/ʧ/, /ʃ/ and /k/

9.2 **A** How do you pronounce *ch* in these words? Listen and repeat.

character charge chef choice choir orchestra

ch

ch is usually pronounced /ʧ/ (as in *cheese*). But there are also a few words where *ch* is pronounced /ʃ/ (as in *mustache*) or /k/ (as in *chemist*).

B Find and underline *ch* in these sentences. Then write /ʧ/, /ʃ/ or /k/ above each example.

/ʧ/

1. My children didn't go to school today – they both had bad stomachaches.
2. If I were a mechanic, I might be able to fix this machine, but I don't know anything about technology.
3. My sister is a chemist; she's doing some research into new techniques for recycling harmful chemicals.

9.3 **C** Listen and check.

D SPEAK Work in pairs. Practice saying the sentences. Listen and check your partner's pronunciation.

SPEAKING HUB

A Work in groups. Discuss ideas for an immersive theater performance. Think about:

- story: Will you use an existing story or create your own?
- location: Where will it take place? How could you make use of the location?
- interactivity: How will the actors interact with the audience?

B PLAN Choose your best idea and add more details. Follow the advice in *The best (and the worst) of immersive theater* on page 100.

C PRESENT Present your idea to the class.

D REFLECT Which immersive play would you most like to watch? Why?

Suggest improvements to a proposal

Plan an arts event

9.2 Tell me a story

- Report a conversation
- Create a collaborative story

G – reported speech   V – reporting verbs   P – using your voice to make a story more interesting
S – listening for definitions of new words

Francis Scott Key Fitzgerald (1896–1940) was one of the most important American writers of the 20th century. His best-known novel, *The Great Gatsby* (1925), is an American classic. It paints a powerful portrait of life in 1920s America, a period known as the Jazz Age. For many young people in America, this was a time for partying and having fun, with new types of music, new ways of dancing and new fashions.

READING

A Work in pairs. Read about F. Scott Fitzgerald and look at the pictures. Have you read *The Great Gatsby*? Why do you think it is 'an American classic'?

I haven't read the book but I have seen the movie starring Leonardo DiCaprio.

9.4 **B** Listen to a conversation between two friends, Joe and Nadia. Answer the questions.

1 Who is Jay Gatsby?

2 Why doesn't Joe want to borrow the book? Why does he change his mind?

3 Why does Nadia like the book?

CHAPTER 3: I MEET GATSBY

PART 1

One day, I was invited to one of Gatsby's parties. As soon as I arrived, I began to look for Gatsby to thank him for his invitation. But no one knew where he was.

As I went to get a drink, I saw Jordan Baker. I walked toward her, glad to see someone I knew.

'I thought you might be here,' Jordan said.

We took our drinks and sat down at a small table under a tree. Jordan began to talk to a girl in a yellow dress.

'Do you come to these parties often?' Jordan asked her.

'I come when I can,' the girl said. 'No one cares what I do, so I always have a good time. Last time I was here, I tore my dress. Do you know, Gatsby sent me a new one! It cost him 265 dollars!'

PART 2

Supper was now being served. Jordan and I left our table and went to look for Gatsby.

People were dancing now. The voices and the laughter were very loud. The moon was high in the sky.

Jordan and I sat down at a table with a well-dressed man of my own age. I was enjoying myself, now. The music stopped for a moment. The man at our table looked at me and smiled.

'I think I know your face,' the man said. 'Weren't you in France during the War?'

'Yes, I was.'

'Me, too,' he said. We talked about the War for a few minutes. Then the man told me that **he had a new motorboat.**

'Want to go out with me in the morning, old sport?' he asked.

'Sure, what time?'

'Let's say nine o'clock.'

I looked at the yard and smiled.

'This is an unusual party,' I told the man. 'I haven't seen my host yet. Gatsby sent me an invitation this morning. I ought to thank him.'

The man stared at me in surprise.

'I'm Gatsby,' he said. 'I thought you knew, old sport. I'm not a very good host, am I?'

Gatsby smiled. He had a pleasant smile. His smile made me feel important. I looked at Gatsby with interest. He was a tough-looking young man, but he had beautiful clothes and beautiful manners.

PART 3

A few guests were standing near Gatsby. I went up to him to say goodbye.

'Don't forget we're going out in the boat, old sport,' he said. 'At nine o'clock.'

Gatsby smiled at me.

'Goodnight, old sport, goodnight.'

I walked across the lawn in the moonlight. The cars drove away. The yard was quiet and empty.

All alone, Gatsby stood on the white steps, waving goodbye.

Glossary

old sport (phrase) a popular way of saying 'my friend' in the 1920s

C READ FOR DETAIL Read *The Great Gatsby*, Chapter 3, Part 1. Are the sentences true (T) or false (F)? Correct the false sentences.

1 Gatsby invited Nick Carraway (the storyteller) to his party. ___
2 Nick already knew most of the people at the party. ___
3 Jordan was surprised to see Nick. ___
4 Gatsby is very careful with his money. ___

D Read Part 2. What do we learn about Gatsby? Write notes on:

1 his appearance (= his clothes and the way he looks).
2 his manners (= the way he treats other people).
3 his background (= what he has done in the past).

E Read Part 3. Why do you think Gatsby has so many parties?

GRAMMAR
Reported speech

A WORK IT OUT Look at the phrase in bold from *The Great Gatsby*, Chapter 3, Part 2. What do you think Gatsby actually said?

Direct speech: 'I ________________ a new motorboat.'

B Complete the examples in the correct tense.

Direct speech	Reported speech
Simple present 'My name's Jay Gatsby.'	Simple past He told me his name 1 ________________ Jay Gatsby.
Present progressive 'I'm really enjoying the party.'	Past progressive I told him I 2 ________________ really enjoying the party.
Present perfect 'I've never met Gatsby.'	Past perfect He said he 3 ________________ never met Gatsby.
Simple past 'Gatsby sent me a new dress.'	Past perfect She said Gatsby 4 ________________ sent her a new dress.
can 'I can't see the host.'	*could* I told him I 5 ________________ see the host.
will 'We'll have a great time on my boat.'	*would* He said we 6 ________________ have a great time on his boat.

C Go to the Grammar Hub on page XII.

D Report the sentences (1–5) from *The Great Gatsby*.

1 'Do you come to these parties often?' Jordan asked her.
Jordan asked the girl if she came to these parties often.

2 'I come when I can,' the girl said.
____
____

3 'I think I know your face,' the man said.
____
____

4 'This is an unusual party,' I told the man. 'I haven't seen my host yet.'
____
____

5 'Gatsby sent me an invitation this morning.'
____
____

E SPEAK Work in pairs. Use your imagination to tell the next part of the story. Report the conversation between Jay and Nick the next morning.

SPEAKING

A Think about the questions below. Write notes.

1 Do you read a lot of novels? What sort of books do you enjoy? Which books would you recommend? Why?
2 Do you ever read books in English? What have you read? Did you find it easy or difficult? Do you need to understand every word or can you simply relax and enjoy the story?

B Work in pairs. Ask and answer the questions from Exercise A. Ask follow-up questions and give examples.

C Work with a new partner. Tell your new partner about your conversation.

LISTENING

A SPEAK Work in groups and discuss the questions.

1 What are some situations where people tell each other stories?
2 Are stories just for fun, or do they have a serious purpose?
3 Do you like telling stories? What kind of stories?
4 What skills do you need to tell great stories? When was the last time you told a story?
   - Where were you?
   - Who did you tell it to?
   - Why did you tell it?
   - What was the story about?

9.5 **B LISTEN FOR GIST** Listen to the conversation between two friends, Zoe and Jacob. They are talking about storytelling. Put the pictures (a–c) in the order that they discuss them (1–3).

1 ___ 2 ___ 3 ___

Glossary

dice (n) a small block of wood or plastic with six sides marked with spots that you roll or throw to play a game

end up (with) (phrasal verb) to be in a particular place or state after doing something or because of doing it

a

b

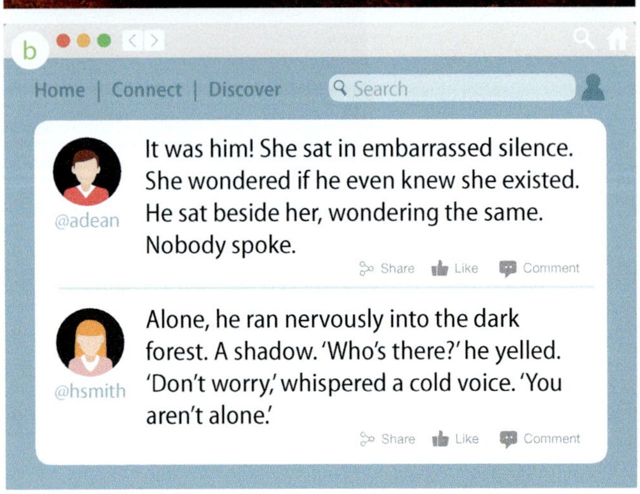

9.5 **C LISTEN FOR KEY WORDS** Listen again and complete the definitions of the new words. Use the strategies in the box to help you.

Listening for definitions of new words

Speakers usually pause before and after an important new word. They usually place extra stress on the word itself.

When you hear an important new word, listen carefully for a definition or explanation.

1 Flash fiction: A story with a word limit, usually ________________ words.
2 Micro-stories: These are stories on social ________________ sites (e.g. Twitter). A whole story told in a ________________-character message.
3 A twist: When something happens in the story that you didn't ________________.
4 Collaborative stories: Stories that are created by a large group of people working ________________.
5 Pass the paper: You write one line of a ________________ on a sheet of paper, fold it down and pass it to the next player, who writes the next ________________, and so on.
6 Add a word: You sit in a ________________. The first person says the first ________________ from a sentence, and then the next person says the next word.
7 Story dice: A set of ________________ dice, and each one has six ________________, one on each side.

D SPEAK Work in groups. Play *Add a word*.

E DISCUSS Work in groups and discuss the questions.

1 Have you ever played any of the games or tried any of the story techniques mentioned in the conversation? Would you like to?
2 Do you think word limits make it easier or harder to write a good story?
3 Do you prefer working collaboratively or by yourself?

c

VOCABULARY

Reporting verbs

A Look at the examples of micro-stories in Listening Exercise B, picture b. Which verbs are used instead of *say* and *think*? Why?

B Look at the information in the box. Use a dictionary to check any new verbs.

> **Reporting verbs**
>
> Instead of using *say* and *tell*, we can use more interesting and descriptive reporting verbs.
>
> verb (+ *that*) + reported speech: *add, admit, agree, argue, explain, insist, mention, predict, promise, repeat, reply, say, yell, warn, whisper*
>
> verb + somebody (+ *that*) + reported speech: *advise, persuade, promise, remind, tell, warn*
>
> verb + reported question: *ask, explain, wonder*
>
> verb + infinitive: *agree, ask, promise, refuse*
>
> verb + somebody + infinitive: *advise, ask, persuade, promise, remind, tell, warn*

C Choose the best reporting verbs to complete the sentences from the conversation between Zoe and Jacob.

1. Zoe asked how Jacob's creative writing class was going, and he ***added / reminded / replied*** that it was going really well.
2. Zoe ***agreed / mentioned / wondered*** whether Jacob was joking about micro-stories.
3. Jacob ***persuaded / warned / whispered*** Zoe that it's usually better if the writer provides less information.
4. Zoe ***agreed / insisted / predicted*** that the second story was really powerful.
5. Zoe ***added / explained / persuaded*** how 'Pass the paper' works.
6. Zoe ***agreed / promised / yelled*** that Jacob would enjoy playing 'Pass the paper', but Jacob ***admitted / insisted / refused*** to play.
7. Jacob ***admitted / predicted / yelled*** that most of the stories are trash.
8. Zoe ***argued / explained / mentioned*** that she had been a student in California.
9. Jacob ***argued / predicted / reminded*** Zoe that the story could have up to 1,000 words.
10. Jacob ***insisted / warned / whispered*** Zoe that it wouldn't be easy to write the story.

PRONUNCIATION

Using your voice to make a story more interesting

9.6 **A** Listen again to Jacob reading the two micro-stories. How does he use his voice to make the stories sound more interesting? Think about:

- speaking quickly, slowly, loudly or quietly.
- showing emotions.
- pausing.

B SPEAK Work in pairs. Look at the audio script on page XXXII. Take turns reading the two stories aloud. Try to use your voice to make the stories sound more interesting.

C SPEAK Look at the story you wrote in Listening Exercise D. How can you use your voice to make it sound more interesting? Read your story to the class.

D REFLECT Work in groups. Which is the best story? Which storyteller used his/her voice most effectively?

SPEAKING HUB

A You are going to tell a story based on four pictures. Student A – go to the Communication Hub on page XIX. Student B – go to the Communication Hub on page XXI. Look at the pictures and spend one minute thinking about your story. Do not worry if your story is not very good yet!

B SPEAK Work in pairs. Take turns telling your story. While your partner is talking, listen carefully to his/her story. You can help if your partner runs out of ideas.

C PLAN Work together to improve your stories and make them longer. Can you join your two stories together into a single story? Use these ideas to help you:

- Who exactly were the people?
- What were the characters trying to do?
- How did they feel?
- What did they say?
- What happened next?

D PRESENT Share your stories with the class. Use your voice to make them as interesting as possible.

E REFLECT Work in groups. Which story did you like best? Why? Who was the best storyteller?

- Report a conversation
- Create a collaborative story

9.3 Leaving London

F– talk about movies and books P– words connected to movies

COMPREHENSION

A Work in pairs and discuss the questions.

- What kind of movies do you like and dislike?
- Do you ever cry at movies? When was the last time?
- Do you prefer reading a book or watching the movie based on the book?

B Think of a movie you have seen recently and answer the questions.

1 What kind of movie was it? Romantic comedy, horror, etc?

2 Who was in it?

3 What kind of ending did it have?

C 00:00–03:36 Watch the first part of the video and answer the questions in Exercise B. Why is Gaby so emotional?

D 03:36–05:03 Watch the second part of the video with the volume turned off. What do you think is happening? Discuss with a partner and then watch with the volume turned up and check your ideas.

FUNCTIONAL LANGUAGE

Talking about movies

Match the two halves of phrases you can use to talk about movies. Watch the video again and check your ideas.

Talking about movies

1	If you like sad and romantic films,	a	sad ending.
2	It's got Jessica Brune in it.	b	tearjerker.
3	It's a real	c	where he writes the letter to her.
4	That was a really	d	reading.
5	It's really worth	e	amazing performance.
6	I thought the plot was good	f	Oh really, she's a brilliant actor.
7	What an	g	then this is the one for you.
8	I loved the scene	h	and it felt like real life.

USEFUL PHRASES

A Match the useful phrases (1–6) with the phrases that have a similar meaning (a–f).

1 Yeah, right!

2 Things don't always work out perfectly.

3 There's something I've been meaning to tell you.

4 We're going to miss you.

5 Do you want a hand?

6 Just finishing up here.

a There isn't always a happy ending.

b I've almost done all my work.

c We don't believe you.

d I've been waiting for the right time to say this.

e We don't want you to leave.

f Can I help you?

B How do you say these useful phrases in your language?

Glossary

brilliant **(adj.) (British)** = great/fabulous/excellent **(adj.) (American)**
film/s **(n) (British)** = movie/s **(n) (American)**

MILLY

SAM

NEENA

ZAC

GABY

PRONUNCIATION

Words connected to movies

9.7 **A** These are some of the words connected to movies that appear in the video. Put them in the correct column according to the word stress. Listen and check your answers.

actor amazing brilliant comedy ending horror movie performance ~~review~~ romantic tearjerker terrible

oO	Oo	oOo	Ooo
review			

B Work in pairs. Complete the sentences so that they are true for you. Compare with your partner.

1 The most terrible movie I've ever seen was ...
2 My favorite comedy is ...
3 The most fabulous actor in my country is ...
4 I'd give the Oscar for the most amazing performance to ...
5 The best place to read movie reviews is ...

SPEAKING

A Think of your favorite movie of all time and write notes.

1 What's the title of the movie?
2 What kind of movie is it?
3 Who stars in the movie?
4 What happens and how does it end?
5 What do you particularly like about the plot and characters?
6 How did the movie make you feel?

B **DISCUSS** Work in pairs. Take turns describing your favorite movie.

Talk about movies and books

➤ Turn to page XXVII to learn how to write a review.

Unit 9 Review

A Correct the four mistakes in the sentences.

1 I'd feel really strange if one of the actors start talking to me.

____

2 If I had a little more time, I'll come and watch the movie with you, but I'm much too busy.

____

3 If I'd know the answer, I'd tell you, but I don't so I can't.

____

4 You'd be a better actor if you can remember your lines!

____

B Change the direct speech into reported speech.

1 'My daughter is a talented artist.'
He said that ______________ a talented artist.

2 'Immersive theater is becoming a lot more popular all the time.'
She said that immersive theater ______________ a lot more popular all the time.

3 'Do you prefer reading books or watching movies?'
He asked me ______________ reading books or watching movies.

4 'I can't paint, but I can draw fairly well.'
She told me she ______________ fairly well.

5 'How much will the tickets cost?'
She asked me ______________.

6 'Be quiet! We're trying to rehearse!'
They told me ______________ because they ______________ to rehearse.

7 'Have you ever seen a famous band live in concert?'
He asked me ______________ a famous band live in concert.

VOCABULARY

A Complete the sentences with the words in the box.

choir display gallery orchestra scene spectators

Reviews

1 We went to an amazing classical music concert last week. The ______________ had over 50 musicians!

2 The play was very smart. There was an unexpected twist in the final ______________.

3 The Japanese Culture Week ended with a wonderful ______________ by a group of traditional dancers.

4 I'm a member of a ______________. There are 30 of us, and we practice singing three times a week.

5 I'm really excited. There's going to be an exhibit of my paintings at the local ______________!

6 It was such an amazing tennis game. The ______________ clapped for ten minutes!

B Read the conversation and choose the correct verb to complete the idioms.

A: So? What did you think of my short story?

B: Well, I thought it was a little too complicated. I couldn't [1]***stay* / *keep*** track of who was who.

A: Really? So do you think I should [2]***get* / *go*** rid of some of the main characters?

B: Yes, that would be much better. And some of your characters were too similar to each other. It needs to be much easier for the reader to [3]***tell* / *talk*** the difference between them.

A: OK, that's a good point. I'll try to [4]***hold* / *pay*** attention to things like that in future. Anything else?

B: The beginning was excellent, and I loved the fact that the whole story [5]***takes* / *starts*** place on a train, but then you didn't really [6]***do* / *make*** use of that idea later in the book. I think you should definitely try to [7]***take* / *make*** advantage of the train trip more.

A: OK. What did you think of the ending?

B: I thought the ending was fairly weak, so the story kind of [8]***falls* / *keeps*** flat at the end. But … apart from that, it was great.

C Match the beginnings of the sentences (1–7) with the endings (a–g).

1 'Shhh! Don't talk during the play,'
2 'You must keep your promise and come to watch the show,'
3 'The gallery might be fairly crowded tomorrow,'
4 'Don't forget to buy a ticket,'
5 'Yes, you're absolutely right,'
6 'I didn't write my story – I copied it from the internet,'
7 'Where is everybody?'

a she reminded him.
b he admitted.
c she predicted.
d he insisted.
e she wondered.
f he agreed.
g she whispered.

FUNCTIONAL LANGUAGE

Choose the correct words to complete the conversation.

A: I want to go to the movie theater tonight, but all the new movies look a little boring.

B: Really? What about *Silly Story 2*? I thought the lead actor, Max Connor, was great [1]***at* / *in* / *on* / *with*** it. If you like funny movies, it's definitely the movie [2]***by* / *for* / *of* / *to*** you.

A: Oh, yes, I saw the ad for it. But I didn't like *Silly Story 1*. The plot was really difficult to [3]***follow* / *mention* / *predict* / *record***, and it was very sad at the end.

B: Yeah, I know what you mean. But this one's much better, and it really [4]***had* / *did* / *made* / *took*** me laugh. And it has a really happy [5]***ending* / *finishing* / *starting* / *stopping***.

A: Don't tell me how it ends! You'll spoil it for me!

B: OK, sorry, but I think it's really [6]***worth* / *love* / *miss* / *recommend*** seeing. Definitely watch this movie.

10 PSYCHOLOGY

The purpose of psychology is to give us a completely different idea of the things we know best.

Paul Valéry

A hiker watches a storm approach in New South Wales, Australia.

OBJECTIVES

- talk about different versions of past events
- talk about past mistakes
- talk about your wishes and regrets
- plan a to-do list
- make and accept apologies
- write a report

Work with a partner. Discuss the questions.

1 Look at the picture. Where do you go when you want to think?

2 Look at the quote. Do you agree?

3 Work in pairs. Tell your partner what you do when you need to reflect on a problem.

10.1 Making up your mind

- Talk about different versions of past events
- Talk about past mistakes

V – psychology verbs; expressions with *mind*
P – third conditional
G – third conditional; *should have* + past participle
S – listening for phrases that support an argument

READING

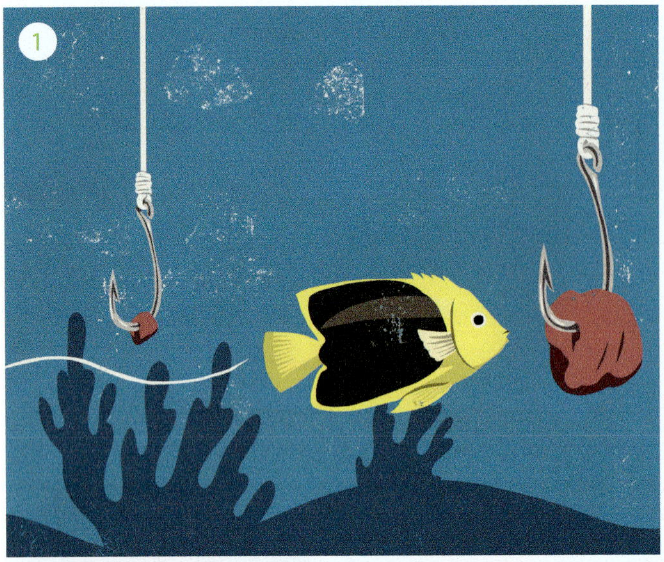

A SPEAK Work in pairs. Go the Communication Hub on page XXIII.

B READ FOR MAIN IDEA Read *Do you think you think rationally? Think again!* What is the connection between the three sub-headings and pictures 1–3 above?

C READ FOR DETAIL Read again. Are the sentences true (T) or false (F)? Correct the false sentences.

1. New research has shown that we're good at making rational decisions. ___
2. After we've thought about a hook number, it's easy to think of a number that's a long way from that hook. ___
3. We would probably make better decisions if we ignored hook numbers. ___
4. If we were more rational, we would worry more about buried costs. ___
5. In the example about the weekend break, the money you've spent on the hotel and travel is a buried cost. ___
6. Filtering involves presenting a situation in a way that makes it sound better (or worse) than it really is. ___

D SPEAK Work in pairs. Can you think of any examples of hook numbers, buried costs or filtering from your own life? Tell your partner.

DO YOU THINK YOU THINK RATIONALLY? THINK AGAIN!

For centuries, psychologists assumed that people think rationally and make decisions based on facts. But we're actually much less rational than we think.

HOOK NUMBERS

Look again at the quiz. Question 1a is clearly nonsense: of course we have more than 70 thoughts per day! So it shouldn't affect our answers to question 1b. But for most people, the number 70 acts as a hook. It encourages us to think of a number that isn't too far from 70. But if the hook number had been much higher, say 70 million, it would have made us think of a number in the millions. And if we hadn't seen a hook at all, we might have chosen a more likely answer: around 70,000 thoughts per day.
Sales people use hook numbers to persuade us to spend much more than we should, for example, by tricking us into believing a watch must be worth thousands of dollars.

BURIED COSTS

A buried cost is time, money or effort that we've already spent and can't get back. It would be rational to ignore buried costs when making decisions; they're gone, so we should forget about them. But for most of us, waste feels like physical pain, and we usually spend even more time, money and effort trying to avoid that pain. Look back at question 2 in the quiz. The money you've spent is gone. Instead of regretting the past, we should forget it and focus on the future. When you're sick, you should stay home and get better.

VOCABULARY

Psychology verbs

A Match the beginnings of the definitions (1–8) with the endings (a–h). Use *Do you think you think rationally? Think again!* to help you.

1 If something **affects** or **influences** you,
2 If you **assume** that something is true,
3 If something **attracts** you,
4 If you **avoid** doing something,
5 If you **encourage** or **persuade** somebody to do something,
6 If you **regret** something,
7 If something **tempts** you,
8 If somebody **tricks** you into doing something,

a you say something that makes him/her want to do it.
b you feel bad about something you did (or didn't do) in the past.
c they make you do it by lying or hiding the truth.
d you believe it although you haven't checked for sure.
e you are careful not to do it.
f you want it, even though it might be bad for you.
g it changes the way you think or behave.
h you like it and want to have it.

B Choose the correct verbs to complete the questions.

1 How do marketers and advertisers ***avoid*** / ***tempt*** us to buy things we don't really want or need?
2 When you go shopping, which things ***attract*** / ***influence*** your decision to buy something? Is it possible that the stores use psychological tricks to affect your choices?

C SPEAK Work in pairs. Ask and answer the questions in Exercise B.

FILTERING

In question 3 from the quiz, were you tempted by School A? That 75 percent pass rate sounds great, doesn't it? What about School B, with all those failures? No, thanks! Of course, your rational side knows that School B is better – a 20 percent failure rate means there's an 80 percent pass rate. But we can't help being influenced by words like *pass* and *fail*.
We're strongly attracted to positive words like *success*, *save* and *free*. But negative words are even more powerful. We hate *losing*, *wasting* or *missing* things. So if you see an ad that warns, 'Don't miss your last chance to save,' remember that someone is trying to trick our irrational minds.

Glossary

bury (v) to put something in the ground and cover it with earth
filter (v) if you filter a photo, you change or improve the appearance of the image before posting it on social media
hook (n) a curved piece of metal or plastic fixed to a pole or with a handle at the other end, used for catching hold of something

GRAMMAR

Third conditional

A WORK IT OUT Work in pairs. Look at the sentence from *Do you think you think rationally? Think again!* Then choose the correct words to complete the rules.

If the hook number had been much higher, say 70 million, it would have made us think of a number in the millions.

Third conditional

1 We use the third conditional to talk about imaginary situations in *the past / the present*.
2 Conditional sentences usually have *two / three* clauses: the *if*-clause and the result clause. To make a third conditional sentence, we use:
if + past perfect, *would* + *have* + past participle
3 We *can / can't* use *might* or *could* instead of *would* in the result clause.

B Find and underline another third conditional sentence in the article.

C Go to the Grammar Hub on page XIV.

D SPEAK Work in pairs. Write three third conditional sentences that are true for you. Tell your partner about the situations in your sentences.

PRONUNCIATION

Third conditional

10.1 **A** Listen and repeat the third conditional sentence. What do you notice about the pronunciation of *had*, *would* and *have*?

If I'd thought about it more carefully, I'd have made a better decision.

B SPEAK Work in pairs. Practice saying the sentences you wrote in Grammar Exercise D. Listen and check your partner's pronunciation.

SPEAKING

Work in pairs and discuss the questions.

1 Think of a time in the past when you paid too much for something or bought something you didn't really want or need. What happened? Why? What would have happened if you'd thought more carefully?
When I bought my first car, I thought it was perfect. But I didn't check whether it actually worked properly! In the end, I spent a lot of money fixing it and sold it again. If I'd …
2 Think of a time in the past when you made a bad decision because you didn't have enough information or experience. What would you have done differently if you'd known then what you know now?
I received an email from my bank last week telling me to click on a link to change my password. Luckily, I noticed that the link was to a completely different site. But if I hadn't noticed …

LISTENING

A SPEAK Work in groups and discuss the questions.

1 Do you find shopping relaxing or stressful? Why?

2 When you're shopping for clothes and shoes, do you find it easy to decide what to buy?

10.2 **B LISTEN FOR MAIN IDEA** Listen to a conversation between two friends, Robert and Vicky. What do they say about the items in the pictures (a–d)?

Glossary

common sense (n) the ability to use good judgment and make sensible decisions

paradox (n) a statement consisting of two parts that seem to mean the opposite of each other

perfectionist (n) someone who always wants things to be done perfectly

a

b

c

d

10.2 **C** Listen again. How does Robert support his arguments? Use the strategies in the box to help you.

Listening for phrases that support an argument

Sometimes when you listen, you need to decide how strong a person's arguments are. Pay attention to the techniques they use to support their argument.

Common sense:

- *Surely, Of course, Obviously, Clearly, As you can imagine, …*

Facts and statistics:

- *In fact, …; The researchers found that …*

Examples and details:

- *For example, …; For instance, …*

Expert opinions:

- *According to Professor Schwartz …; He's shown that …*

10.2 **D LISTEN FOR DETAIL** Listen again. Complete the notes about the conversations.

1 **The Paradox of Choice:** According to Professor Barry Schwartz (an __American__ psychologist), too many ______________ makes us ______________.

2 **Shampoo company:** Cut choices from ______________ to ______________. Sales went up by ______________ percent.

3 **Robert's experience of buying a laptop:** He went to a small store with ______________ laptops to choose from. Took ______________ minutes to choose and buy a laptop.

4 **Perfectionists regret their choices:** Vicky bought ______________ different pairs of shoes, but took each pair back to the store.

5 **Quick deciders don't worry about perfection:** When Robert finds jeans that are ______________ enough, he buys them and stops worrying. Only takes them back to store if they're ______________.

E SPEAK Work in groups and discuss the questions.

1 Have you ever experienced the Paradox of Choice? Think about the following situations:
   - shopping
   - choosing what to watch on TV or online
   - making important life decisions
   - cooking or eating

2 Are you a perfectionist or a quick decider? What about other people in your family?

3 How can stores, websites and other businesses help us deal with the Paradox of Choice?

GRAMMAR

should have + past participle

A WORK IT OUT Look at the sentences from the conversation between Vicky and Robert. Then choose the correct words to complete the rules.

So with your laptop, you **should have gone** to a smaller store.

I realized that they weren't perfect and I **shouldn't have bought** them.

should have + past participle

1 We write *should* (*not*) + *have* + past participle / base form.

2 We use *should have done* to talk about mistakes that we *make* / *made* in the past and imagine how we could have avoided those mistakes.

B Go to the Grammar Hub on page XIV.

C SPEAK Work in pairs. Use *should/shouldn't have done* to talk about these situations.

1 Angela went shopping for a new coat. She found a great coat in the first store, but she went to ten more stores to make sure it was the best one. When she went back to buy it, somebody else had bought it.

2 Kasia bought a used computer five years ago, but it didn't work properly. Although she had enough money to buy a new one, she kept using the old one for years.

VOCABULARY

Expressions with *mind*

10.2

A Complete the sentences (1–8) from the conversation with the expressions in the box. Then listen again and check your answers.

all in the mind | bear in mind | change my mind | of two minds | made up my mind | never mind | put your mind to | would you mind if

1 ________________ I borrowed your laptop for a few minutes?

2 Just ________________ that it's really slow.

3 I found two that I liked, but I was ________________ and I couldn't decide which one to buy.

4 But ________________. I still have my old computer, so it isn't so bad.

5 Once I've ________________, I stick with my decision.

6 You think it's impossible, but maybe it's ________________.

7 I think you can become a quick decider – you just need to ________________ it!

8 But what if I ________________ later?

B SPEAK Work in pairs. What do you think the expressions in Exercise A mean?

C SPEAK Work in pairs and discuss the questions.

1 Quick deciders are generally less stressed, but there are some dangers connected with making quick decisions. What should they **bear in mind** before making a decision?

2 How long does it usually take you to **make up your mind** about whether you can trust somebody? What might make you **change your mind** about them?

SPEAKING HUB

A Read the sentences about regrets. Do you agree or disagree with them? Why?

1 You should never regret anything. Your mistakes are part of who you are.

2 You should regret the things you haven't done more than the things you have done.

B Think about two or three mistakes you have made in the past. What did you do? What did you not do? What should or should you not have done?

C Work in pairs. Tell your partner about some of the mistakes you have made. While your partner is talking, listen carefully, and then ask questions to find out more information.

Finding out more information

Really? So what did you do? Why did you do that?

What do you think you should have done?

But if you hadn't done that, what do you think would have happened?

D Work in pairs and discuss the questions.

1 What can you learn from the mistakes you have made in the past?

2 What would you do differently if you were in the same situation in the future?

3 Is it good to talk about past mistakes?

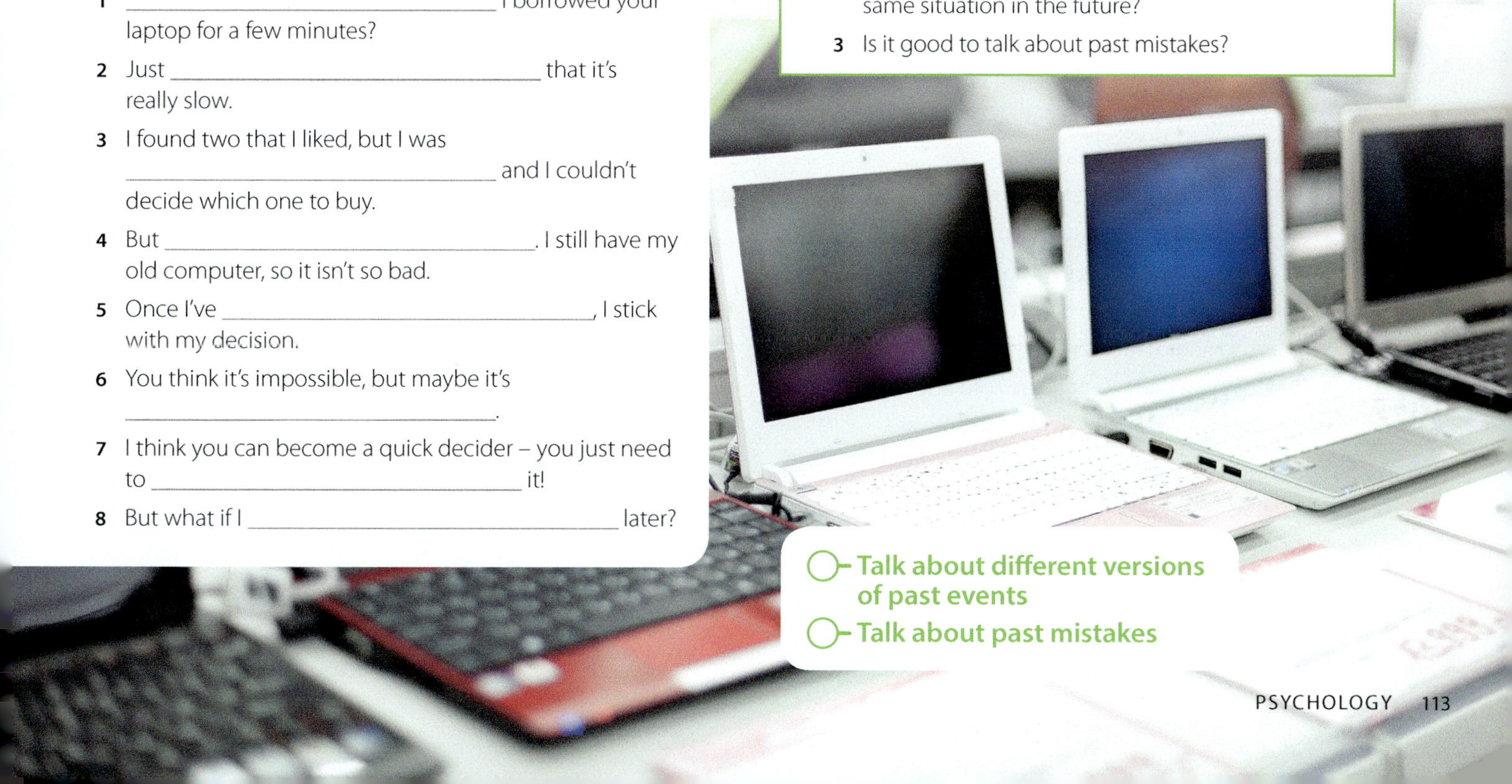

- Talk about different versions of past events
- Talk about past mistakes

10.2 Wish lists

- Talk about your wishes and regrets
- Plan a to-do list

V – reflexive verbs; staying organized
S – bridge sentences
P – emphasis and reflexive pronouns
G – hopes and wishes

LISTENING

A SPEAK Work in pairs and discuss the questions.

1. Do you have any habits that you'd like to stop?
2. Are there any good habits that you'd like to start?
3. How easy is it to change your habits?
4. Look at the diagram. What do you think it shows?

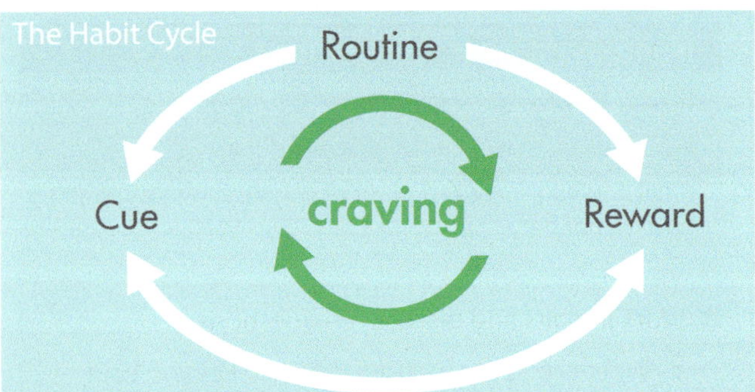

10.3 **B LISTEN FOR GIST** Listen to a radio show about habits. Which habits in the pictures do the speakers talk about?

10.3 **C LISTEN FOR DETAIL** Listen again and choose the correct answers.

1. What is David's main cue for eating fast food?
   a. He sees a sign while he's driving.
   b. He smells food in a shopping mall.
2. What happens when a routine is part of a true habit?
   a. You can follow the steps without thinking.
   b. You do it although you don't want to.
3. Why are cravings dangerous?
   a. Because you don't want the reward any more.
   b. Because you feel that you need the reward.
4. What's the only way to change a habit?
   a. Change the routine.
   b. Change the reward.
5. Why does Leo make coffee when he arrives at work?
   a. Because he loves the taste of coffee.
   b. Because he's tired and he needs a break.

D SPEAK Work in pairs and discuss the questions.

1. What are some cues for bad habits? What routines and rewards can we use to change those bad habits?
2. What cues and rewards can we use to start good habits?

VOCABULARY

Reflexive verbs

10.4 **A** Complete the sentences from the conversation (1–8) with the words in the box. Then listen and check your answers.

blame	control	get	help	make	reward	set	treat

1. When I drive past a sign for a fast-food restaurant, I ________________ myself to a snack from the package.
2. 'Can I try one of those?' 'Sure! ________________ yourself.'
3. I wish I could stop, but I can't ________________ myself.
4. I always ________________ myself a cup of coffee before I check my emails.
5. I suppose I could ________________ myself a glass of water.
6. I always ________________ myself goals, but nothing seems to work.
7. First of all, Alice, don't ________________ yourself.
8. How will you ________________ yourself for being good?

Reflexive verbs

A reflexive verb is a verb + a reflexive pronoun (*myself, yourself, himself, herself, itself, ourselves, yourselves, themselves*).

Some reflexive verbs have a special meaning:

Help yourself! = Please take as much as you want; there's no need to ask.

B Go to the Vocabulary Hub on page XVIII.

C **SPEAK** Work in pairs and discuss the questions.

1 Where do you see yourself in ten years?
2 How do you amuse yourself when you're on a long trip?
3 Can you think of any situations where you can't trust yourself?

PRONUNCIATION

Emphasis and reflexive pronouns

10.5 **A** Listen to the sentences from the radio show. For each sentence, decide if the reflexive pronouns are stressed or unstressed.

1 I treat myself to a snack from the package.
2 I always make myself a cup of coffee before I check my emails.
3 Don't blame yourself.
4 How will you reward yourself for being good?

B Now choose the best word or phrase to complete the rules.

Emphasis and reflexive pronouns

1 When a reflexive pronoun follows a verb, the pronoun **is / is not** usually stressed.
2 But when we want to emphasise the subject at the end of a clause, we **can / can't** stress the pronoun.

C **SPEAK** Work in pairs. Practice saying the sentences in Exercise A. Listen and check your partner's pronunciation.

GRAMMAR

Hopes and wishes

A **WORK IT OUT** Match the sentences from the conversation (1–5) with the explanations (a–d).

1 **I wish I'd known** about all this a few years ago! But I guess it's too late for me now.
2 **I hope your new routine works** for you, Leo.
3 **I wish we had time** to talk about your other seven cups of coffee, but we need to go to our next caller.
4 **I wish I could** run a marathon next year.
5 I really **wish I were** better organized.

a The speaker is talking about something that's likely to happen in the future.
b The speaker is talking about something that's unlikely to happen in the future.
c The speaker is imagining a different present situation.
d The speaker is imagining a different past situation.

Hopes and wishes

When we talk about hopes and wishes, we use very similar structures to the first, second and third conditionals.

	Conditional sentences	Hopes and wishes
Likely future	It'll be good if your idea works.	I hope your idea works.
Unlikely future	I'd be happy if I could find a new job. (or: … if I found a new job.)	I wish I could find a new job. (NOT: I wish I found a new job.)
Unreal present	It would be nice if I were taller.	I wish I were taller.
Unreal past	It would have been better if you'd told me.	I wish you'd told me.

B Go to the Grammar Hub on page XIV.

C Complete the sentences with *hope* or *wish*. Then choose the correct words to complete the hopes and wishes.

1 I ______________ you *have* / *had* / *could have* a great time on vacation next week.
2 I started playing tennis last year and I love it, but I'm too old to become a top player. I ______________ I *start* / *started* / *'d started* playing when I was younger.
3 It's great that you're coming to my city next week. I ______________ I *met* / *could meet* / *'d met* you while you're here, but unfortunately I'll be away all week.
4 I'm a little worried about Frank and Donna. They should have arrived an hour ago. I ______________ they *arrive* / *'d arrived* / *arrived* soon.
5 I never have time to do all the things I need to do each week. Sometimes I ______________ there *were* / *are* / *had been* eight days in a week!
6 My main regret is that I didn't spend enough time with my children when they were younger. I ______________ I *don't spend* / *didn't spend* / *hadn't spent* so much time working in those days!
7 My dream is to be the first person to travel to Mars! I really ______________ I *went* / *could go* / *'d gone* there one day, but I know it's never going to happen.

SPEAKING

Work in pairs and discuss the questions.

1 Do you have any regrets about your habits? What do you wish you'd started earlier? What do you wish you'd never started?
2 What do you wish you could change about yourself?
3 What are your hopes for the future? Think about next week, next month and next year.
4 What are your dreams for the future? What do you wish you could do one day?

READING

A SPEAK Work in pairs and discuss the questions.

1 What is a to-do list? What information does it contain?
2 Why do you think psychologists are interested in to-do lists?
3 Do you keep a to-do list? Why/Why not?

B READ FOR GIST Read *The psychology of to-do lists*. Match the headings (a–g) with the paragraphs (1–7).

a Organization, motivation and satisfaction
b The benefits of forgetting
c Not as difficult as it sounds
d An experiment over dinner
e Keeping tasks small and simple
f Using to-do lists to cut stress
g The stress of not finishing things

The psychology of to-do lists

1 ___

One day in the 1920s, a large group of psychologists were having a meal at their favorite restaurant. They were discussing the waiter's amazing memory: he always remembered everybody's orders perfectly, but he never wrote anything down. One of the psychologists, Bluma Zeigarnik, decided to try an experiment. She told everyone to cover their plates. Then she asked the waiter to come back to the table, and to try to remember what was on each plate. Amazingly, he couldn't remember anything, even though he himself had put the plates on the table only a few minutes earlier. How was it possible that a man with such an amazing memory had forgotten everything a few minutes later?

2 ___

Zeigarnik realized that there was in fact nothing special about the waiter. In fact, we're all good at remembering current tasks – things that we still need to do. But as soon as they're finished, we forget all about them. The 'Zeigarnik effect', as it's now called, is our brains' way of cleaning up and sorting information. If we had to remember everything forever, our brains would soon run out of space.

3 ___

But there's a dark side to the Zeigarnik effect. Studies have shown that people perform badly in tests when they're worrying about other unfinished tasks. It seems that we can't stop thinking about what we still need to do. This makes us stressed and prevents us from focusing on new tasks.

4 ___

Is there anything we can do about this problem? Recent research suggests that we can reduce our stress levels by keeping a record of all our current tasks in a to-do list. This simple action tells our brains to stop worrying about the task, which means we can give our full attention to other tasks.

5 ___

To-do lists have three additional benefits. First, they help us to stay organized. Second, they are a useful record of what we've achieved and when. It can be highly motivating to look back at our past achievements – especially because the Zeigarnik effect usually makes us forget them. However, the best thing about to-do lists is the satisfying feeling you get when you cross each item off the list.

6 ___

The key to successful to-do lists is to break large objectives into smaller action points. Instead of writing 'Learn to drive' on your list, focus on small and practical jobs that you can achieve very quickly, such as 'Find a list of driving schools in my city' and 'Read a website with reviews of different schools'. The smaller the tasks, the better. Dave Allen, a time-management expert, also recommends an archive to store all the things you might need and a system of 43 folders to schedule when to do each task.

7 ___

If that sounds like too much hard work, think again. With a good system, life is much easier. You can relax and enjoy the rest of the day, happy in the knowledge that everything is under control.

Glossary

archive (n) a place where you store documents and records

C Read the box about bridge sentences. What is the connection between bridge sentences and topic sentences (see Unit 8)? What's the difference between them?

Bridge sentences

The first sentence in a paragraph is usually a bridge sentence, which shows how the paragraph is connected to the previous paragraph. For example, it might use words like *however* to introduce a contrast, or words like *another* to add extra information.

Not all paragraphs have a bridge sentence.

D READ FOR KEY INFORMATION Read the first sentence in each paragraph again. Which five are bridge sentences? Underline the words and phrases in the sentences that refer back to the previous paragraph. What exactly do they refer to?

E SPEAK Work in pairs and discuss the questions.

1 Have you ever experienced the Zeigarnik effect? Think about:
- preparing for a test.
- learning a speech, a song or a poem.
- remembering people's names and faces.

2 Do you ever look back at your past achievements? Would you find it motivating?

VOCABULARY
Staying organized

A Look at the underlined words in *The psychology of to-do lists*. Find words or phrases that mean the following.

1 a job that you need to do
a t a s k
2 to keep something in a safe place
to _ _ _ _ _ something
3 to put things back in the right places
to _ _ _ _ _ up
4 to plan exactly when you will do something
to _ _ _ _ _ _ _ _ _ something
5 a small thing that you're going to do
an _ _ _ _ _ _ point
6 to put things in the right order
to _ _ _ _ things
7 a large thing that you want to achieve
an _ _ _ _ _ _ _ _ _
8 to write something down
to keep a _ _ _ _ _ _ of something

B SPEAK Work in pairs and discuss the questions.

1 How many **tasks** are on your to-do list?
2 Do you **keep a record** of the tasks you need to do? Would you like to start?

SPEAKING HUB

A PREPARE Write a short wish list. Use the ideas below or your own ideas.
- a problem that you would like to solve
- a good habit that you hope you will start / wish you could start
- a way to become less stressed or better organized
- how you'll continue learning/using English after this course

B PLAN Work in groups. Discuss your wish lists. As a group, choose the most interesting items from your wish lists and create a to-do list. Try to:
- plan cues, routines and rewards for any habits you want to change.
- turn your objectives into tasks and action points.

C PRESENT Stand up and tell the class what you plan to do and when. When others are speaking, listen carefully and be positive about their plans.

D REFLECT Work in groups and discuss the questions.

1 How will you make sure you'll do the things on your list?
2 How will you motivate each other to do those things?

Talk about your wishes and regrets
Plan a to-do list

10.3 Come home

F– make and accept apologies P– vowel sounds

COMPREHENSION

A When was the last time you had to say goodbye to someone? How did you feel? How long was it before you saw that person again?

B Number the pictures in the order you think they happened. What do you think happened?

a ☐

b ☐

c ☐

d ☐

e ☐

f ☐

C ▶ 00:00–02:25 Watch the first part of the video and check your ideas. How do you think the video will end?

D ▶ 02:25–04:29 Complete the letter that Sam wrote to Gaby by choosing the correct words below. Watch the second part of the video and check your answers. Does the video end how you predicted?

1 leaving / in / over
2 words / time / pen
3 should / usually / never
4 city / life / home
5 business / Madrid / yourself

Dear Gaby,

I've just heard that you're [1] _______________ London and … I wish I had said this to you in person, but I just couldn't find the [2] _______________. I'm so sorry, but I [3] _______________ know the right thing to say. I know you've already made your mind up about leaving, and I'm going to miss you so much. The thought of not having you in my [4] _______________ hurts because … I love you. I always have. I just didn't know how to say it before. Take good care of [5] _______________.

MILLY

SAM

NEENA

ZAC

GABY

FUNCTIONAL LANGUAGE

Making and accepting apologies

A Put the words in the correct order. Then put each phrase under the correct heading in the table.

1 quickly / leave / sorry / to / so / I'm / really

____

2 you'll / worry / be / don't / fine

____

3 apologize / need / no / there's / to

____

4 worry / don't / it / about

____

5 just / things / of / those / one / it's

____

6 OK / all / to / be / it's / going

____

7 my / it's / fault

____

8 not / fault / fault / it's / it's / my / your

____

9 nothing / about / worry / there's / to

____

10 great / is / this / to / be / going

____

Making an apology	Accepting an apology	Giving reassurance
I'm really sorry to leave so quickly.		

B Watch the video again and check (✓) each phrase as you hear it.

Glossary

housemate **(n) (British)** = roommate **(n) (American)**

USEFUL PHRASES

A Match the useful phrases (1–5) with the phrases that come before or after them (a–e).

1 It's time to go.
2 I wish I had said this to you in person.
3 I'm such an idiot!
4 I've changed my mind about leaving.
5 I'm scared.

a What about your plane? You're going to miss it.
b I can't believe that I missed her.
c You'll be fine; don't worry.
d But I just couldn't find the words.
e There's nothing to worry about.

B How do you say these useful phrases in your language?

PRONUNCIATION

Vowel sounds

A Match words with the same vowel sounds from boxes A, B and C.

A airport roommate <u>mind</u> person sorry worry

B apologize <u>guys</u> hurt love strangely thought

C gone <u>my</u> of course paying under words

10.6 **B** Listen, check and repeat the words. Copy the sounds.

SPEAKING

A Work in pairs. Write conversations about the following situations or your own ideas. Student A – apologize. Student B – accept the apology and reassure Student A.

arrive late / for meeting break / chair
forget / to call miss / party spill / coffee

A: I'm really sorry about breaking your chair.
B: Oh, don't worry about it – it's not your fault. It's just one of those things.

B **PRESENT** Act out your conversations. Take turns being Student A and Student B.

Make and accept apologies

➤ Turn to page XXVIII to learn how to write a report.

Unit 10 Review

GRAMMAR

A Complete the third conditional sentences. Use the correct form of the underlined verbs.

1 The waiter forgot our order because he didn't write it down.
If the waiter ___had written___ down our order, he ___wouldn't have forgotten___ it.

2 You didn't finish anything on your to-do list. Maybe it's because all the items were too big.
You might ______________ some things on your to-do list if they ______________ a little smaller.

3 I saw a sign for a fast-food restaurant, so I felt a need to eat.
If I ______________ a sign for the fast-food restaurant, I ______________ a need to eat!

4 I didn't have time to try on these jeans, but I bought them anyway.
I ______________ these jeans if I ______________ them on first! They're much too small!

B Write sentences with *should/shouldn't have done*.

1 I wish you'd been more careful.
You ___should have been more careful___.

2 I regret buying these shoes.
I ______________.

3 Why didn't they listen to us?
They ______________.

4 It was a mistake to go out yesterday.
We ______________.

C Complete the conversation with the correct form of the verbs in parentheses.

A: Hey! I'm having a dinner party tomorrow night. I hope you [1] ______________ (*can come*). It's going to be excellent.

B: Oh, I wish I [2] ______________ (*can come*), but I can't. I have tickets for a soccer game tomorrow, and it's the final.

A: Oh, I didn't know it's the final tomorrow! I wish I [3] ______________ (*know*)! I'd have arranged the party for a different night. Anyway, I hope your team [4] ______________ (*win*)!

B: Well, my team isn't in the final. I wish we [5] ______________ (*be*)! But we lost in the semi-final last week. I wish I [6] ______________ (*not buy*) a ticket – then I could come to your party!

VOCABULARY

A Choose the correct verbs to complete the sentences.

1 I got an email from somebody who tried to ***persuade / trick*** me into giving my bank account number.

2 I didn't want to buy a camera at all, but the saleswoman ***affected / persuaded*** me to buy one.

3 Whenever I walk past a fast-food restaurant, I'm ***regretted / tempted*** to go inside.

4 For a long time, businesses ***assumed / influenced*** that more choice meant more sales.

B Find and correct one mistake in each underlined phrase.

[1]Would you mind that I asked you for some advice? You see, I want to go somewhere new this weekend, but I'm [2]of three minds about where to go. This morning, I [3]made my mind and decided to go bike riding in the forest, but then I heard the weather is going to be horrible, so I [4]changed the mind and decided to go to the new museum instead. But ... I don't really like museums. What should I do? [5]Bear to mind, I don't have a car, so it needs to be somewhere with good bus connections.

C Match the beginnings of the tips for staying organized (1–5) with the endings (a–e).

1 Don't do everything at once. Focus
2 Remember to schedule
3 Use a to-do list to keep
4 Break big objectives into smaller action
5 Use an archive to store

a a record of your tasks.
b important old documents.
c some time to relax!
d on one task at a time.
e points.

D Choose the correct reflexive verb to complete the sentences.

1 You shouldn't ***blame / control*** yourself. It's not your fault.

2 ***Help / get*** yourself to anything you want.

3 I always go into fast food restaurants when I see them. I can't ***make / control*** myself.

4 He's trained so hard for the race. Why doesn't he ***treat / set*** himself to a night off and just relax?

FUNCTIONAL LANGUAGE

Complete the conversation with the words in the box. There are two extra words.

about apologize blame fault not so those worry

Dimitri: Hey, Igor! Have you eaten my pizza?

Igor: Don't [1] ______________ me! I've been out all day. I don't know anything about it.

Dimitri: Oh ... I'm [2] ______________ sorry. I shouldn't have blamed you.

Igor: It's OK. Don't [3] ______________ about it. So I wonder who ate your pizza ...

Rob: Uh, sorry, but it's my [4] ______________. I was really hungry when I got home last night and I hadn't gone to the store!

Dimitri: Oh, there's no need to [5] ______________. It's just one of [6] ______________ things.

Endmatter Contents

Grammar Hub

Vocabulary Hub

Communication Hub

Writing

Grammar Hub

6.1 Modals of obligation

should

	Positive	Negative
I/you/he/she/it/we/they	**I should choose** the best team.	**We shouldn't yell** at the players.

must

	Positive	Negative
I/you/he/she/it/we/they	**They must find** a better place to train.	**You must not be** so aggressive on the field.

have to

	Positive	Negative
I/you/we/they	**You have to wear** a helmet.	**They don't have to play** the game on the computer.
he/she/it	**She has to perform** well today.	**He doesn't have to win** every match.

- We use *should/shouldn't* when we describe what is or is not a good idea now, in the future or generally.
- We use *must* and *have to* when we describe rules and situations that are necessary.
- There is sometimes no difference between them. However, we usually use *must* and *must not* in written rules, and *have to* in speech.
- We use *must not* when we describe something that is not allowed.
- We use *don't/doesn't have to* when we describe things that aren't necessary, but you may still do them.
- There is a difference in meaning between *must not* and *don't have to*.

  must not *= not allowed*

  don't have to *= not necessary*
- In questions, we use *have to* instead of *must*.
- We can use *don't/doesn't need to* instead of *don't/doesn't have to* when we describe things that aren't necessary.

6.2 Present perfect and present perfect progressive; *had to / needed to*

Present perfect

Positive	Negative	Question
I've joined a sailing club.	**They haven't made up** their minds about joining the league.	**Have you met** your opponent yet?

- We use the present perfect for actions completed during a period of time that continues to now.
- We also use the present perfect for actions completed before now when we don't say exactly when.
- See Grammar Hub 2.1 for more information about the present perfect.

Present perfect progressive

	Positive	Negative
I/you/we/they	**I have been collecting** stamps for years.	**We haven't been doing** our best in every game.
he/she/it	**She's been training** hard every single day.	**Zain hasn't been training** hard enough.

Question	Positive short answer	Negative short answer
Have they been playing tennis for long?	Yes, **they have**.	No, **they haven't**.
Has Anika been watching the game on TV?	Yes, **she has**.	No, **she hasn't**.

- We use the present perfect progressive to talk about an action that started in the past and continues in the present. It can be a single or a frequently repeated action.

  He has been cooking all afternoon.
- We can use both the present perfect and the present perfect progressive to describe a recently completed activity.

  She has posted the videos on social media. She has been posting the videos on social media all morning.
- We use the present perfect progressive to find out the duration of an activity.

  How long have you been waiting for your teammates?
- We do NOT use the present perfect progressive with state verbs.

  I have known my coach for years.

had to / needed to

	Positive	Negative
I/you/he/she/it/we/they	**They had to** practice for four hours each day. **He needed to wear** safety equipment.	**You didn't have to train** for the snowball fight. **She didn't need to buy** a new helmet.

Question	Positive short answer	Negative short answer
Did you have to take a lesson first?	Yes, **I/we did**.	No, **I/we didn't**.

- We use *had to* and *needed to* to talk about things that were necessary in the past. They mean the same thing.
- We don't use *must* to talk about the past.

  They had to pay for the skiing lessons last winter.
- We use *didn't have to* and *didn't need to* to talk about things that were not necessary but possible in the past.

6.1 Modals of obligation

A Choose the correct option.

1 We *don't have to* / *must not* be competitive to have fun playing sports.
2 He *must* / *doesn't have to* wear a helmet. It's required.
3 I *must* / *must not* eat a massive meal before playing a sport.
4 They *shouldn't* / *don't have to* practice today because the coach isn't going to be here.
5 *Do you have to* / *Must you* train every day?

B Complete the sentences with the correct words and phrases from the box.

don't have	doesn't have	has
must not	don't need	should

1 You ______________ to buy a ticket. Dad's bought them already.
2 She ______________ ask her coach for advice on how to play better.
3 I ______________ to go to practice today. It's been canceled.
4 For a helmet to work, it ______________ to fit on your head properly.
5 You ______________ run while holding the ball. It's against the rules.
6 He ______________ to wear protective gear because his sport isn't dangerous.

C Choose the correct option to complete the dialogue.

Anna: I'm excited about Saturday's game. It starts at 1 pm. I think we [1] ______________ meet in front of the entrance, shouldn't we?

Vincenzo: I [2] ______________ take my little sister to her lesson first, so I might be a little late. You [3] ______________ wait for me outside. Just go on inside and I'll find you.

Anna: Well, I don't mind waiting for you outside. I [4] ______________ be in my seat when the game starts. Besides, it's a big place. We [5] ______________ go in together so we don't get lost.

Vincenzo: OK, fine.

	a	b	c
1	don't need to	must	should
2	have to	should	don't have to
3	must	don't have to	have to
4	should	must	don't have to
5	must	should	don't need to

➤ Go back to page 63.

6.2 Present perfect and present perfect progressive; *had to / needed to*

A Choose the correct option.

1 I've never *played* / *been playing* racquetball before. Is it fun?
2 Have you *been watching* / *watched* sports on TV all day?
3 I've just *finished* / *been finishing* a really difficult exercise class.
4 Sorry about my appearance. I've *run* / *been running*.
5 Do you think he's *understood* / *been understanding* the rules yet?
6 Lee hasn't *worked out* / *been working out* for a long time but he's already *increased* / *been increasing* his muscle strength.

B Complete the sentences in the present perfect or progressive with the correct form of these verbs. Sometimes more than one tense is possible.

follow	join	stay	lose	play	spend

1 Tom has ______lost______ interest in playing soccer.
2 The coach has ______________ a lot of time with the players lately.
3 Have you ______________ the tennis competition? It's getting good!
4 Georgia has ______________ in shape these days using a new exercise program.
5 Eli and Greta haven't ______________ the club yet.
6 I've ______________ this video game all day and there's still a lot left.

C Correct the mistakes.

1 He had to left the game because he broke his leg.
2 I must yell so the other players could hear me.
3 You hadn't to yell. I couldn't hear you on the field.
4 I didn't needed to tell my friend about the game.
5 **A:** Why they didn't have to buy a paddle?
B: Because they already had one.

➤ Go back to page 69.

Grammar Hub

7.1 Modals of speculation and deduction

- We use *could*, *might* or *may* when we think something is possible, but we are not sure.

  This dish is very hot – it could contain a lot of chilies.
  Carla might be allergic to nuts – don't add any walnuts.
  Paul may want sugar in his coffee.
- In the negative, we use *might not* and *may not* but NOT *could not*.

  This restaurant may/might not be very good.
  NOT ~~This restaurant could not be very good.~~
- We use *must* when we are sure something is true because we have strong evidence for our belief.

  This cake is burned – it must taste horrible!
- We use *can't* when we are sure something is not true because we have strong evidence for our belief.

  These cookies are white – they can't be chocolate chip cookies.
- We don't use *must* and *can't* for facts we are 100% sure about.

7.2 Comparatives and superlatives; *the …, the …*

Comparatives and superlatives

	Comparative	Superlative
Short adjectives (one syllable)	adj + *-er* (+ *than*) cheap → cheap**er**	*the* + adj + *-est* cheap → **the** cheap**est**
Longer adjectives	*more* + adj (+ *than*) popular → **more** popular	*the most* + adj popular → **the most** popular
Irregular adjectives	good → **better** (+ *than*) bad → **worse** (+ *than*)	good → **the best** bad → **the worst**
Adverbs	*more* + adv (+ *than*) quickly → **more** quickly	*the most* + adv quickly → **the most** quickly
Irregular adverbs	badly → **worse** far → **farther/further** fast → fast**er** hard → hard**er** well → **better**	badly → **the worst** far → **the farthest** / **the furthest** fast → **the** fast**est** hard → **the** hard**est** well → **the best**
Countable nouns	many nutrients → **more** nutrients few nutrients → few**er** nutrients	many nutrients → **the most** nutrients few nutrients → **the** few**est** nutrients
Uncountable nouns	much protein → **more** protein little fiber → **less** fiber	much protein → **the most** protein little fiber → **the least** fiber

- We use comparative adjectives and adverbs to say how two or more things or actions are different.
- We use superlative adjectives and adverbs to say that something is the top or bottom of a group.
- For adjectives ending in *-e* or *-y* the rules differ a little.

  Your meal is larger than mine, but Harry's is the largest.
  Carrot soup is tastier than pea soup, but chicken soup is the tastiest of all.
- For adjectives which end with one vowel and one consonant, we double the final consonant before adding *-er* or *-est*.

  These melons are ***bigger*** *than those ones.*
- To make negative comparatives and superlatives, we use *less* instead of *more* and *the least* instead of *the most*.
- We never use *more* or *the most* together with *-er* or *-est*.

  I think juice is healthier than coffee. NOT ~~I think juice is more healthier than coffee.~~
- We only use *than* when it is followed by the thing we are comparing.

  This dish is good but this one is better. NOT ~~This dish is good but this one is better than.~~
  This dish is better than that dish.

the …, the …

the + comparative adjective + noun, *the* + comparative adjective + noun	**The fresher** the ingredients, **the better** the dish.
the + comparative adjective + clause, *the* + comparative adjective + clause	**The more tasty** it is, **the more satisfied** they will be.
the + comparative adverb + clause, *the* + comparative adverb + clause	**The faster** it boils, **the more quickly** it will be ready.
the + *more/less* + noun + clause, *the* + *more/less* + noun + clause	**The more recipes** you learn, **the more food** you can cook.
the + *more/less* + clause, *the* + *more/less* + clause	**The more I practiced**, **the less I needed** a cookbook.

- We use *the …, the* to show that two changes are closely connected. As one thing changes, the other thing changes too.
- Sometimes we use the very simplest form of this structure, using comparative adjectives only, and no verb.

  The more, the merrier.
- We don't have to use only the forms shown in the table above. We can also combine different parts of the structures.

  The more complicated the recipe, the longer it takes.
  The less we spend on food, the more money we have.

7.1 Modals of speculation and deduction

A Decide if the statements are true or false.

1 'Kitty may serve fruit salad for dessert tonight.'
Dessert will definitely be fruit salad. **True / False**

2 'I've been invited to three pot-luck dinners. They must be popular.'
Pot-luck dinners are popular. **True / False**

3 'This can't be tomato soup – it isn't red!'
It almost certainly isn't tomato soup. **True / False**

4 'Bitter chocolate could be good in a cake.'
The speaker really doesn't like bitter chocolate. **True / False**

5 'If you left the milk out all night, it could be sour.'
It's possible that the milk is sour. **True / False**

B Choose the correct option.

1 **A:** 'Are you going to order soup?'
B: 'No, I'm very hungry and it ***must not / might not*** be very filling.'

2 **A:** 'Lara said she wants chicken.'
B: 'But she doesn't eat meat. She ***can't / must not*** want chicken.'

3 **A:** 'What's 'scampi'?'
B: 'I don't know really. It ***could / can*** be some kind of fish.'

4 **A:** 'Dinner is at seven tonight.'
B: 'I ***could / may*** not get there in time because I have to work late.'

5 **A:** 'Look at that man! He's ordered three pizzas!'
B: 'He ***can / must*** really like pizza!'

6 **A:** 'I've ordered sushi for lunch.'
B: 'Hector ***might / could*** not eat that but we'll see.'

➤ Go back to page 77.

7.2 Comparatives and superlatives; *the …, the …*

A Complete the sentences with the correct form of the adjectives and adverbs in parentheses.

1 The ______________ (*fast*) the pizza delivery man can get here is 15 minutes.

2 You can buy cheese ______________ (*cheaply*) in the street market than in the stores.

3 The food in the airport was bad, but the meal on the plane was ______________ (*bad*).

4 I made the soup with ______________ (*few*) ingredients than it says in the recipe.

5 The ______________ (*good*) way to serve this dessert is with a little cream.

6 I would prefer to try a ______________ (*mild*) sauce than the one you're eating.

B Complete the sentences with the words and phrases in the box.

less meat	more times	more quickly	the better	the more money	the sweeter	you disagree

1 The ______________ you eat, the healthier it is for your heart.

2 The more sugar you add, ______________ the sauce will be.

3 The ______________ you eat your salad, the sooner you'll have dessert!

4 The more ______________ with me, the less likely I am to change my mind!

5 The ______________ you reheat food, the more unsafe it becomes.

6 The less food we throw away, ______________ we'll save.

C Correct the mistakes in each sentence.

1 The peas will cook more fast than the potatoes.

2 I think the most sourest taste of any food is vinegar.

3 Salad is the least filling than pasta.

4 First prize in the competition will go to the person who cooks the more creatively.

5 I put very little sugar in Jim's coffee, but he wanted even little!

6 Chia seeds have much protein than some foods, but quinoa has the most.

D Write one word in each blank to complete the sentences.

1 Is fast food ______________ popular than home cooking in your country?

2 My old mixer worked fairly well, but this one works much ______________.

3 Water is the ______________ fattening drink you can have because it has zero calories!

4 Raw food is generally healthier ______________ cooked food.

5 All these curries are spicy, but this one is the hottest ______________ all!

6 The older the wine is, ______________ better it gets.

7 The salad plates are pretty large, but the dinner plates are ______________.

8 Mmm! This is ______________ most delicious meal I've ever had!

➤ Go back to page 80.

Grammar Hub

8.1 Adjective clauses

Essential adjective clauses

	Relative pronoun	
Person	who/that	The person **who/that** first had the idea was named Smith.
Thing	which/that	The thing **which/that** stops it being a success is the price.
Possession	whose	The man **whose** design won first prize was from China.
Place	where	The company **where** I work makes a difference to people's lives.
Time	when	Early in the morning is the time **when** I have my best ideas.

- We use an essential adjective clause to give information about and identify a noun (person or thing).
- We use *who* or *that* for people, and *which* or *that* for things.
- With *who*, *which* and *that*, we can leave out the relative pronoun if it's followed by a subject + verb rather than just a verb.

The design (that) he suggested was very good.

- When the relative pronoun is the subject of the adjective clause, we don't add another pronoun.

*Do you know the name of the man **who invented** this?* NOT ~~*Do you know the name of the man who he invented this?*~~

Non-essential adjective clauses

	Relative pronoun	
Person	who	Carol Taylor, **who** presents science programs, is a university professor.
Thing	which	The idea, **which** I first read about in the newspaper, is really very simple.
Possession	whose	Miriam, **whose** dad is a designer, would like to become an inventor.
Place	where	London, **where** her grandparents live, is where Sophie would like to find work.
Time	when	On Sundays, **when** Andrew isn't working, he likes to catch up with his reading.

- We use a non-essential adjective clause when we want to include two pieces of information in the same sentence. The adjective clause is usually an additional piece of information and is always separated by commas.
- We do not use *that* with non-essential adjective clauses.
- When we remove a non-essential adjective clause, the sentence still makes sense.

8.2 Zero and first conditionals; Conditionals with modals and imperatives

Zero conditional

Condition	Result
If **you listen**,	**you learn**.
If **you like** science,	**it helps**.

Question	Positive short answer	Negative short answer
If **I win**, **do I get** a prize?	Yes, **you do**.	No, **you don't**.
Does it help if you like science?	Yes, **it does**.	No, **it doesn't**.

- We use the zero conditional to talk about things that are always true.
- We can put the *if*-clause or the result clause first. The only difference is we do not use a comma if we begin with the result clause.
- We can use negatives and *unless* (which means *if not* or *except if*) in the zero conditional.

If you don't pay attention, you make mistakes.
= Unless you pay attention, you make mistakes.

First conditional

Condition	Result
If **you try** hard,	**you'll succeed**.
If **it doesn't work**,	**we'll start** again.

Question	Positive short answer	Negative short answer
If **we win** the award, **will we be** famous?	Yes, **we/you will**.	No, **we/you won't**.
Will we be famous if **we win** the award?		

- We use the first conditional to talk about possible situations in the future.
- We can put the *if*-clause or the result clause first. The only difference is we do not use a comma if we begin with the result clause.
- We can use negatives and *unless* (meaning *if not* or *except if*) in the first conditional.

If you don't listen, you won't understand.
= Unless you listen, you won't understand.

- We never put *will* in an *if*-clause.

Conditionals with modals and imperatives

- We can use other modal verbs (e.g. *can*, *could*, *might*, *should*) instead of *will*.

*If you work hard enough, you **can** do it!*
*I **might** visit the science museum if it's open tomorrow.*

- We can use an imperative instead of a result clause.

*If you see smoke, **call** for help.*
***Call** me if you have any questions.*

8.1 Adjective clauses

A Choose the correct option.

1 There are a lot of students ***which*** / ***who*** have great ideas.
2 The last century was the time ***when*** / ***where*** technology really progressed.
3 The magazine ***who*** / ***that*** I like best is called *New Scientist*.
4 Princeton is the place ***where*** / ***which*** I studied for my degree.
5 I want to find a job ***that*** / ***who*** helps others.
6 John is the boy ***who*** / ***whose*** father is a doctor.
7 I don't know anyone ***who*** / ***which*** works in technology.
8 He was born at a time ***when*** / ***where*** computers didn't exist.

B Match to make sentences.

1 California is where ___b___
2 The computer is an invention ___
3 Steve Jobs was the person who ___
4 The experiences ___
5 Myra is the woman ___
6 My phone is the one thing ___
7 I really enjoyed the time ___

a started Apple Computers.
b most software industries started.
c which I would hate to lose.
d which has changed many people's lives.
e that I had were more important than the money I made.
f when I was studying at college.
g who helped me choose my career.

C Join the two sentences to make one. Use non-essential adjective clauses.

1 My aunt is a scientist. She lives in Boston.
My aunt, who lives in Boston, is a scientist. / My aunt, who is a scientist, lives in Boston.
2 The invention is very simple. It has made a big difference to people's lives.
______
3 Justin is 23. He has just won a prize.
______
4 Carl spoke to us from Lisbon. He lives there.
______
5 The invention won first prize. It is sold in many countries.
______
6 Marie loves inventing things. Her husband is also an engineer.
______
7 Next week the results come out. We'll see if you win anything.
______

➤ Go back to page 87.

8.2 Zero and first conditionals; Conditionals with modals and imperatives

A Find and correct the mistakes with the zero conditional.

1 If you ~~will~~ read a lot, you understand things better.
2 It's better if you called me in the evenings.
3 Unless you don't try, you don't learn.
4 The roads will more dangerous if it rains.
5 It doesn't work if you won't turn it on.
6 I'll never go out if it's cold.

B Complete the first conditional sentences using the information in parentheses.

1 The machine will not work *if you don't press this button.*
(*you / not / press this button*)
2 If you find it at the right price, ______
(*you / buy it?*)
3 What will we do ______
(*it / not work?*)
4 How will you get home ______
(*you / miss the bus?*)
5 If it rains tomorrow, ______
(*you / still / play soccer?*)
6 If you take an umbrella with you, ______
(*it / keep you dry*)
7 I won't help him ______
(*he / not ask*)

C Choose the correct option.

1 If you see Jimmy, ______
a will give him this note.
(b) give him this note.
2 You will save money if ______
a you can wait a few months.
b you will wait a few months.
3 If you don't like it, ______
a you can go home.
b will you go home.
4 If you have any problems, ______
a will call me.
b call me.
5 If I feel like it,
a I might go to the pop concert.
b I can go to the pop concert.
6 Ask me if there's anything ______
a you don't understand.
b you won't understand.
7 If you want to have a good time, ______
a you will come and join us on Saturday night!
b come and join us on Saturday night!

➤ Go back to page 93.

Grammar Hub

9.1 Second conditional

Condition	Result
If **you submitted** a proposal,	**they would accept** it.
If **she didn't teach** music,	**she'd be** a full-time musician.
If **the show were** expensive,	**I wouldn't go** to it.
If **we didn't have** an art venue,	**we wouldn't see** much art.

Question	Positive short answer	Negative short answer
If **you had** more free time, **would you spend** it creatively?	Yes, **I would**.	No, **I wouldn't**.
Would you spend your free time creatively if **you had** more of it?		

- We use the second conditional to talk about present situations that aren't real and future events that are unlikely but possible.
- Although it uses the simple past, the second conditional is NOT about the past.
- We use *if* + simple past in the *if*-clause and *would* + base form in the result clause.
- We can use *might* or *could* in the result clause if we are not sure of the result.

  If she rehearsed every day, she might improve her skills.

  We could display community art if we had a local arts venue.
- With the verb *be*, we generally use *were* instead of *was* with all subjects, including *I*.

9.2 Reported speech

Direct speech	Reported speech
simple present	simple past
'**We enjoy** live concerts the best.'	They said (that) **they enjoyed** live concerts the best.
present progressive	past progressive
'**We are learning** how to write a short story.'	They said (that) **they were learning** how to write a short story.
will	*would*
'**I will** read my book later.'	She said (that) **she would** read her book later.
may	*might*
'**Elle may** sing in the play.'	He said (that) **Elle might** sing in the play.
can	*could*
'**We can** film our daily lives.'	They said (that) **they could** film their daily lives.
should	*should* (no change)
'**He should try out** for that role.'	She said (that) he **should try out** for that role.
For commands and instructions	*tell* + object (+ *not*) + infinitive
'**Rehearse** the scene again.'	He told them **to rehearse** the scene again.
'**Don't look** at the camera.'	She told me **not to look** at the camera.

- We use reported speech to report what people say. We use a reporting verb in the simple past (e.g. *said*, *asked*, *told*).
- When we report what someone says, the reported verb usually goes back one tense.
- When we report questions, the subject comes before the verb (the same as in sentences).

  *Alain: 'Where **is he acting**?' → Alain asked where **he was acting**.*
- With yes/no questions, we start the reported question with *if* or *whether*.

  *Chloe: 'Will Tom attend the show?' → Chloe asked **if/whether** Tom would attend the show.*
- We change some pronouns from direct speech to reported speech depending on the speaker (*I* to *he/she*, *you* to *me*, *my* to *his/her*, etc).

  *Kieran: 'I've given **you my** ticket already.' → He said **he** had given **me his** ticket already.*
- We sometimes also need to change words which refer to time and place.

Direct speech	Reported speech
tomorrow	*the next day / the following day*
today	*that day*
here	*there*
this	*that/the*

- We usually don't change the verb tenses if we are reporting facts that are still true in the present.

  *Our coach said that acting **requires** a great deal of time and effort.*

9.1 Second conditional

A Choose the correct option.

1 If I *knew* / *know* the words to the song, I would sing it.
2 If she had a better idea for the story, she *uses* / *would use* it.
3 If we *would hold* / *held* an art competition, many people would take part.
4 The public *liked* / *might like* his proposal if he presented it to them.
5 If you *invite* / *invited* Monique to the play, would she come?
6 If they allowed the public behind the stage, the actors *weren't* / *wouldn't be* pleased.
7 I'd study art at Kingston University if I *were* / *am* you.

B Correct the mistakes in these second conditional sentences.

1 If you ~~get~~ got rid of your guitar, you would miss it later.
2 If we bought cheaper tickets, we would saved a lot of money.
3 If they interact with the audience, the play would be more exciting.
4 I won't be terribly upset if my bandmates and I didn't make up.
5 Will Chanda enjoy it more if she spent more time in her studio?
6 If the show took place outdoors, more people can come.
7 Everyone would be very unhappy if it rains the day of the concert.

C Write the correct form of the verbs in parentheses. Use *would* if necessary.

1 If the city __built__ (*build*) a new theater, many people would attend it.
2 If we rehearsed every day, we ________ (*become*) the best!
3 If my favorite musician ________ (*perform*) for free, thousands would go to see it.
4 Jean-Philippe ________ (*sell*) millions of copies if he recorded his songs.
5 The public would be disappointed if the gallery ________ (*close*) its doors.
6 If I ________ (*be*) a famous artist, could I sell my paintings for $1 million?
7 If you ________ (*tell*) your story, I think people would show an interest in it.
8 Most people ________ (*not like*) it if I sang in public!

➤ Go back to page 99.

9.2 Reported speech

A Choose the correct option.

1 Maya: 'I'm going to an outdoor concert tonight.'
She said she *is* / *was* going to an outdoor concert that night.
2 Dan and Tracy: 'We're rehearsing all day tomorrow.'
They said they *were rehearsing* / *will rehearse* all day the following day.
3 Joe to Lyn: 'I can give you my proposal.'
He said he *can* / *could* give her his proposal.
4 Nadia to me: 'I will ask the doorman to let you in for free.'
She said she *asked* / *would ask* the doorman to let me in for free.
5 The teachers: 'We've chosen a local warehouse.'
They said they *will choose* / *had chosen* a local warehouse.
6 Me: 'I'm not writing a review of the play this evening.'
You said you weren't writing the review *this* / *that* evening.
7 John to Isabel: 'Come to the concert hall at 7 pm.'
John *said* / *told* Isabel to come to the concert hall at 7 pm.

B Report the statements.

1 Hanna: 'I'm performing at the theater tomorrow.'
She said __(that) she was performing at the theater the next/following day.__
2 Alexis: 'I've never written a novel before.'
He said ________
3 Marcia: 'I'll buy my tickets online.'
She said ________
4 Davide and Maria: 'We're meeting a famous actor today.'
They said ________
5 Anastasiya: 'I can't hear from the back row.'
She said ________
6 Hussein: 'I gave Sonia my seat.'
He said ________

C Choose the correct option.

1 Sara: 'When is the concert?'
She asked ________.
a if the concert was today
b when the concert was
c when is the concert
2 Elena to Jim: 'You'll love Paulina's performance.'
She promised that Jim ________ Paulina's performance.
a loves
b will love
c would love
3 Soraya to me: 'Have you read *The Great Gatsby*?'
She asked me ________ *The Great Gatsby*.
a whether I read
b if I had read
c why I had read
4 Georgia and Hans: 'Are our seats at the front?'
They asked ________.
a if our seats are at the front
b if our seats were at the front
c if their seats were at the front

➤ Go back to page 103.

Grammar Hub

10.1 Third conditional; *would have* + past participle

Third conditional

Condition	Result
I would have made a better decision	if **Daniel had done** the research.
If **I had known** all the facts,	**he wouldn't have made** his discovery.

Question	Positive short answer	Negative short answer
If **you had thought** about it more, **would you have made** the same decision?	Yes, **I would (have)**.	No, **I wouldn't (have)**.
Would they have passed the exam if **they had answered** correctly?	Yes, **they would (have)**.	No, **they wouldn't (have)**.

- We use the third conditional to imagine a situation in the past that didn't actually happen.

  If I had set my alarm clock, I wouldn't have been late for work. (= I ***didn't*** *set my alarm clock and I* ***was*** *late for work.)*
- As with other conditionals, we only use a comma when the *if*-clause comes first.
- We can use *could have* or *might have* instead of *would have* to express possibility.

  I could have answered correctly if I'd had more time.
- In answer to a third conditional question, we can use either *I would* or *I would have*.

  Would you have made the same decision if you'd known all the facts?
  Yes, I would. / Yes, I would have. / No, I wouldn't. / No, I wouldn't have.

would have **+ past participle**

should have **+ past participle**

Positive	Negative	Question
I would have told her about my exam results.	**He wouldn't have bought** me such an expensive gift.	**Why would they have left** the house already?
She should have bought the first pair.	**You shouldn't have spent** so much money.	**Should I have changed** my mind?
They should have offered more choice.	**I shouldn't have bought** these shoes.	How much **should they have paid**?

- We use *should/shouldn't have* + the past participle of the main verb to talk about mistakes that we made in the past. We regret those actions and try to imagine how we could have acted differently.

  She shouldn't have changed her mind. (= She ***did*** *change her mind and this was a mistake.)*
- We always put the past participle of the main verb after *should/shouldn't have*.

  They should have thought about their decision more carefully. NOT ~~They should have think about their decision more carefully.~~

10.2 Hopes and wishes

wish + simple past	imagining a different present situation (unreal present)	**I wish she were** more organized. **I wish I weren't** so hungry! **He wishes he knew** the answer.
wish + past perfect	imagining a different past situation (unreal past)	**We wish our son had won** the race. **They wish they hadn't eaten** so much.
wish + *could*	imagining an unlikely future possibility (unlikely future)	**I wish I could stop** drinking coffee.
hope (that) + simple present/ present progressive	imagining a likely future possibility (likely future)	**I hope that you enjoy** yourself tomorrow. **I hope that you are enjoying** yourself on vacation! **We hope that she doesn't make** the wrong decision.

- We can use *wish* to talk about ourselves or other people.

  I wish I had more friends. / I wish Sarah had more friends. / Sarah wishes her brother had more friends.
- We usually use *were* instead of *was* after *I wish* or *He/She wishes*.

  I wish I were better organized.
- We use *wish* + *could* to talk about something that we want to be different in the future. However, by using *could*, we express a belief that our wish probably won't come true.

  I wish I could treat myself to a vacation. (= I know that I won't be able to do this because I don't have the money, time, etc.)
- Although *hope* refers to the future, it is followed by a verb in the present tense. You can include the word *that*, but it is usually omitted.

  I hope (that) the snacks aren't too salty.
  We hope (that) the fast food restaurant is open tomorrow.
- We use the negative for the verb which **follows** *wish* or *hope*.

  I hope it doesn't rain tomorrow.
  NOT ~~I don't hope it rains.~~
  I wish I hadn't spent so much money.
  NOT ~~I don't wish I had spent so much money.~~

10.1 Third conditional; *Would have* + past participle

A Read the sentences and choose the option which is true.

1 He should have made a decision based on the facts.
  a He considered the facts. b He didn't consider the facts.
2 She could have avoided the other car if she'd stopped in time.
  a She avoided the other car. b She didn't avoid the other car.
3 If you had listened to me, you wouldn't have made a foolish decision.
  a You made a foolish decision. b You didn't make a foolish decision.
4 If David had gone to a smaller store, he would have felt less stressed.
  a David went to a small store. b David went to a big store.
5 You shouldn't have encouraged her to spend all that money!
  a She spent a lot of money. b She didn't spend a lot of money.
6 We wouldn't have bought this house if we'd known it was so noisy here.
  a We bought the house. b We didn't buy the house.

B Correct the mistakes in each sentence.

1 I shouldn't paid so much for this cell phone.
2 If our teacher gave us time to review, we would all have earned better grades.
3 Will the show have attracted more people if we had advertised it better?
4 I'm sorry – I would have listened to your advice.
5 If you have bought your shoes in the first store, you would have saved time!
6 Should we have count the sunk costs?
7 Would you had agreed to take part if you had known it was a trick?
8 I should realize that the watch was made of plastic!

C Choose the correct option.

The sneakers were fashionable, attractive and cheap, so I bought them. However, I [1]***shouldn't / wouldn't*** have been so easily influenced by the saleswoman. A few days later, I searched for that brand online and discovered that they were made by child workers! If I [2]***had known / would know*** that they were made by children, I would never [3]***buy / have bought*** them. In fact, I [4]***had avoided / would have avoided*** that store completely! If I [5]***would discover / had discovered*** the truth sooner, I would have complained to the store. And of course I [6]***hadn't encouraged / wouldn't have encouraged*** my friends to buy them either! It's really important that, as shoppers, we act responsibly. I've found an online group which persuades customers not to buy products like these. I joined it right away. If I [7]***had heard / heard*** about it sooner, I [8]***would / will*** have joined months ago!

➤ Go back to page 111.

10.2 Hopes and wishes

A Match the situations to the people's comments.

1 Brett's too short for the basketball team.
2 Dad is always losing his keys.
3 I don't know any of the answers.
4 Josh's drive to work takes 90 minutes.
5 I want to stop eating sugar completely.
6 Phoebe feels lonely.
7 Anna is really tired.

a 'I wish I didn't have to drive so far.'
b 'I wish I had studied more.'
c 'I wish I had more friends.'
d 'I wish I were taller.'
e 'I wish I hadn't stayed up all night.'
f 'I hope you achieve your goal.'
g 'I wish I wasn't so disorganized.'

B Choose the correct option.

1 I ***wish / hope*** to achieve everything on my to-do list.
2 Do you wish you ***don't give / hadn't given*** in to your cravings?
3 The children wish they ***could stay / stayed*** up late to watch the movie.
4 I wish I ***have / had*** more money to spend on clothes.
5 Kate wishes her husband ***is / were*** more focused on his career.
6 They wish they ***didn't live / couldn't live*** near a noisy shopping mall.
7 Jared ***wishes / hopes*** he could take a vacation.
8 I wish you ***didn't persuade / hadn't persuaded*** me to eat this burger – it's horrible!

C Complete the sentences with the correct form of the verb in parentheses.

1 I never have enough time. I wish there ____________ (*be*) more hours in the day!
2 I hope this snack ____________ (*not / be*) high in salt.
3 The children are full of energy. I wish they ____________ (*not / eat*) so many sugary snacks!
4 My children wish I ____________ (*not / work*) such long hours.
5 I hope Pam ____________ (*not / change*) her mind!
6 Alisha wants to buy a laptop but wishes she ____________ (*know*) more about them.
7 I wish my best friend ____________ (*be*) here to help me make the right choice!
8 She ____________ (*wish*) she could give up drinking sugary drinks but says it's very difficult.

➤ Go back to page 115.

6.2 Hobbies and free time activities

Complete the texts with the verb phrases in the box.

collect escape from daily stress get you out of the house is a fan is into is relaxing isn't my thing joined a society keeps you in shape lost interest in took up

My brother [1] ________________ soccer. He [2] ________________ of Liverpool Football Club and he goes to almost all their games. To be honest, soccer [3] ________________, so I've only been to one game with him. I like to [4] ________________ stamps. I've recently [5] ________________ for that, and I'm going to my first meeting with the other members now. Who says stamp collecting doesn't [6] ________________?!

Last year, I [7] ________________ sailing as a hobby. I live in the city, and sailing is a great way to [8] ________________. Being out on the lake with the wind in your hair [9] ________________, and it [10] ________________ too because you have to do a lot of physical work. I used to go to the gym, but I soon [11] ________________ that. The running machines were too boring!

➤ Go back to page 66.

7.1 Phrasal verbs

Work in pairs. Match the underlined phrasal verbs (1–9) with the definitions (a–i) .

1 I can't <u>figure out</u> what ingredients you've used here. What are they?

2 A: 'Maybe I'll start studying for my exams next week …'
B: 'Don't <u>put it off</u>! Start today!'

3 We've eaten out every night this week. Let's <u>stay in</u> this evening and cook some food at home.

4 Sorry to <u>let</u> you <u>down</u>, but I can't come to your party.

5 I asked everybody to be quiet for a few minutes, but most people just <u>kept on</u> talking.

6 Can you <u>turn</u> the oven <u>down</u> to 150°C in ten minutes? If you leave it at 220°C for too long, the food will burn.

7 I don't mind cooking, but can you <u>clean up</u> afterward?

8 Can you <u>put</u> your phone <u>away</u>, please! It's really rude to check your messages while we're eating dinner!

9 Great job! <u>Keep up</u> the good work!

a continue without stopping

b take something that's in the wrong place and put it in the right place

c continue at the same high level

d make everything clean and neat again after making a mess

e not go out

f find the answer by thinking carefully

g decide to do something later, not now

h make something lower/colder/quieter

i make somebody feel sad because you don't do something that you promised to do

➤ Go back to page 75.

7.1 Adjectives to describe food

A Complete the sentences with the adjectives in the box.

delicious   disgusting   filling   mild   savory   sour

1 Our bakery sells a mix of sweet products, like cakes and fruit pies, and ________________ products, like bread and meat pies.

2 Do you prefer strong flavors or ________________ flavors?

3 Mmm … I love this meal. It's absolutely ________________!

4 I love ________________ food like lemons, grapefruit and pickled cabbage.

5 Ugh! How long has this milk been in the fridge? Two weeks? It tastes ________________!

6 This meal is great but it's very ________________ – I feel completely full already.

B Label the pictures with the adjectives in the box.

bitter   raw   rich   spicy

1

____

2

____

3

____

4

____

➤ Go back to page 76.

8.2 Positive adjectives

Choose the best adjectives to complete the sentences.

1 A: My dog pressed six buttons in the right order!
B: That's so ***unique*** / ***impressive***!

2 I just want an umbrella that's ***incredible*** / ***practical*** – if it keeps me dry, I'm happy.

3 I read a ***fascinating*** / ***gorgeous*** article about the dangers of technology.

4 The party was ***sensible*** / ***unforgettable*** – I'll remember it for the rest of my life.

5 It's ***unique*** / ***incredible*** that people waste so much money on stupid gadgets!

6 It looks like a normal umbrella, but it contains very ***sophisticated*** / ***gorgeous*** electronics.

7 The CleverPet is ***sophisticated*** / ***suitable*** for small pets, like cats and dogs, but not large animals, like horses.

8 A: I lost my Oombrella. I forgot to take my phone with me.
B: Well, that wasn't very ***sensible*** / ***unique***, was it?

➤ Go back to page 90.

9.1 Verbal idioms

A Complete the sentences with the underlined verbal idioms in *The best (and the worst) of immersive theater.*

1. I can't really **tell** ________ ________ ________ immersive theater and interactive theater. Aren't they the same?
2. I tried to tell a joke, but it **fell** ________. Nobody understood it.
3. If you agree to help people all the time, they might **take** ________ ________ your kindness. You need to say 'no' more often.
4. Do you still have your old guitar, or did you **get** ________ ________ it?
5. Immersive plays usually **take** ________ in unusual locations.
6. They have a nice big yard, but they don't really **make** ________ ________ it.
7. Six actors **took** ________ ________ the play: four adults and two children.
8. I always write down the money I spend to help me **keep** ________ ________ my finances.
9. Everything is **going** ________ today! My computer stopped working and my car broke down!
10. If you don't **pay** ________ ________ your teacher, you won't learn very much.

B Complete the verbal idioms with the words in the box.

attention friends fun note sure true

1 I've always dreamed of being a chef, but I'm not sure my dream will ever **come** ________.
2 You shouldn't **make** ________ **of** other people's mistakes. They aren't funny at all.
3 When someone gives you good advice, always **take** ________ **of** what they say.
4 I **made** ________ **with** Alissa when we were at school, and we've liked each other ever since.
5 I didn't notice the sculpture in the corner. They should put it in the middle of the room to **draw** ________ **to** it!
6 I think I know the answer, but I need to check the internet to **make** ________.

➤ Go back to page 101.

10.2 Reflexive verbs

Complete the sentences with the correct reflexive pronouns. What do you think the reflexive verbs mean?

1 Can you all please behave ________! You're making too much noise!
2 Daisy bought ________ a box of chocolates this morning and ate every single one!
3 Where do you see ________ ten years from now, Hannah? Will you still be doing the same job?
4 Many people find it difficult to express ________ when they're speaking a foreign language. They know what they want to say, but they can't say it.
5 Look at that dog! It's having a good time playing in the water! It's really enjoying ________!
6 I want to do some exercise every day, but I don't trust ________. I'll probably give up after a week!
7 I need to go out for half an hour. Can you all amuse ________ while I'm gone?

➤ Go back to page 115.

6.2 Student A

Look at the table. Do you currently do these things? Complete the table so it is true for you. Then ask your partner questions and write down his/her answers.

	You		Your partner		
Activities	**Yes/No?**	**How long?**	**Yes/No?**	**How long?**	**Other details**
Use an app to study English					
Follow a celebrity on social media					
Regularly go to a favorite café					
Play a sport					
Collect something					
States					
Be a member of an online-only group					
Know someone from another country					
Have a desktop computer					
Have a car					

➤ Go back to page 67.

9.2 Student A

➤ Go back to page 105.

Communication Hub

7.2 Students A and B

1 a about a week
  b 8–10 months
  c 4–5 days
  d 18–24 months
  e about 3 days
  f about 2 days

2 a False. You should only reheat food once.
  b True. After the best if used by date, the food may lose some taste or color, but it's probably still safe to eat for a little longer.
  c True. Rice sometimes contains very strong bacteria which aren't killed by cooking. So after cooking, put any leftover rice in the fridge and eat within 24 hours.

➤ Go back to page 80.

8.3 Student A

Use the pictures and notes to write instructions for making a paper airplane. Use sequencing phrases. Then read out your instructions so that Student B can make a paper airplane.

How to make a paper airplane

Put a piece of paper on the table.

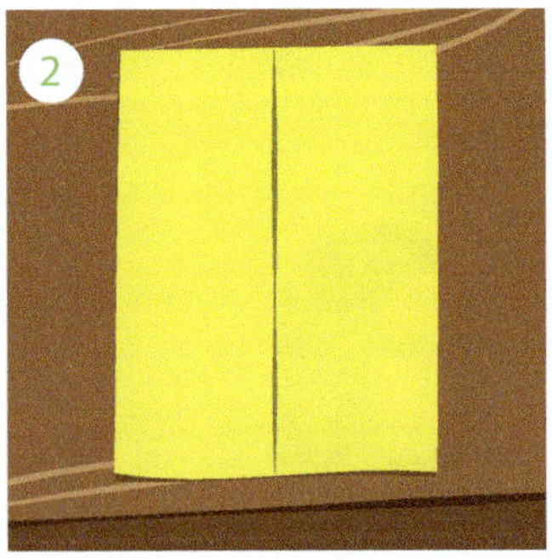

Fold the piece of paper in half lengthways, then unfold it.

Smooth it down.

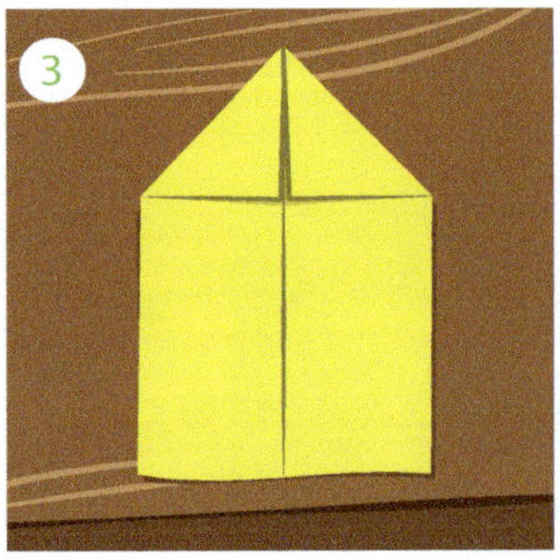

Form a point at the top of the paper.

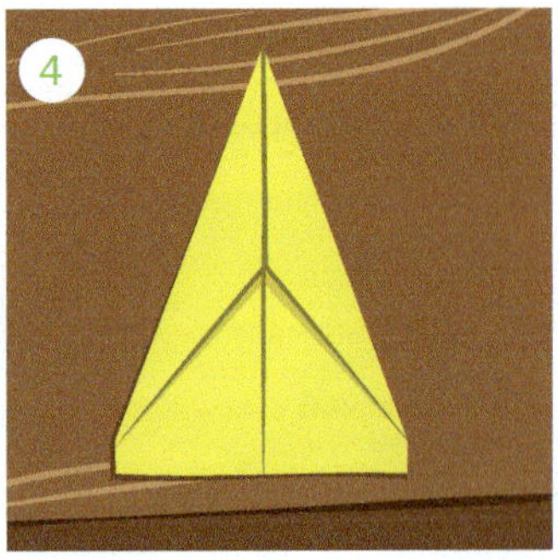

Fold the edges again.

Smooth down the edges with a ruler.

Fold the right side of the paper over the left side.

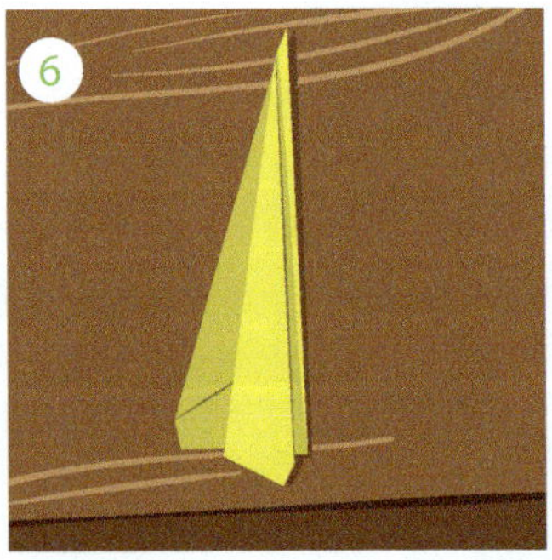

Create the wings.

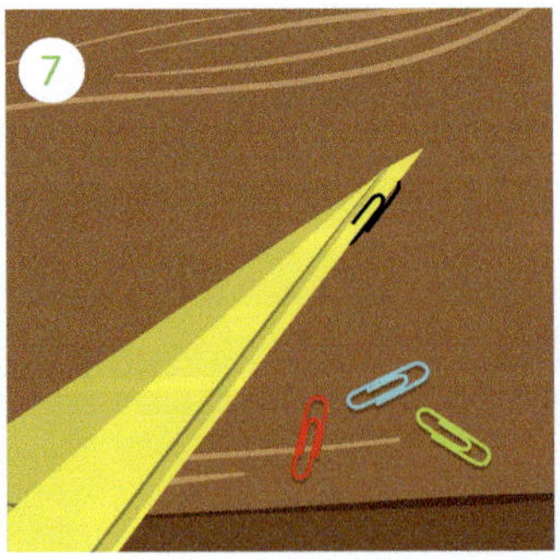

Attach a paperclip to the nose of the airplane – it will make it fly better.

Unfold the wings and you're ready for takeoff.

➤ Go back to page 95.

9.1 Student B

Proposal 2: Immersive theater

Costs (= money going out)		Income (= money coming in)
Building work: $100,000	Marketing: $150,000/year	Ticket sales: $1,500,000/year Sponsorship: $500,000/year
Equipment: $150,000	Other costs (e.g. electricity): $150,000/year	
Employees: $500,000/year		

- Sponsorship: Companies pay for their names/logos to be in the theater, on posters, etc.
- Ticket prices: $50–$100
- 80–100 tickets/performance; 400 performances/year (evenings and weekends only)
- No plans to help the community (e.g. free tickets for schools)

➤ Go back to page 99.

9.2 Student B

➤ Go back to page 105.

9.1 Student C

Proposal 3: Modern art gallery

Costs (= money going out)	Income (= money coming in)
Building work and equipment: $150,000	Gift shop and snack bar: $150,000/year Sales of paintings, etc: $200,000–$500,000/year
Employees: $150,000/year	
Marketing: $50,000/year	
Other costs (e.g. electricity): $100,000/year	

- Two major exhibits each year (international artists, etc.)
- Smaller exhibits each month (local artists, etc.)
- Free entry for all people to all exhibits
- The gallery will take 40 percent of the sale price of any paintings (e.g. by local artists) that it sells.

➤ Go back to page 99.

8.3 Student B

Use the pictures and notes to write instructions for making a paper heart. Use sequencing phrases.
Then read out your instructions so that Student A can make a paper heart.

How to make a heart

You will need a square piece of paper.

Fold the piece of paper in half both ways, and unfold it so that you see the fold marks.

Turn the piece of paper around so that the point is at the top, and fold the top corner down to the middle.

Fold the bottom corner to the top.

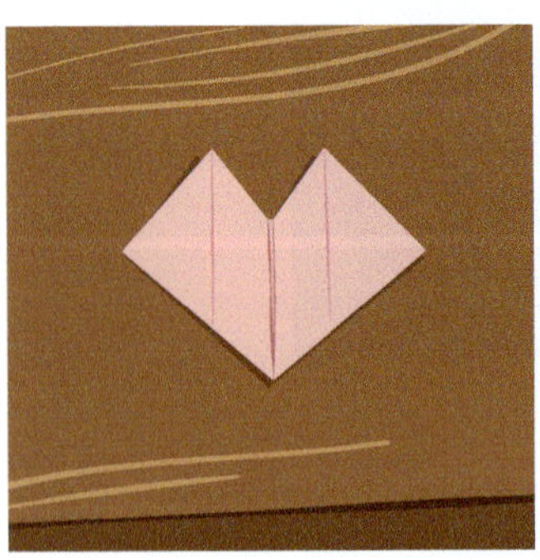

Fold the bottom edges to the middle.

Turn the paper over and fold the two top corners down.

Fold the corners down on both sides.

The heart is ready.

➤ Go back to page 95.

10.1 Students A and B

Take the quiz.

Psychology quiz

1 a Do we have more than 70 thoughts per day or fewer than 70?

b How many thoughts do we have each day?

2 You have paid for a weekend break in an expensive hotel. On the morning of your long journey, you feel sick and you just want to stay in bed. But it's too late to cancel your trip and get your money back. What do you do?

3 You're choosing a language school to help you pass an important exam. You know that 75 percent of School A's students passed the exam last year. You also know that 20 percent of School B's students failed the exam. Which school sounds better?

➤ Go back to page 110.

6.2 Student B

Look at the table. Do you currently do these things? Complete the table so it is true for you. Then ask your partner questions and write a note of his/her answers.

	You		Your partner		
Activities	Yes/No?	How long?	Yes/No?	How long?	Other details
Use an app to order food					
Write a blog					
Regularly go to a favorite movie theater					
Play a musical instrument					
Work for a company					
States					
Be a member of a club or society					
Know someone famous					
Have a laptop computer					
Have a pet					

➤ Go back to page 67.

W– introductory clauses

A Work in pairs. Read the magazine ad. Then look at the free time activities in the box. Which three do you think would be good subjects for an article? Why?

Share your stories with Life & *Style*.

In our Free time section, we're going to publish a new series of reader's articles, called *'Why everyone should …!'*

Send us your short articles about ideas for free time activities and hobbies – things that you think everyone should try doing at least once in their lifetime.

arts and crafts playing soccer skydiving stamp collecting stargazing (astronomy) team video gaming

B Read *Why everyone should … go stargazing!*. Put the sentences (a–f) in the order they are mentioned in the article (1–6).

a It is a good way to meet people. ___
b It is a simple hobby to start. ___
c Stargazing events at night are enjoyable. ___
d Cellular digital technology is useful. ___
e There is a place to go to use good equipment. ___
f You can join a club. ___

Why everyone should … go stargazing!

Wow! That's all I can say as I look at the rings of Saturn, or see a shadow pass across the sun. I'll never regret taking up stargazing.

Besides the wonder of discovering the universe, the great thing about stargazing is that it is an easy hobby to take up. You only have to look up into the sky at night and you've already become a stargazer. The cool thing is that there are many cell phone apps to help you when you start, telling you exactly what you are looking at.

It is also easy to visit your local observatory. The wonderful thing about going there is that you can use powerful telescopes to see deep into the universe. You'll see the mountains of Mars, the moons of Jupiter and the stardust of the Milky Way.

A nice thing about stargazing is that it is actually very sociable. There are local societies all over the country, and enthusiasts frequently meet up for 'star parties'. They are like having a picnic at night and are a lot of fun. One thing to remember is that you should bring hot chocolate rather than juice – it's important to keep warm!

Everyone wants to put a little 'wow!' into their lives, and stargazing is a surprisingly simple, inexpensive and enjoyable way to do that. There's so much to discover in the universe, so isn't it time to start exploring?

C Read the tips on writing articles. Then look at the article again. Which tips did the writer follow? Give examples.

Top tips for writing a magazine article

1 In the introduction, clearly give the topic, and grab the reader's attention and interest.
2 Use a more relaxed and personal style than in a newspaper report.
3 Show your passion for the subject.
4 Give each paragraph a clear topic.
5 Use direct quotes from interviews.
6 Use humor.
7 In the conclusion, summarize the key points in the article.
8 Finish with a memorable sentence, giving the reader something to think about.

D Look at the box. Find and underline the introductory clauses in the highlighted sentences in the article.

Introductory clauses

We can begin a sentence with an introductory clause that provides, and draws attention to, the topic for the rest of the sentence.

E Work in pairs. Complete the sentences with information about a hobby, sport or activity that you do. Then compare your answers with a partner.

1 One good thing about ________ is that ________.
2 Something that I like about ________ is that ________.
3 A good reason to ________ is that ________.
4 One problem with ________ is that ________.
5 One thing to remember is that ________.

WRITING

A PREPARE You are going to write a short magazine article. Choose a hobby, sport or free time activity as the subject of your article. Why do you think everyone should try it?

B PLAN Write notes for your article. Read the tips in Exercise C again to help.

C WRITE Write an article (150–200 words).

D REVIEW Work in groups. Read the other students' articles. Which activities would you choose to do? Why?

Write a reply in an online discussion forum

W comparing and recommending

A Work in pairs and discuss the questions.

1 Have you ever …

a read an online discussion forum?

b asked a question on an online discussion forum?

c written a reply to somebody on an online discussion forum?

2 What kind of online discussion groups are you interested in? Use the ideas in the box and your own ideas.

current affairs financial matters food health and fitness music and movies personal matters product reviews and recommendations travel

3 What's good about using these websites? What's bad about them?

B Read the forum post and the three replies. Which reply offers the best advice? What is the worst advice?

Message from Jo493

Hi. We have some relatives from another country coming to stay next week. I want to take them out to eat when they arrive after their long flight. I'm not sure whether to take them to an expensive restaurant or a fast-food joint.

I've asked them which they prefer, and they say they don't mind … but maybe they're just being polite. What do you recommend?

3 Comments

Reply from Miss Orange

It depends. Expensive restaurants serve better food, but of course they're much more expensive than fast-food joints. On the other hand, I like fast food because it's a lot faster than food from a restaurant. Why don't you ask them what they want to eat? Or how about cooking a meal for them instead?

Reply from hungry_al

I strongly recommend taking them for a good meal at an expensive restaurant. It'll make them feel special and welcome, and it should make an excellent first impression on them. They might be stressed after their flight, so they might want to go somewhere quiet and relaxing. You could always take them to a fast-food joint later during their stay with you – it's a nice thing to do with somebody you already know well. But for that first meeting, an expensive restaurant is far better.

Reply from Stewpot

I think you should take them for some fast food. After a long flight, they'll be tired and hungry, so they'll want to eat as quickly as possible. Another thing to remember is that your visitors might not feel very fresh and clean after their flight, and they may not have suitable clothes for a fancy restaurant. So you'll have to take them home first so they can change their clothes … and that could take hours. It's much quicker and easier if you take them for some simple food at a fast-food joint. After all, you can always take them to your favorite restaurant the next day. Good luck!

C Read again. Which reply or replies …

1 started with a clear recommendation?

2 ended with a clear recommendation?

3 introduced a third option?

4 thought about how the visitors will feel after their trip?

5 missed some important information in the original message?

6 gave reasons to explain why their recommendation is better?

7 suggested a way of using both options?

D Look at the box. Choose *Do* or *Don't* for each rule.

Comparing and recommending

1 **Do / Don't** start with a clear recommendation. (I think you should …; I strongly recommend …)

2 **Do / Don't** say it depends. The writer is asking you for a recommendation, so don't make their decision more complicated.

3 **Do / Don't** use comparatives to show why your option is better. (It's much quicker and easier …)

4 **Do / Don't** just talk about what you prefer.

5 **Do / Don't** show that you have thought about the people in the situation. (They might be stressed after their flight, so …)

6 **Do / Don't** give reasons for your recommendation.

7 **Do / Don't** add extra suggestions.

8 **Do / Don't** end with a clear recommendation. (… is far better.)

WRITING

A PLAN Read the forum post. What are the two options? Write notes on some arguments for and against each option.

I want to organize a dinner party for about 20 people from work and their families. I like the idea of a pot luck dinner party, but I've heard they don't always work well. Maybe I should just cook all the food myself. What do you recommend?

B WRITE Which option will you recommend? Write your reply (100–150 words).

C REVIEW Work in groups. Read each other's replies. Did everyone follow all the rules in the skills box? Who wrote the best recommendation?

Write a biography

W – using linking words to show contrast

A SPEAK Work in pairs. Read the short biography *Sal Khan, founder of the Khan Academy*.

1 Who is Sal Khan?
2 What are the main events in his life?
3 How innovative is he? Why?

Sal Khan, founder of the Khan Academy

1 Sal Khan is one of the most innovative people in education today. The Khan Academy, which he started in 2006, makes free online videos to teach people around the world about math, science and many other things.
2 Sal was born near New Orleans, US, in 1976. After college, he found a well-paid job in finance. However, he soon realized there was more to life than money.
3 Sal's life changed in 2004, when he started giving math lessons to members of his family. To save time, he decided to record his lessons and post them on YouTube. Despite the simple quality of the videos, they soon became popular around the world. Suddenly, he was teaching millions of people and making a real difference to their lives.
4 Although Sal didn't invent video-based learning, he helped make it popular and successful. His main innovation was to give everything away for free. As a result, he can really help those people who need it.
5 Sal's story teaches us that we don't need to be an inventor to be innovative, and we don't need to be powerful to change the world. In fact, we just need to do something we love. Hopefully, we can help other people along the way.

B Read again. Are the sentences true (T) or false (F)? Correct the false sentences.

1 You can only watch the videos in the US. ___
2 Sal's first job was as a teacher. ___
3 He made videos because he wanted to be famous. ___
4 Sal was the first person to teach using YouTube videos. ___
5 The writer thinks that Sal loves his work. ___

C A good biography usually has five sections. Match the sections (1–5) with the explanations (a-e). Use the biography of Sal Khan to help you.

1 introduction
2 backstory
3 turning point
4 impact
5 conclusion

a the story of the person's early life: family, education, first jobs, etc.
b why the person is special; how they changed the world
c lessons for our own lives
d who you are writing about and that person's biggest achievements
e something happened that changed the person's life

D Look at the box. Add an example of each linking word from Sal Khan's biography.

Using linking words to show contrast

We use linking words (*although*, *despite*, *however*) to link two different or contrasting ideas, one of which is unexpected, surprising or seems to be contradictory.

although + subject + verb

- ***Although*** *Sal Khan isn't an inventor, he's very innovative.*
- *Sal Khan is very innovative,* ***although*** *he isn't an inventor.*

1 ________________________________

despite + noun

2 ________________________________

despite + (*not*) + verb + *-ing*

- ***Despite*** *not being an inventor, Sal Khan is very innovative.*

despite the fact that + subject + verb

- ***Despite the fact that*** *he isn't an inventor, Sal Khan is very innovative.*

however

- *Sal Khan isn't an inventor.* ***However,*** *he's very innovative.*
- *Sal Khan is very innovative;* ***however,*** *he isn't an inventor.*

3 ________________________________

E Complete the sentences with the correct linking words.

1 ________________ the fact that he had no experience as an engineer, he solved an extremely difficult engineering problem.
2 Nobody was interested in her ideas at first, ________________ they became a lot more popular later.
3 Her invention was gorgeous and extremely innovative. ________________, it was far too expensive at first.
4 She ended up changing the world ________________ some very serious challenges at the beginning.
5 ________________ he was only 14 at the time, he managed to win the design competition.

WRITING

A PREPARE You are going to write a short biography of a famous innovator or an innovative friend or family member.

B PLAN Use the five-section plan in Exercise C to help you.

C WRITE Write your biography (about 200 words). Try to use linking words to show contrasting ideas. Use the skills box to help you. Check your grammar and spelling.

D REVIEW Work in groups. Read the other students' biographies. Which biography is about the most innovative person?

9 Writing

Write a review

W – using colons to introduce explanations

A Look at the pictures and read the reviews. Which event was better, the exhibit or the concert?

Robert Gonsalves exhibit at the TACA

One of my favorite artists is Robert Gonsalves (1959–2017). I fell in love with his incredible paintings years ago, so I was delighted to visit an exhibit of his work last month at the Toronto Academy of Contemporary Art.

His paintings show beautiful scenes with a twist: they all show two different worlds coming together. This means you can enjoy the paintings on two levels: first as objects of beauty, and then as amazing ideas to help you see the world differently.

However, I visited the exhibit on a Saturday afternoon, when it was extremely crowded. At times, it was difficult to get close to the paintings. Also, the space felt too small for so many paintings. If there were only one painting on each wall, it would create a much more powerful impression.

Overall, I would strongly recommend the exhibit, but you should go when it is less crowded.

Mel Montuno in concert at the City Arena

Last night I attended a concert by Mel Montuno, one of today's most exciting young musicians.

I became a fan of Mel's music two years ago, when I saw her performing live for an audience of 30. Now she is an international star – she usually has audiences of 10,000!

Although Mel is still an incredible songwriter with a beautiful voice, I definitely preferred her before she was famous. Last night's concert felt 'too big': she looked uncomfortable with such a large audience and hardly interacted with her fans at all.

More seriously, the music was too loud and the lights were painfully bright. After half an hour, I had to leave, to give my ears and eyes a break!

Mel Montuno is currently on an eight-city tour of the country. If you like huge concerts, you might want to buy a ticket. But if, like me, you prefer calm, beautiful music, I recommend buying Mel's new CD, *My Jazz Age*, instead.

B Read again and answer the questions.

1 Why did the writer decide to go to the exhibit/concert?
2 What did the writer like?
3 What wasn't so good?
4 What does the writer recommend? Why?

C What is the purpose of the paragraphs in each review? How are the two reviews similar? How are they different?

D Read the advice about writing reviews. Find examples of each piece of advice in the reviews.

1 Add a personal touch to describe how you felt.
2 Include practical information.
3 Don't be too negative – write about how you would do things differently or why people might not mind the problems.
4 Avoid repeating words like *beautiful* or *amazing*. Try to include a range of words instead.
5 Always end with a clear recommendation for your readers.

E Look at the box. Find three colons in the reviews. Underline the explanations after each colon. Circle the key phrase before each colon.

Using colons to introduce explanations

We can use colons (:) to join two sentences together and show how they are connected. The information after the colon provides an explanation for the key phrase before the colon.

F Match the beginnings of the review writers' sentences (1–3) with the endings (a–c).

1 There were three problems with the restaurant:
2 My recommendation couldn't be clearer:
3 When I arrived at the festival, I got an unpleasant surprise:

a go and buy tickets for this concert immediately.
b the food was bad, the service was slow and the prices were too high.
c half of the musicians had canceled their live shows because of the bad weather.

WRITING

A PREPARE You are going to write a review of an art event. Write about a real event that you attended or invent one.

B PLAN Write notes. Think about:

1 What was good about the event?
2 What would you improve? How?
3 Would you recommend the event to other people?

C WRITE Write your review (150–200 words).

D REVIEW Work in groups. Read some of your classmates' reviews. Which events would you like to attend?

W writing a report

A Work in pairs and discuss the questions.

1 Why do people write reports? What are some situations where non-business people write reports?
2 Why do people read reports? What information do they need?

B Read the *Report on charity auction* and answer the questions.

1 Why has the writer written the report?
2 What went well with the auction? What went wrong?
3 What did the writer learn from the experience?

REPORT ON CHARITY AUCTION

Summary:
On December 15, we held a charity auction to raise money for the local hospital. The auction raised less money than expected. This report explores what we did wrong.

Background:
We asked 24 local celebrities (e.g. sportspeople, TV presenters) to donate gifts for our auction. We received 55 gifts, including many valuable items (e.g. a signed soccer ball, a beautiful painting). We expected to raise around $5,000. 720 people attended our auction event. The auction only raised $322. Many of the items were not sold.

Analysis:
1 **Paradox of choice:** There were too many items, so people could not decide. If we had limited the auction to around ten items, we would probably have made more money.
2 **Hook numbers:** We wanted to attract large numbers of people to the auction, so in our marketing materials, we showed pictures of the best items with low starting prices, e.g. $2 for the signed soccer ball. We shouldn't have done this because it encouraged people to make offers of a few dollars, not hundreds of dollars.

Recommendations:
- For future auctions, limit the number of items to around ten.
- In marketing materials, show the value of the items (e.g. *Worth over $500*) rather than the starting price.

Glossary

auction (n) a public occasion when things are sold to the people who offer the most money for them

donate (v) to give something such as money or goods to an organization, especially to a school, hospital, political party or charity

C Look at the box. Match the features of a report (1–8) with the explanations (a–h). Find examples in the report.

Writing a report

A report describes a past event or a present situation and ends with recommendations for the future.

1 title
2 summary
3 headings
4 bullet points
5 numbered lists
6 full forms
7 facts and figures
8 examples

a Use these small black circles to make it easier to read lists of items.
b Your report should include dates, names, numbers, etc.
c In the first paragraph, say briefly what happened and why you've written the report.
d The reader can see immediately what the report is about.
e You can use these to show that the order of items in a list is important.
f Use words like *Analysis* and *Recommendations* to show you're starting a new section.
g Include these to explain important points. You can put them in parentheses: (e.g. ...).
h Reports are usually fairly formal, so it's best to write separate words (e.g. *do not*) instead of contractions (e.g. *don't*).

D Find examples of the third conditional and *would have* or *should have done* in the report. Which section are they in? Why?

WRITING

A PREPARE You are going to write a short report about an event where some things could have been better. Think about:

- will you write about a real event or will you invent one?
- what event will you describe? Something from your work or studies? An accident that you had?
- who will read your report? Why?

B PLAN Write notes under these headings:

- Background: What happened?
- Analysis: What went wrong? Why?
- Recommendations: What should happen differently in the future?

C WRITE Write your report. Remember to use headings, bullet points or numbered lists. When you finish writing the three main sections, write a short summary at the beginning.

D REVIEW Work in groups. Read some of your groups' reports. Do you agree with their recommendations?

Audio scripts

UNIT 6

Lesson 6.1, Listening, Exercise B

6.1 Soccer, // basketball, // golf, // tennis // – four of the world's most popular sports. / They are played by millions / and watched by millions more, / and all four / are in the greatest festival of sports, // the Olympic Games.

However, // there is one sport / that is just as popular as those, / but it still hasn't been accepted in the Olympics, / and indeed, // many people say / that it is not even a sport. / What sport am I talking about? // eSports. / Yes, // electronic sports, / or competitive video gaming.

Now, I guess many of you think video games are just something people play at home or on their phones. In fact, they are played in the same way as any other sport, with teams competing against each other in large venues and stadiums, in front of thousands of paying spectators, and with millions more watching online.

Even if you already know how massive eSports are, maybe many of you think gaming is not actually a sport. But I hope to persuade you that video gaming has all the features that we see in other sports.

First of all, it is clearly competitive. Players and teams compete in national and international tournaments, with a goal to win the final, lift the trophy and become the champions. The will to win is a key part of video gaming.

Also, playing video games requires incredible mental strength and skill. You need to focus for long periods of time and the games are very fast. eSports demand smart thinking, quick decision-making and great communication between team members, just like traditional team sports.

Of course, some people argue that video gaming is not a real sport because it doesn't require physical strength. Now, I accept it isn't the same as soccer or football, for example, but, because the games are long and demanding, professional gamers have to be very fit. If your fitness levels are poor, so is your ability to concentrate. This is why the managers and coaches of professional teams make sure their players spend time training in the gym and have a healthy diet. That all sounds like a sport to me.

So, have I changed your mind yet? Do you now feel that eSports should be in the Olympics? If not, remember that when they choose new sports for the games, they are looking for ones that are popular and have strong youth appeal. That sounds like eSports to me. Online eSports platforms have hundreds of millions of users every week. While the numbers of people playing and watching traditional sports are declining, they are rapidly increasing for eSports, and most of those people are young people.

So, eSports are physically and mentally demanding. They attract young people like no other sport. They are popular all over the world, and, of course, anyone can take part. They have already become a professional success story, with famous top players, great teams, and enthusiastic fans.

Video gaming is not a sport of the future; it is a sport of today, and so, eSports should, undoubtedly, be in the Olympic Games. Now, please excuse me, but I have a game to go and play. Thank you.

Lesson 6.1, Listening, Exercise D

6.2 In fact, they are played in the same way as any other sport, with teams competing against each other in large venues and stadiums, in front of thousands of spectators, and with millions more watching online.

Lesson 6.2, Listening, Exercise B

6.5 **RP = Radio Presenter S1 = Speaker 1 S2 = Speaker 2 S3 = Speaker 3 S4 = Speaker 4 S5 = Speaker 5**

RP: Hobbies. Interests. Pastimes. They're something more than watching TV, and something different from playing a sport. I'm Gavin Ross, and in this week's *Human Behavior*, we're asking you, the public, about what you like doing in your free time. What hobbies do you have? How long have you been doing them? Why do you have them? Let's hear from some of our listeners out on the streets in Boston today.

S1: I'm really into classic or vintage cars. I've been buying them since I was 18, when I first learned to drive and got my first one, a small 1960s sports car. Obviously, it isn't exactly a cheap hobby, what with buying and then repairing them. It means I don't go on expensive vacations like my friends, but I'm not going to give it up. I've just bought an old Mini, so I'll start working on that tomorrow.

S2: Arts and crafts are my thing – jewelry making, painting, woodwork. I've had this interest since I was a child. For the last six months, I've been going to pottery classes. In fact, I've been working in the studio this afternoon – that's why my hands are so dirty. As a hobby, it's relaxing and a great escape from daily stress, and, you know, it makes time fly – a sure sign I'm enjoying myself.

S3: I don't really have a hobby, but my husband is an enthusiastic cyclist. Actually, I think that cycling is an obsession for him, rather than a hobby. If he isn't out on a ride, he's cleaning the thing, or checking out the latest accessories online. He's been doing it since his teens, so I knew what I was getting when I married him. It isn't really my thing, so I leave him to it; it seems to keep him in shape and happy.

S4: I don't know if you can call this a hobby, but I spend most of my time following Danny CJ, the singer – I'm a massive fan. I've been a member of his fan club for a long time, I've been to a lot of his concerts and I collect everything I can about him: all the music, pictures, posters, calendars. It's great following him on social media, too. He even replied to one of my tweets once. Whenever he comes to Boston, my friends and I all hang out outside his hotel. He's in there now – we've been waiting here all day, but we haven't seen him yet. Hold on, is that him? Danny! Danny! Over here!

S5: Do I have a hobby? Well, you might say my hobby is having hobbies. I tend to get really into something, like, at first, I get really obsessed with it, but then I soon lose interest. I don't know why. I've always been like this. Recently, I've been getting into bird watching – I've bought all the kits and a bunch of books, and I've joined two local societies. No idea how long this will last though. I might start cooking classes soon, or take up sailing. Anything that gets me out of the house.

RP: Those are just some of the people I've met while making this show, and I'd like to hear from even more of you. Visit our show's website to see how you can take part in this series of *Human Behavior*. The address is www.radiotalk.nett/humanbehavior …

UNIT 7

Lesson 7.1, Listening, Exercise C

7.2 **V = Vicky C = Charlie T = Tina M = Markus**

V: Charlie! You're here at last!

C: Hi, Vicky. Sorry I'm a little late.

V: No problem. You're only … 20 minutes late. Welcome to pot luck night.

C: Thanks. Am I the last person here?

V: No, actually, there's only one other person so far. He arrived half an hour early!

C: Oh, that must be Felipe, right? He's always early.

V: True. But it was good because he helped me make my dish: a cheese and chilli salad.

C: Ach … I'm allergic to dairy products. Oh, well. Never mind.

V: Hmm. Wow … those looks delicious, Charlie. What are they?

C: Spicy buffalo wings. They're a traditional dish from New York made with a hot sticky sauce.

V: Wow. That's … different.

C: Yes, that's what I thought. Uh … can I heat them up in the oven? They just need 15 minutes.

V: Sure, but you'll have to wait ten minutes. I'm heating up Felipe's dish right now.

C: OK, no problem.

V: Great. Let me take your dish. Go and join Felipe – he's waiting in the backyard.

C: OK, thanks.

V: Aha … Tina. Welcome to pot luck night!

T: Thanks. Is everyone else here already?

V: No, not yet. But Felipe's here, and Charlie.

T: Those look nice. What are they?

V: Buffalo wings. Charlie brought them. Hmm … I've never eaten buffalo meat before. I wonder what it tastes like.

T: Hang on … that can't be right. They can't be buffalo wings. Buffaloes don't have wings!

V: No, you're right. But they're definitely wings. They could be chicken or something like that.

T: Aha … yes. Isn't there a city called Buffalo in New York? The name must come from the city, not the animal.

V: Good thinking. Anyway, what have you brought?

T: It's my own recipe. It's called cheesy chicken pasta surprise.

V: Oh, right. What's the surprise?

T: Ah … you'll have to wait and see. Can I just heat it up in the oven?

V: Well, uh … you'll have to wait for Charlie's dish … and Felipe's dish. It's chicken curry in a creamy sauce.

T: Oh, yes, so that's what smells so good. I love hot, spicy food.

V: Great. So let me take your dish to the kitchen. Go and join the others out in the backyard.

V: Markus! Great to see you. Come on in.

M: Thanks. I'm so sorry I'm late … again! You must think I'm so disorganized!

V: No, don't worry. Most of the others have just arrived, too. So … what have you brought?

M: Cream of chicken soup. I hope that's OK.

V: Uh … yeah, I hope so, too. But I don't have any soup bowls, so it might be a little difficult. I suppose we could drink it from cups. Uh … do I need to heat it up?

M: No, don't worry. I heated it up before I left. That looks great. What is it?

V: It's Tina's cheesy chicken pasta surprise.

M: Ah. It smells great, but … what are those red things?

V: They look like they might be chilies.

M: Oh, I hope not! I hate spicy food.

V: Well, they might not be chilies. They may be red peppers or something.

M: No, they're definitely chilies. Oh, well – hopefully there are some other dishes that I can eat.

V: Uh … you may have a problem there. We also have Felipe's spicy chicken curry and Charlie's spicy chicken wings.

M: Oh, no! Well, at least I have my chicken soup. And it means there will be more food for you.

V: Uh … not really. I don't like chicken.

7.5 Lesson 7.2, Listening, Exercise B
H = Host MT = Mrs. Taylor Mr.T = Mr. Taylor P = Philip A = Alison

H: Hello and welcome to *The Food Fad Show*. Today, we're talking about food waste. Did you know that globally, we waste a huge amount of the food we produce. The average person, just one person, wastes $200 of food every year. Can you believe that? $200!

H: In the studio today we have the Taylor family. A year ago, they decided to reduce the amount of food they waste every year by 50 percent. Tell us more, Mrs. Taylor.

MT: Well, I've been interested in food waste for a long time. But the more I researched the topic, the more I realized that we aren't just throwing away food; we're also throwing away hundreds of dollars per year – enough to pay for a nice family vacation. That's when I decided we needed to cut our own waste dramatically.

H: OK, so what have you done to save money?

MT: Let me give you an example. Ugly carrots taste just as good as beautiful carrots, but in our local grocery store, they cost less than half as much. As far as I'm concerned, the uglier, the better! Also, my grocery store always lowers the price of meat or dairy products that are getting close to their best if used by date. So it's usually possible to buy food a lot more cheaply by checking those dates carefully. As long as you eat the food soon after buying it, it's completely safe.

H: Right. So it's all about money, then, Mr. Taylor?

Mr.T: No, not really. Food production has a massive impact on the environment: first to produce the food and distribute it, and then to get rid of any waste. I always thought the best way to save the planet was to reduce the amount of garbage we throw away and to reuse and recycle as much as possible. But in fact, the food itself has a much greater impact than the packaging it comes in. For example, throwing away a head of lettuce harms our planet 100 times more than throwing away the plastic bag.

H: Really? That's amazing. Why?

Mr.T: Well, just think of all the water needed to grow it, the electricity to keep the greenhouse at just the right temperature, and then the environmental cost of keeping it fresh all the way from the farm to your fridge. It all adds up!

H: Wow! I'd never thought of that!

Mr.T: Here's another example. It takes 100 buckets of water to bake one loaf of bread. A hundred! Think about that the next time you throw away some one-day-old bread. If we could end all food waste around the world, it would be like taking one quarter of the world's cars off the roads. As far as I'm concerned, the less food we throw away, the better.

H: OK, so what have you done to cut down on food waste? Alison?

A: Yes, well, before our experiment, Mom or Dad always served up a large plate of food for each of us, but it was usually too much for me. So half of it always went in the garbage can. These days, we all help ourselves to food from a serving dish in the middle of the table. It's great because now we only take what we want – and we eat everything on our plates. It's much better because the less we cook, the less we waste.

H: OK, great. And what about leftovers?

A: When we started off, we had a rule that we had to eat yesterday's leftovers before any fresh food. But it was awful, so we stopped it. I mean, yesterday's leftovers are disgusting! Who wants to eat those? But now we use those leftovers to make soup or a stew. It's still a little strange, but the longer we do it, the more normal it feels.

H: Yes, I'm sure. OK, and what about Philip? Can I ask you a question or are you too busy playing on your phone?

P: Don't worry – I'm not playing. I wanted to show you a cool cell phone app. It helps us keep track of exactly what food we have in the house – and when that food will go bad.

H: Oh, OK. Sorry. So … how does it work?

P: Well, you need to type in all the numbers whenever you buy – or eat – anything. Some people might find that to be a waste of time, but I like that sort of thing. Of course, you don't need to count every single potato, for example, but the more carefully you count things, the more accurate your results will be. It's really fascinating when you study the numbers. Now, whenever we're in the grocery store, we can check what we need and what we don't. The app also sends us a notification when something is getting close to its best if used by date. That's really useful.

H: Yes, I'm sure.

P: And it even suggests delicious meal ideas to use up the ingredients we have, instead of buying new ones all the time. I never enjoyed cooking before, but thanks to the app, it's a lot more fun. And best of all, the app tells us exactly how much money we're saving every day.

H: Oh, yes. Tell us about the money, Mrs. Taylor.

MT: Well, so far, it's been a great success. According to Philip's app, we've managed to save $730 in food bills alone over the past year. And guess what? We're going on vacation next week to celebrate our excellent achievement.

H: Wow! Congratulations!

UNIT 8

Lesson 8.1, Listening, Exercise B

8.3 **C = Caroline T = Toby**

C: Hey, Toby. Do you want some coffee?

T: No, thanks. I'm in a hurry. I need to go to the library to work on my project for college.

C: Really? What's the project?

T: We have to invent 'something that will make a difference to people's lives'. But I'm terrible at coming up with ideas. They didn't teach us how to be creative in school when I was younger! But you, you're so creative. I mean, you write amazing stories; you design beautiful clothes. How do you do it?

C: Well, you can actually learn to use your imagination better. I've read a lot of books about creativity, and I've learned some great techniques from them.

T: Really? Can you give me an example?

C: Well, whenever I feel like I have too much work, I always stop working for an hour or so.

T: But I don't have time to stop. I'm really busy!

C: I always thought the same. But when I tried it, I found that a break actually boosted my creativity. When I'm relaxed, I have lots more creative ideas, and I'm much more productive after a break – I get more work done in less time. Tell me, how do you fill your time in the evenings?

T: Uh, I usually just watch TV or play games on my phone. I'm too tired to do anything else.

C: Aha. So that's what's blocking your creativity: you're filling your brain with information all the time. You need to unplug completely. Instead of watching TV, go for a run. You need to let your mind wander freely.

T: OK, I guess I can watch less TV. But I hate running!

C: Well, it doesn't have to be running. You could go dancing or swimming, or get some other type of physical exercise. They're all good for generating new ideas.

T: OK. I love swimming, so I guess I could go to the swimming pool once a week.

C: Great. Swimming's actually perfect because the water is blue.

T: Uh, sorry? What does that have to do with creativity?

C: Well, I read recently that the color blue makes us more creative. Whenever I need to think outside the box, I go to the beach and look at the sky and the ocean. It always helps.

T: OK, but it doesn't really help me with my project. I need to start work on it right now. I'm actually getting stressed about it.

C: Well, maybe that's the problem: you're letting your emotions block your creativity. You should look at a problem from the outside, to take away the emotions. Then it's much easier to find a solution. That's why it's easier to solve other people's problems than your own – because you can focus on the problems, not the emotions.

T: OK, but …

C: So another good technique is to discuss your ideas with other people – and listen to what they say. The best solutions usually come from group discussions and brainstorming sessions. And if there's nobody you can talk to, you can imagine having a conversation with a friend. Look at the problem through someone else's eyes.

T: OK, yes, I know what you mean. But what about my project? I need to come up with an invention right now. But I don't have any ideas at all. My mind's gone blank!

C: Well, there's one last trick I usually use when I really have no ideas. I call it the alphabet technique. OK, so tell me three letters of the alphabet.

T: Uh, W, G and P.

C: Perfect. So your invention needs to solve a problem, and that problem needs to start with your first letter, W.

T: Water? It isn't really a problem, is it?

C: Well, let's use your second letter to help us. What was it?

T: G for – grass. Hmm, water, grass. Aha, maybe the invention could be a better way of watering the grass in people's yards when they're away on vacation. I mean, just pouring water onto the grass all day and all night is really wasteful. But what's the solution?

C: I don't know. But it needs to start with your third letter, which was …?

T: P – for plastic bottles. Aha, I could use old plastic bottles, filled with water. Then I could make tiny holes in the bottles, so the water comes out really slowly, over a week or two.

C: Sounds good!

T: Hmm. I need to think about this carefully. OK, I'm going for a long walk along the beach to figure out the details. See you later.

C: OK. Call me if you need any help! Good luck!

Lesson 8.2, Listening, Exercises B and C

8.4 **L = Leo T = Teresa**

L: Hello, and welcome to this week's *Must-have Gadgets* podcast. I'm Leo Kovalski.

T: And I'm Teresa Martinez. Now, earlier this week I went to the International Gadget Show, where I saw some really amazing gadgets. And I've brought two along today to show you, Leo.

L: Sounds great. So what do you have for us?

T: Well, let's start with a very sensible invention: the Oombrella. What do you think, Leo?

L: Uh … it just looks like a normal umbrella. I mean, the design is gorgeous, really nice, but … it isn't exactly innovative, is it?

T: Oh! But this Oombrella is unique. It's the world's first umbrella that's connected to the internet.

L: What? Why on earth do I need an umbrella that connects to the internet?

T: Well, did you bring an umbrella to work today?

L: No, unfortunately. I forgot to check the weather forecast, so I didn't know it was going to rain.

T: Aha. Well, you can borrow my Oombrella today. It'll check the weather forecast for you. If the forecast says it's going to rain later, Oombrella will send a message to your cell phone.

L: OK, but why do I need a special umbrella just to send weather forecasts to my phone?

T: Well, the Oombrella is especially suitable for forgetful people, like you, who forget to check the weather forecast on their phones.

L: Yes, well, I am a fairly forgetful person. But what do forgetful people do all the time? They leave their umbrellas behind in cafés, or on the bus! What if I lose your Oombrella tonight?

T: Well, if you leave it behind, you'll get a message on your phone. They call it the unforgettable umbrella because you can't forget it.

L: OK, yes, that is pretty practical, I suppose.

T: Yes. And the Oombrella also has lots of sophisticated electronics: if you go for a long walk in the rain tonight, the app will send you a weather report when you get home. So you can read all about the weather during your walk.

L: Hmm … I'm not sure I need an Oombrella. I never go for a walk unless the sun's shining. The big question for me is: will it keep me dry if there's a storm tomorrow morning when I'm coming to work?

T: Absolutely! It's made of super-strong materials, so it won't break. You'll be able to use it for years.

L: Really? Well that is impressive. My umbrellas always break after five minutes in a storm. So if this Oombrella lasts for years, I'll be very happy.

T: Well, I only said you could borrow mine. I'd like to have it back tomorrow.

L: Oh, yes, of course. So … what else do you have?

T: Well, the second gadget is called CleverPet. It's a food bowl for dogs and cats.

L: Great. And don't tell me … it's connected to the internet, right?

T: Yes! How did you guess? Do you have any pets, Leo?

L: Yes, I have a dog named Henry.

T: And what does Henry do all day, while you're at work?

L: Uh … not much. He sleeps most of the day, but sometimes he chews the furniture in my apartment.

T: Well, that's because he's bored. Of course he chews your furniture if he has nothing else to do all day.

L: OK. And what does this have to do with your incredible internet-connected dog food bowl?

T: Well, it isn't just a bowl. It's a puzzle.

L: A puzzle? For dogs?

T: Yes. There are three buttons with lights. When a light flashes, the dog has to press a button. If he presses the right button, the light goes on again and he wins something to eat.

L: OK.

T: Then, over the next few days, weeks, even years, the puzzles get more and more difficult. The dog has to remember lots of information and press the buttons in the right order.

L: Oh, right. And, uh, do dogs enjoy puzzles?

T: Absolutely! They love them. It keeps them busy for hours, which means they never get bored. And if they don't get bored, they don't chew the furniture.

L: Well, I must admit, it sounds fascinating.

T: It is. And it really helps pets stay active. Scientists have shown that pets stay healthier and they live longer if they keep busy. You should definitely get one for Henry.

L: Yes, I think I might!

T: Great.

L: OK, so that's all from today's podcast. We'll be back next time with more must-have gadgets. Thanks for listening.

UNIT 9

Lesson 9.1, Listening, Exercise B

9.1 **C = Chair L = Leon V = Violet F = Florian**

C: Welcome to the final of the Warehouse Project competition. Now, we received hundreds of excellent ideas, but there can only be one winner. Today, the three finalists are here to present their proposals before the public vote later this evening. But for now, let's hear from the first finalist, Leon MacGregor.

L: Thank you. I'd like to present my proposal to turn the warehouse into a community music center, with modern recording studios, rehearsal rooms and a performance area for live concerts. If the proposal is successful, people will be able to use the center free of charge. I believe music can make a big difference to our community, especially for older people who have retired from work. If we open a community music center, it will change thousands of people's lives, by giving them opportunities to go out, meet new people and learn new skills. Won't that be wonderful for our city?

My dream is for the people of this city to join music classes with professional musicians, to learn how to sing or to play a musical instrument. They'll work together to form bands, orchestras and choirs. They'll have the space and equipment they need to rehearse and create new music. And they'll be able to perform live in front of an audience. If you share my dream, vote for my proposal to help it come true. Music … for the community.

C: Thank you, Leon. Our next finalist is Violet Spring.

V: Thank you. As an actor, I love the theater. And I'm not alone – tens of thousands of people all over the country visit the theater every day. But not in this city. Since the Grand Theater closed down ten years ago, theater-lovers have had nowhere to go. They have to travel to theaters in other cities – and spend their money there instead of here. But I'm convinced that if we had a good, modern theater in this city, it would be extremely popular. What do I mean by a modern theater? Well, I firmly believe that the future is immersive theater.

Immersive theater is where the audience becomes part of the performance. There's no stage – just one shared space for actors and spectators alike. You don't just watch a play – you experience it. Immersive theater works best in a large open area, where groups of audience members can move around to watch different scenes of the play in different parts of the theater. And I think the city's warehouse would make a wonderful immersive theater. But it isn't just about art. Immersive theater is also a great business. The best shows attract rich international tourists who are prepared to pay premium prices. If we turned the warehouse into a theater, it would make a lot of money. This money could be spent on schools, roads and other important things for the city. If you like the sound of that, please support my proposal.

C: Thank you, Violet. Very interesting. Our final finalist is Florian Quirk.

F: Thank you. Let me ask you a question. What … is the purpose … of art? To keep bored people busy? To make money from rich tourists? No, I don't think so. Art is about opening your mind to new experiences, new emotions. It's about losing yourself … and finding yourself. Great art makes you laugh; it makes you cry; it makes you think. It helps you see things you've never seen, feel things you've never felt, understand things you've never understood. In short, the purpose of art … is to give a purpose … to life. That's why I'd like to turn the warehouse into a gallery of modern art. A place where audiences can view the works of today's best artists, including exhibits by some of the talented artists from this city. And if we make it free of charge, all the people of this city can enjoy the exhibits, displays and live performances. So if you really want to use this space for the arts, then forget about business plans and community projects. Let's create a gallery that will change the way the people of this city think … forever. Thank you.

C: OK, thank you. Well, I must say, all three proposals sound excellent! If the city council had three warehouses, maybe we could do all of those wonderful things. But we only have one warehouse, unfortunately, so we need to make a choice. I'd like to call a 15-minute break now so we can …

Lesson 9.2, Listening, Exercise B

9.5 **Z = Zoe J = Jacob**

Z: So, Jacob, how's your creative writing class going?

J: Really well, thanks, Zoe. This week, we've been writing flash fiction. That's where you have to write stories within a word limit, usually 1,000 words. It's really difficult.

Z: Really? Why?

J: Because you have to make every word count. It makes you think hard, and that makes you more creative.

Z: Yes, I see what you mean, but 1,000 sounds very extreme.

J: Well, it isn't as extreme as micro-stories. They're stories on social media sites like Twitter. A whole story told in a 140-character message.

Z: You're joking, right?

J: No, I'm not. Do you want to hear one of my favorites? 'It was him! She sat in embarrassed silence. She wondered if he even knew she existed. He sat beside her, wondering the same. Nobody spoke.'

Z: OK. It isn't much of a story, is it? I mean, nothing happened.

J: No. But it's about creating a powerful scene, and characters with real emotions.

Z: Characters? You just said 'he' and 'she'.

J: Well, it's usually better if the writer provides less information, so that you, the reader, can create the missing information from your own imagination.

Z: Uh, OK.

J: OK, so here's another one. 'Alone, he ran nervously into the dark forest. A shadow. "Who's there?" he shouted. "Don't worry," whispered a cold voice. "You aren't alone."'

Z: Oh, that's better. I see what you mean about using your imagination. I like the twist at the end.

J: What do you mean by 'twist'?

Z: It's when something happens in the story that you didn't expect. I mean, you think he's alone, but then he isn't. It's really powerful, isn't it?!

J: Yeah, I think so. There are also some groups on social media that write collaborative stories: stories that are created by a large group of people working together. So for example, I'll write the beginning of a story, in one 140-character message, and then you'll write the next part of the story, and so on. Eventually, we'll end up with an amazing story.

Z: Ah. It reminds me of a game we played when I was a child. We called it 'Pass the paper'. You write one line of a story on a sheet of paper, fold it down and pass it to the next player, who writes the next line, and so on. We could play it now, if you like. You'll enjoy it!

J: No, thanks. It isn't my kind of thing. But there are actually websites now that do similar things. You write a sentence online, and then someone else writes the next sentence, and so on. I know some people in my class use websites like those to give them ideas. Of course, most of the stories are trash, but it's all about opening your mind to new ideas.

Z: Yes, I'm sure.

J: And there's another one where each person can just write three words. Some of the stories are really funny.

Z: Oh, yes. That reminds me of another game we frequently played when I was a student in California, 'Add a word'. Do you know it? It's when a group of you sit in a circle. The first person says the first word from a sentence, like 'My'. And then the next person says the next word. For example …

J: Favorite?

Z: OK, yes. So, my – favorite, uh, frog.

J: Lives?

Z: Uh, under.

J: My.

Z: Uh, bed?

J: OK. Uh, because.

Z: He.

J: Can't.

Z: Afford.

J: A.

Z: Hotel?

J: Yeah, why not. Hey, that's a great game for collaborative stories, Zoe. You see! When you work together, you come up with ideas that you'd never have if you were on your own.

Z: Sure. So is that how you always come up with new ideas?

J: Not always, no. I sometimes use story dice.

Z: Story dice?

J: Yes. I have a set of 12 dice, and each one has six pictures, one on each side.

Z: OK.

J: So if I'm figuring out an idea for my story, I throw six dice. Then I have to use all six pictures in my story. Let's say the pictures on my dice show a castle, the color blue, an angry face, a bag of money, a motorcycle and a fish. So I have to write my story so that it includes all those things.

Z: Wow! So how about 'My fish was angry because he crashed his expensive motorcycle into a blue castle'?

J: Well, that's very creative, but it has to sound natural and believable. The story can have up to 1,000 words, remember.

Z: Cool. OK, I'm going to try to write it.

J: Great. It won't be easy … but it should be fun!

UNIT 10

Lesson 10.1, Listening, Exercise B

10.2 **R = Robert V = Vicky**

R: Would you mind if I borrowed your laptop for a few minutes?

V: No, of course not. Go ahead. Just bear in mind that it's really slow and it keeps crashing all the time.

R: Sounds like you need a new one.

V: Yeah, I know. I'm trying to buy one, but … it's difficult.

R: What do you mean?

V: Well, I went to the electronics store last week. They had over 100 laptops to choose from. After about three hours in the store, looking at every single laptop, I found two that I liked, but I was of two minds and I couldn't decide which one to buy. It was horrible. In the end, I gave up! But never mind. I still have my old computer, so it isn't so bad.

R: Ah. Sounds like the Paradox of Choice.

V: What's that?

R: Well, the name comes from an American psychologist, Professor Barry Schwartz. According to Professor Schwartz, most people assume that having lots of choices is always a good thing. But he's shown that in fact too many choices is bad for us. It makes us stressed, so we can't make decisions.

V: Uh … OK. So why do stores give us so many choices? Surely they'd sell more if they reduced the number of choices?

R: Exactly. The problem is, most companies still think more is better. But a few smart companies have realized that they'll sell more if they offer fewer choices. I read recently that a shampoo company cut the number of shampoo choices from 26 to 15. Everyone thought they'd lose sales, but in fact, their sales went up by ten percent.

V: Really? Wow! So fewer choices is better.

R: Yes, in general. But of course it's better to have some choice than no choice at all – that's just common sense.

V: Right.

R: So with your laptop, you should have gone to a smaller store. If you'd done that, you'd have had fewer choices, but your decision would have been much easier. The store where I bought mine had just three laptops to choose from. One was too expensive; one was too basic; the third one was absolutely fine, so I bought it. It took me five minutes. And I'm very happy with it.

V: Wow! I could never do that. I'd be worried that I'd missed the chance to buy a better computer somewhere else.

R: That's because you're a perfectionist.

V: A perfectionist? What's that?

R: It's a person who always looks for the perfect thing to buy. You can't relax unless you're sure you've studied every option and chosen the best one. And even after you've made a decision, you still worry that you've made the wrong choice.

V: Yeah, that definitely sounds like me! For example, I went shopping for some new shoes last week. After about six hours, I finally bought a pair. But when I got them home, I regretted my decision immediately. I realized that they weren't perfect and I shouldn't have bought them. So I took them back to the store to get my money back. Then I bought a different pair of shoes, but I took them back to the store a few days later. In the end, I bought the first pair again.

R: Yes, you're definitely a perfectionist. I, on the other hand, am what I call a 'quick decider'.

V: What's that?

R: It's a person who makes quick decisions without worrying about perfection. When I'm shopping for new jeans, for instance, and I find some jeans that are good enough, I buy them and stop worrying about them. And I never take them back to the store – unless they're damaged, of course. Once I've made up my mind, I stick with my decision.

V: Wow! You're so lucky. I could never do that!

R: Well, you think it's impossible, but maybe it's all in the mind. I think you can become a quick decider – you just need to put your mind to it! It'll make life much easier.

V: Yes, you're right. I'll definitely do that! From now on, I'm going to be a quick decider. But, uh, what if I change my mind later?

Lesson 10.2, Listening, Exercise B

10.3 **D = David B = Barbara A = Alice L = Leo**

D: Hello, and welcome back to *All in the Mind*. On today's show, we're talking about habits. I'm joined by Professor Barbara Janovich, an expert in habits. Welcome to the show, Professor.

B: Thanks, David.

D: So, Barbara, why do we develop bad habits? And why are they so hard to break?

B: Well, the best way to understand habits is to break them into four parts. First, there's a cue, which might be something that you see or hear or feel. So in your example with fast food, the cue might be that you're driving in your car and you see a sign for a fast-food restaurant. Or maybe you're walking through a shopping mall and suddenly you smell the fast food.

D: Oh, yes. That smell always makes me want to eat fast food, even when I'm not hungry! I wish it didn't, but it does!

B: Exactly. So the next stage is the routine – the actions you always take. So this is where you go into the fast food restaurant, order your food and eat it. In a true habit, you can do all of this without really thinking – it kind of happens to you, and your brain almost shuts off.

D: OK.

B: And then the third part is the reward: something nice happens. In this case, the sugar and salt in the food cause your brain to produce feel-good chemicals.

D: OK, so the cycle is cue, routine, reward. But you said there are four parts. What's the fourth part?

B: Well, this is the dangerous part: the craving. Let me explain. If you repeat the cycle a few times, your brain produces those feel-good chemicals earlier and earlier in the process. So instead of being part of the reward, you get that nice feeling at the cue stage – when you see the restaurant sign, for example, or you smell the food and you know the reward is coming soon. And now you have a problem: you've had the good feeling, but you haven't had the reward yet. This creates the craving – a powerful need to get your reward. Now you can't relax until you have your reward.

D: Ah. I wish I'd known about all this a few years ago! But I guess it's too late for me now. Is there anything I can do to break the cycle?

B: Yes, but isn't easy. You can't stop the cues, and you still need the reward. So the trick is to change the routine. So for example, I always keep a package of low-fat salty snacks in my bag. That means that when I drive past a sign for a fast-food restaurant, I treat myself to a snack from the package.

D: Uh, can I try one of those?

B: Sure! Help yourself.

B: So the cue is the same, and the reward is similar – salty food – but I've changed the routine. Of course, salty snacks aren't perfect, but they're a lot cheaper and healthier than a burger and fries.

D: Sounds good. OK, so earlier we asked our listeners to call in to tell us about their bad habits. Our first caller is Leo. Leo, what's your habit?

L: Hello. Well, it's coffee. I drink about eight cups a day, but I don't even like it very much! I wish I could stop, but I can't control myself.

B: OK. Well, let's start with the first cup of coffee each day, Leo. What's your cue for drinking it?

L: It's when I arrive at work. I always make myself a cup of coffee before I check my emails.

B: How long does it take to get to work?

L: About an hour. Why?

B: Well, it sounds like the reward isn't really the coffee, but a five-minute break after your long, tiring trip.

L: Uh, yes, maybe.

B: So now we know the cue and the reward, the question is: is there a different routine that would give you the same reward after your trip to work?

L: I suppose I could get myself a glass of water and go for a quick walk around the office.

B: Sounds good.

D: OK, great. I hope your new routine works for you, Leo. I wish we had time to talk about your other seven cups of coffee, but we need to go to our next caller, Alice. What's your bad habit, Alice?

A: Well, actually, I'd like some help creating a new habit. You see, I wish I could run a marathon next year. I go running from time to time, but I want to get into the habit of running every day. I always set myself goals, but nothing seems to work. I really wish I were better organized.

D: Thanks for that, Alice. Professor?

B: Well, first of all, Alice, don't blame yourself. This is a very common problem. If you want to create a new habit, again you need to think about cues and rewards: what will make you remember to go running at the same time every day? How will you reward yourself for being good? So let's start by creating your cue, Alice. When would be a good time of day to go running?

Notes

Macmillan Education
4 Crinan Street
London N1 9XW
A division of Macmillan Education Limited

Companies and representatives throughout the world

American Language Hub Level 3B Student's Book ISBN 978-1-380-04725-0
American Language Hub Level 3B Student's Book with Student's App
ISBN 978-1-380-04719-9

Written by Jeremy Day and Gareth Rees.

With thanks to Signature Manuscripts for the Grammar Hub pages.

First published 2020

Designed by emc design ltd
Illustrated by Rasmus Juul represented by Lemonade Illustration Agency, Daniel Limon (Beehive Illustration)
Cover design by Restless
Cover photograph by Peathegee Inc/Getty Images
Picture research by Emily Taylor and Victoria Gaunt
Café Hub videos produced by Creative Listening
Café Hub video scripts written by James and Luke Vyner

The authors and publishers would like to thank the following for permission to reproduce their photographs:

Alamy Stock Photo Samuel Bay p62(tl,tr), Chris Howes/Wild Places Photography p68(cl), Maskot p100(tr), Mladen Mitrinovic pXIX(tr), roibu p98(t), Kurt De Leon Wulf p104(r); **Bridgeman Images** Passengers in the dining room aboard the airship LZ 127 'Graf Zeppelin' during the trip from Germany to America, 1928 (b/w photo)/© SZ Photo/Scherl p116(b); **Corbis** 94-95(background); **DIGITALVISION** pp82(b), 118(background), Uwe Krejci p114(tl); **Eden Full Goh** p86(r); **Getty Images** pp62(bl), 68(bl), 71(background), 97, 112(a), Alija pp100(br), 101, al_irfan78 pXXI(bl), Alexandros Maragos pp105-106(background), AMe Photo p112(c), Arterra/Contributor p80(3), Jose A. Bernat Bacete p86(l), Ezra Bailey pXXVI, Thomas Barwick p112(d), Caspar Benson pXXI(br), Blend Images – KidStock p65, Bloomberg/Contributor p91(b), Warren Bolster 61, 67(r), brunorbs p78(tcr), cristianoalessandro pXXVII(t), Daisy-Daisy p80(1), Peter Dazeley p67(l), Steve Debenport p98(bc), Nick Dolding p64(br), DrAfter123 p88(t), Blasius Erlinger p109, JackF p112(b), Marlene Ford p68(cr), franckreporter p104(l), Alena Gamm/EyeEm p76(c), JGI/Jamie Grill p117, Mike Harrington pXXIV(tl), Hero Images pp 69, 85, XXIV(cl), Hoffmann Photography p100(tl), iStockphoto pp110-111, iStockphoto/97 p113, iStockphoto/LUHUANFENG p79(br), Thinkstock Images/Monkey Business Images Ltd pXVII(br), iStockphoto/pilipphoto p115(tl), iStockphoto Thinkstock Images/photoncatcher pp106(b)-107(b), iStockphoto/Stevo24 p103(bl), iStockphoto/yang5i pXIX(bl), iStockphoto Thinkstock Images/Gary Blakeley pXVI(b), iStockphoto Thinkstock Images/Gabrielle Morehead p83(background), iStockphoto Thinkstock Images/fleurdrz pXVII(bl), iStockphoto Thinkstock Images/kasto80 pXXI(tl), iStockphoto/Thinkstock Images/tolokonov p105, thejokerstrick pp70(background, t), Chaithanya Krishna Photography p74(c), Mads Perch p97, PictureIndia RF/Asia Images Group p114(tr), David Madison p62(br), maxchu pXXIV(tr), Anik Messier p66(r), Dean Mitchel pp98, 99(b), moisseyev p80(2), Kelvin Murray p78(tcl), Richard Newstead pp92-93, PhotoDisc p 63(br), Quiet Noise Creative pXXI(tr), Ingrid Rasmussen/Design Pics p80(4), Lew Robertson pp79(cl),(t) Douglas Sacha p78(bcl), shironosov p66(m), Cultura RM Exclusive/BRETT STEVENS p76(t), Hulton Archive/Stringer 102(tr), SuperStock p68(br), Hindustan Times/Contributor p74; **Gilaxia** XXVII(b); **Imagesource** pXVII(tl); **PhotoDisc** pp94(br), 95(cl,b), Getty Images pXIX(br), Getty Images/Anthony Saint James p71(background-Tennis); **REX/Shutterstock** Oombrella/Bournemouth News p90(r), Bazmark Films/Warner Bros./Kobal p103(br), Flyte/Solent News p90(l); **Science Photo Library** SPUTNIK p116(t); **Shutterstock** Chesky p80(6), Olga Danylenko p66(l), Gorodenkoff p64(bl), SpeedKingz p80(5), thodonal88 p114(tm); **Springer Nature Limited** Paul Bricknell pXVII(tr); **Thinkstock Images** Klaus Vedfelt pXVI(t), vchal p81, vichie81 p100(bc), vladislavnosick p76(b), Westend61 pp62(bl), 73, Ross Woodhal p68(tl), Kathrin Ziegler p89, zodebala p74(b), p75: **Westend61** p115(b); **123RF**/ belchonock pXXVIII, handmadepictures p78(bl), Somchai Jongmeesuk p115(tm), Nadezda Murmakova pXIX(tl), raptorcaptor p78(br).

Commissioned photographs in the Café Hubs by Creative Listening.

Printed and bound in Mexico
by Compañía Editorial Ultra, S.A. de C.V.

2021 2020
04 03 02 01

American Language Hub

LEVEL 3B
Workbook

with Key + access to Audio

macmillan education

Macmillan Education
4 Crinan Street
London N1 9XW
A division of Macmillan Education Limited

Companies and representatives throughout the world

American Language Hub Level 3B Workbook with Key ISBN 978-1-380-04729-8
American Language Hub Level 3B Workbook with Key + access to Audio
ISBN 978-1-380-04723-6

Written by Signature Manuscripts

Signature Manuscripts has asserted their right to be identified as the author of this work in accordance with the Copyright, Designs and Patents Act 1988.

First published 2020

Designed by SPi Global based on original design by emc design ltd
Cover design based on original design by Restless
Cover image by Getty Images/Peathegee Inc

The authors and publishers would like to thank the following for permission to reproduce their photographs:

AlamyJaroszpilewski p55, Alamy/Jorge Tutor p64(tl); **Getty Images** pp42, 43, 56, Getty Images/All Canada Photos p48, Getty Images/AzmanJaka p69, Getty Images/Ezra Bailey p62, Getty Images/Bloomberg p54, Getty Images/Justin Case p40, Getty Images/Cultura Exclusive p72, Getty Images/Cultura RF p49, Getty Images/Steve Debenport p70(tr), Getty Images/Dougal Waters Photography Ltd p63, Getty Images/ERproductions Ltd p53, Getty Images/FatCamera p45(tl), Getty Images/GK Hart/Vicky Hart p56(tr), Getty Images/Hero Images p44(c), Getty Images/Image Source p60, Getty Images/iStockphoto p50(b), 57(tm), Getty Images/Lucy Lambriex p50(a), Getty Images/Maskot p67, Getty Images/Mediaphotos p46, Getty Images/Liam Norris p73, Getty Images/Science Photo Library RF p50(c), Getty Images/Skynesher p39, Getty Images/South_Agency p51, Getty Images/Nikola Spasenoski p45(b), Getty Images/Kevin Steele p64(tr), Getty Images/The Image Bank p68, Getty Images/Thomas M. Barwick INC p44(b), Getty Images/Troy House p65, Getty Images/Abel Mitja Varela p66, Getty Images/Westend61 p41; **PhotoDisc** p52; **Thinkstock** p57(tl); **Yellowdog Productions** p58.

Printed and bound in Mexico
by Compañía Editorial Ultra, S.A. de C.V.

2021 2020
04 03 02 01

Contents

6.1 Sports and hobbies

GRAMMAR
Modals of obligation

A Circle the correct answer, a, b or c.

1 You ___ attend soccer practice today – you can come tomorrow if you like.
   a shouldn't
   b don't have to
   c must not

2 You ___ tell the coach if you can't play in Saturday's game or she'll be annoyed with you.
   a must
   b need
   c don't have to

3 Don't disturb him – he ___ concentrate on making the shot.
   a doesn't have to
   b has to
   c should

4 You ___ wear the helmet, but I strongly recommend that you do.
   a must not
   b shouldn't
   c don't have to

5 If you want to improve your performance, you ___ train every day.
   a have
   b should
   c don't need to

6 Hey! You ___ kick the ball – you can only use your hands!
   a must not
   b don't have to
   c don't need to

B Circle the modal verb which *cannot* be used in each sentence.

1 When running a marathon, you ______________ drink water regularly so that you stay hydrated.

   need to / must / shouldn't

2 But, you ______________ drink too much liquid, or you'll get a stomachache.

   don't need to / shouldn't / must not

3 Frank, you ______________ yell; I'm sitting right next to you!

   don't have to / don't need to / must not

4 We ______________ be at the stadium until noon, so we're free until 12.

   must / don't need to / don't have to

5 She ______________ score any more points to win the game – she has enough already.

   doesn't have to / shouldn't / doesn't need to

6 You ______________ hit the other players – it isn't the right way to play.

   don't have to / must not / shouldn't

7 If you're interested in volleyball, you ______________ sign up for the school team.

   should / must / don't need to

8 You ______________ throw the ball into the net to score a point.

   must / have to / don't have to

VOCABULARY
Adjectives ending in *-ive*

A Complete the text with the correct form of the words given in capital letters.

The Olympics are considered the greatest sporting event ever known. However, it takes more than being a [1]__________ athlete to win. **COMPETE**
There is a [2]__________ amount of pressure from the media. **MASS**

Players are sometimes greeted by camera crews when they arrive for practice. The media can be very [3]__________ at times, **AGGRESSION** and this can break a player's concentration. Without a doubt, having this added pressure is not the most [4]__________ way for a player to train. **EFFECT**

Athletes have to employ [5]__________ **CREATE** ways of dealing with the stress, such as meditation, taking long baths or using positive thinking to calm them. All Olympians deserve a medal for their [6]__________ strength in competing **IMPRESS** under these conditions.

B Matching the nouns in the box to the meanings.

champion fan final league medal players spectator stadium tournament trophy

1 A large building, usually without a roof, where people watch sporting events such as soccer games or races. __________
2 Someone who has won an important competition, especially in a sport. __________
3 People who play a particular game or sport. __________
4 The last game, race, etc in a competition. The winner of this is the winner of the whole competition. __________
5 A large silver cup or similar object given as a prize to the winner of a competition, especially a sporting event. __________
6 Someone who likes to watch a particular sports team and wants that team to win. __________
7 A small flat piece of metal that you are given for winning a competition. __________
8 A group of teams or players who regularly compete against one another, put in order according to how many games they have won. __________
9 A series of games in which the winner of each game plays in the next game until there is one player or team left. __________
10 Someone who watches a sporting event. __________

Sports

C Circle the correct option to complete the sentences.

1 Roger is a terrific baseball *spectator / coach*; his team always wins the championship.
2 His shelves weren't tall enough for the *trophy / medal* he had just won!
3 The FIVB is the world *champion / league* of international volleyball teams.
4 The *spectator / stadium* was so packed with fans that there was nowhere to sit.
5 If you don't win this last game, you'll lose the whole *trophy / tournament*.
6 The team's *fans / spectators* arrived at the game wearing red and white scarves.
7 To win the competition, you'll have to compete against last year's *final / champion*.
8 Getting a place on the team is very difficult; they only pick the top *fans / players*.
9 I'd rather play a sport than be a *spectator / champion* – participating is more fun than watching.
10 If he wins this game, he'll be through to the *final / league*.

PRONUNCIATION
Rhythm: pausing

A Read this excerpt from a radio show. Mark (/) where you think the speaker will use a short pause and (//) for a longer pause which is used to add emphasis or drama.

Stay tuned, / folks. We have an exciting show for you today. Later on in the show, Lionel Messi – world famous athlete, considered by some to be the greatest soccer player of all time – will be joining us to talk about his life and career. We'll speak about the challenges he's faced, both on and off the field, and how he overcame them to be who he is today.

6.1 **B Listen and check whether you have placed your pauses appropriately.**

C Practice reading the excerpt aloud with the correct use of pauses.

6.2 Sports and hobbies

VOCABULARY
Hobbies and free time activities

A Circle the correct option to complete the radio interview.

Presenter: Aisha has come on to the show today to tell us about her work as a life coach. Aisha, how do you help people [1]***escape / get*** from daily stress?

Aisha: There are a lot of ways, actually. But, mainly, it's all about finding out what is [2]***relaxing / fitting*** for you, personally. I do think, though, that the best activities are ones that you both enjoy and that [3]***close / get*** you out of the house.

Presenter: I see. I've always really enjoyed [4]***keeping / collecting*** stamps, but I don't think that's a very popular hobby anymore.

Aisha: It doesn't matter what it is, as long as you really enjoy doing it. The real benefits come from having a [5]***close / near*** interest in a hobby. Whatever you [6]***have / are*** into doing is going to have positive results for you.

B Complete the sentences with the words in the box.

active fan hobby member society thing

1 Why don't you join a ________________ to be with other people who share your interest in old books?
2 I decided to take up a ________________ and I've started doing yoga once a week.
3 Going to a gym isn't really my ________________ to be honest.
4 I'm a ________________ of the Rihanna fan club.
5 Cross-training is becoming a very popular way to keep ________________.
6 I'm a huge ________________ of Drake and his music.

GRAMMAR
Present perfect progressive

A Complete the blog post with the present perfect or present perfect progressive form of the verbs in parentheses.

MY SPORTY SISTER AND ME

My sister Samia loves sports. I [1] ______ (*never / know*) anyone as active as her. She [2] ______ (*play*) soccer, tennis, basketball and other sports for years. If you ask her 'How long [3] ______ (*you / take part*) in sports competitions?' She'll tell you that she started as soon as she could walk! This month she [4] ______ (*train*) for another marathon. She [5] ______ (*complete*) two so far. One in New York and one in Chicago. I [6] ______ (*not achieve*) very much all day today, apart from writing this blog post. Not like Samia. She [7] ______ (*just / come in*) very hot and sweaty because she [8] ______ (*work out*) at the gym all afternoon.

B Rewrite each sentence using the present perfect progressive and the word given in capital letters. Write no more than five words.

1 Clara moved here six years ago.

FOR

Clara ______ six years.

2 Seth started playing tennis as a child.

SINCE

Seth ______ he was a child.

3 I go to the gym a lot less recently.

NOT

I ______ to the gym a lot recently.

4 They began to train last year to get ready for the marathon.

A

They ______ year to get ready for the marathon.

had to / needed to

C Find and correct the mistakes in the sentences.

1 I hadn't to buy a yoga mat because my sister lent me hers.

______

2 We have to have lessons before we could jump out of the plane for the first time.

______

3 Julio need to practice a lot before he became good at fly fishing.

______

4 Kayleigh hadn't to watch the ukulele teacher because she already knew how to play the song.

______

5 She didn't had to do anything yesterday so she spent the day relaxing at home.

______

6 I had spend a lot of money to buy this stamp, but I'm pleased that I did.

______

7 The coach said we needed practice more, so we did.

______

8 I had use my friend's Ping-Pong paddle last week because I broke mine.

______

PRONUNCIATION
been: unstressed

6.2 **A** Listen and underline the words the speaker stresses in each sentence.

1 I've never been to India.
2 Tanya's been playing tennis for hours.
3 He's been very quiet all day.
4 How long have you been captain of the club?
5 We've been training since last year.
6 Have you been surfing before?

B Practice saying the sentences in Exercise A. Don't forget that *been* should be unstressed.

READING

A Read three short texts which are all on the same topic. What is that topic?

B IDENTIFY TONE Where would you expect to read the three different texts? Match the texts (a–c) with the sources (1–3).

1 an encyclopedia ......
2 a blog ......
3 a magazine ......

C READ FOR DETAIL Which text mentions …

1 international styles of music?
2 work and free time?
3 children?
4 a life-changing experience?
5 different kinds of instrument?
6 helping others?

D REFLECT Think about the answers to these questions.

1 Do you play a musical instrument? If not, would you like to?
2 How can music help people to overcome a difficult experience?

a Great concert at the Memorial Hall last night – and all for charity! We raised $350 for the Hope Children's Hospital. Wonderful result! Well done everybody – the ladies of the organizing committee, Kingfisher Café who provided the refreshments … AND the band! They were just sensational … so impressive! I loved EVERY MINUTE of the concert. And a special thank you to the kids – it's great to see the young ones getting involved at such an early age. We hope we'll see you again next year, guys!

b A brass band is a musical group generally consisting entirely of brass instruments, frequently accompanied by a percussion section. Some groups include both brass and woodwind instruments, and this combination is typified by the New Orleans-style band. Variations on the make-up of the brass band vary across the world; the Balkan countries have a strong brass band tradition and have a distinctive style influenced by gypsy trumpet music, Turkish marching bands and traditional folk music. A British brass band usually consists of 28 players. The British scene is characterized by a strong competitive element, with annual contests being held to determine the best band in the country.

c Founded in 1917 to give miners something to do in their free time, the Grimethorpe Colliery Band has a long and proud history. The musicians were full-time mine workers, spending their days deep under the ground, digging out coal, and their evenings in music rehearsals. Sadly, the band is all that remains of Grimethorpe Colliery since the government closed it down in 1992. The closure of the pit came as a terrible shock and hundreds of people lost their jobs. At that time, 17 members of the band were working miners. Since then, the band has risen to fame for its part in the award-winning movie *Brassed Off*.

Glossary

colliery (n) a coal mine (place where coal is dug from the ground)
percussion (n) musical instruments which you hit or shake (e.g. drums)
woodwind (adj) musical instruments made of wood which you blow into to produce a sound

6.4 Sports and hobbies

LISTENING

A Look at the pictures (a–c). How could these people make money from their hobbies?

6.3 **B LISTEN FOR MAIN IDEAS** You will hear a talk about how to turn a hobby into a business. Read the main ideas of the talk. Listen and put them in the order (1–6) that they are mentioned.

- **a** Organize your ideas and your time. ____
- **b** Advertise your new business. ____
- **c** Make money from what you enjoy. ____
- **d** Organize the money side of your business. ____
- **e** Don't be scared – it's the right decision. ____
- **f** Use different ideas, not just one. ____

6.3 **C LISTEN FOR DETAIL** Listen again and circle the correct answer, a, b or c.

1 The advantage of turning your hobby into a business is that you will
- **a** learn how to make things.
- **b** have more free time.
- **c** enjoy what you do to earn money.

2 Which statement best describes how people feel after making a business from a hobby?
- **a** I'm too scared of failure to start up my own business.
- **b** I don't regret making this life-changing decision.
- **c** Starting my own business was a mistake.

3 New businesspeople should organize their time by
- **a** practicing how to concentrate.
- **b** setting detailed short-term actions.
- **c** focusing only on positive targets.

4 Why should you use your hobby in different ways?
- **a** To have various ways of making money.
- **b** So you can teach others about it.
- **c** To sell more products.

5 How can you attract customers?
- **a** By using the internet effectively.
- **b** By giving away free products.
- **c** By sharing your ideas.

6 What is the speaker's advice about money?
- **a** Enjoying your hobby is more important than money.
- **b** You must earn more than you spend.
- **c** It's a good idea to consult a professional.

Glossary

entrepreneur (n) person who creates a successful business
profitable (adj) which makes money

D REFLECT Think about the answers to these questions.

1 Do you have a hobby which you could turn into a business?

2 If you turned passion into profit, do you think you would still enjoy your hobby?

FUNCTIONAL LANGUAGE

Expressing your opinion

Complete the conversation with the words and phrases in the box.

another example	brutally honest	don't think
for instance	if you	my opinion	probably right

Leon: I've decided to turn my hobby into a business.

Pam: What – working out at the gym and keeping active?

Leon: Yes, [1] ____________, I could set up an online fitness advice service, or, to give you [2] ____________, I could become a personal trainer.

Pam: [3] ____________ ask me, that's not a good idea.

Leon: Why not?

Pam: In [4] ____________, if you turn your hobby into a business, you won't enjoy it. It won't be fun anymore – it will be stressful and boring.

Leon: I certainly [5] ____________ that's true. I'll just be making money doing something I love, instead of sitting at a desk all day.

Pam: And to be [6] ____________, Leon, I don't think you have what it takes to become a businessman. You need to know about finances and marketing and so on.

Leon: Hmm. You're [7] ____________.

6.5 Sports and hobbies

Your chance to win an adventure vacation with *Pursuits* magazine!

In our **'What to do'** section we're going to publish a series of readers' articles called *Try it!*

Send us your articles about a sport or hobby you think our readers should try doing. At the end of the series, readers will vote for the best article. Get writing!

WRITING

A Read the magazine ad above. Think about the answers to these questions.

1. Which sport or hobby would you choose to write about?
2. The first prize for this competition is an adventure vacation. Would you enjoy that? Why/Why not?

B ORGANIZATION Read *Try it – canoeing*, ignoring the blanks. You will see that each paragraph has a clear topic. Put the topics (a–e) in the order they are mentioned in the article.

- **a** start in a group with others ___
- **b** buying your own equipment ___
- **c** risk-taking or relaxing ___
- **d** taking safety precautions ___
- **e** canoeing in other countries ___

Try it – canoeing

Whether it's paddling slowly along a river or racing down a white-water run, canoeing is one of the most exciting activities I've ever tried.

[1]___ about canoeing is that it can be both relaxing *and* thrilling. If you want excitement, try a white-water run. If you want a quiet day in the countryside, [2]___ and canals is that you can stop off wherever you like to rest.

If you've never done it before, it's best to join a club. [3]___ is that you get basic training and safety tips, and you make a lot of new friends. [4]___ joining a club is you don't have to provide your own canoe.

[5]___ is that you become part of a community. And you don't have to limit yourself to canoeing near home. There are clubs all over the country and … all over the world! Traveling to another country for a canoeing trip is just awesome!

Try it! It's great fun and a good way to meet new people. [6]___, though, is to put safety first and always wear a lifejacket. It isn't just a walk in the park!

C INTRODUCTORY CLAUSES Read the article again and fill in the blanks (1–6) with the introductory clauses (a–f).

- **a** The reason for joining a club
- **b** One thing I especially like about canoeing
- **c** One of the nice things about exploring rivers
- **d** Another good thing about
- **e** The most important thing to remember
- **f** One of the great things

WRITING PRACTICE

A PREPARE You are going to write a magazine article called *Try it!* about a sport or hobby you think other people would enjoy. Write notes about each of the points below.

1. Look back at Writing Exercise A. Which sport/hobby did you choose?
2. Think of three or four reasons why you enjoy it.
3. Think of a way to grab the reader's attention in your first paragraph.
4. Can you think of a memorable closing sentence?

B WRITE Write your article in 150–200 words.

- Use your notes and ideas from Exercise A.
- Remember to give each paragraph a clear topic.
- Don't forget to use introductory clauses.

PRONUNCIATION

Modals of speculation and deduction

A **Complete the conversation with the missing modal verbs. Use one to three words in each space. Then practice the conversation.**

Woman: What do you think of the food?

Man: It's very nice. I'm glad you brought me here … Wait a minute; what's this in my soup?

Woman: I don't know – it [1] ______ a piece of meat.

Man: That [2] ______ right – this is a vegetarian restaurant, remember?

Woman: Right, yeah. It [3] ______ some kind of vegetable. Of course. It [4] ______ a potato. Do you want to ask the waiter?

Man: No, it [5] ______ meat and then I'll look stupid! I'm sure it [6] ______ anyway. It [7] ______ a vegetable, like you said, but I don't recognize the taste. I [8] ______ a look at the menu and see if it says anything there.

Diphthongs

B **Match words (1–7) with words (a–h) which have the same diphthong sounds.**

1 human ___		**a** phone
2 boy ___		**b** choice
3 cry ___		**c** say
4 straight ___		**d** computer
5 no ___		**e** choose
6 brown ___		**f** doubt
7 fruit ___		**g** light

7.1 **C** **Listen and check your answers. Then practice saying the words in Exercise B.**

VOCABULARY

Phrasal verbs

A **Complete the sentences with the correct form of the phrasal verbs in the box.**

give up serve up set up show up start off take off try out

1 Stay for dinner! I've found a new recipe online that I want to ______.

2 I don't mind ______ my place at tonight's meal – I'll go another time.

3 My dad hates it if anyone ______ late for a family meal.

4 Can you call everyone to the table? I'm ready to ______ the food.

5 I know Chinese food is popular here, but it never really ______ in my country.

6 This restaurant ______ as a fast food place but it was sold to a young chef last year.

7 It takes a lot of time and money to ______ a new restaurant.

Adjectives to describe food

B Complete the restaurant reviews with the missing words. The first letter has been given to help you.

To be honest, the meat was [1]d__________ because it was clearly not cooked properly and was [2]r__________ in the middle. The soup was very [3]w__________, too – there was very little in it. We won't be going back there!

They have a great selection of sweet and [4]s__________ snacks, which are so [5]f__________ that you really won't be hungry afterward. We've now tried most things on the menu and have to say that the food is delicious – really [6]t__________!
A word of warning, though – the home-made ice cream is so [7]r__________ and chocolatey that you won't want to move for an hour!

I had a pizza, which was very [8]c__________ (you can never have enough cheese!) and well-cooked with fresh ingredients. My friend had a [9]f__________ chicken dish with apple and banana in it – very unusual! It was [10]s__________ but not too hot. We were very impressed!

C Look at the table below. Put the adjectives from Exercise B in the correct column based on the context of the reviews.

Positive	Neutral	Negative

GRAMMAR
Modals of speculation and deduction

A Find and correct the mistakes in the sentences.

1 That must not be our bill – we only had a snack!

____

2 We should call and make a reservation – there might don't be a table.

____

3 You must to think I'm very rude eating with my fingers!

____

4 You maybe are right about this food – it doesn't taste good.

____

5 Let's try this new restaurant – it could maybe good.

____

6 This place might have not the best food, but it's good enough and very cheap.

____

B Rewrite these sentences using modals of speculation and deduction.

1 I've never tried buffalo wings, but I love all the ingredients so I'm sure they're delicious.

I've never tried buffalo wings, but I love all the ingredients so they *must be* delicious.

2 Allergy warning! It is possible that this snack contains nuts.

Allergy warning! This snack __________ nuts.

3 You've just eaten two whole meals! It's impossible that you want more food!

You've just eaten two whole meals! You __________ more food!

4 That salad looks strange, but maybe it doesn't taste too bad.

That salad looks strange, but it __________ too bad.

5 This sauce is OK, but I'm sure it isn't homemade – surely it's from a store.

This sauce is OK, but it __________ homemade – it __________ from a store.

6 I'm sure you think it's strange that I don't eat meat, but I just don't like it.

You __________ it's strange that I don't eat meat, but I just don't like it.

GRAMMAR

Comparatives and superlatives; *the ..., the ...*

A Complete the second sentence so that it has a similar meaning to the first sentence, using the word given. Write between two and five words.

1 Buy these chips – they don't have as much salt as the others.
Buy these chips – they have ______________ of all the bags. (*the*)

2 David doesn't cook as well as Mark.
Mark ______________ David (*than*)

3 If you add more pepper, the sauce will be spicier.
The more pepper you add, ______________ sauce will be. (*the*)

4 The juice in a carton isn't as fruity as the homemade kind.
The homemade juice ______________ the carton kind. (*tastes*)

5 Does a carrot have as many calories as a potato?
Which has ______________ – a carrot or a potato? (*calories*)

6 I didn't do as badly as Kate on the cooking exam.
Kate did ______________ on the cooking exam. (*me*)

B Circle the correct answer, a, b or c.

1 I find that the longer you leave a fruit on the tree, the ___ it tastes.
a juicy b as juicy c more juicy

2 That was ___ pizza ever! It was delicious!
a tastiest b the tastiest c more tasty

3 I think that curry will be too spicy for me. Do you have anything ___?
a milder b mild c more mild

4 Hank wants to eat ___ than he does now, but he simply doesn't know how.
a more healthy b most healthily c more healthily

5 Goji berries are ___ than strawberries, but they contain fewer calories.
a more expensive
b the most expensive
c expensive

6 I felt full after one bowl. That was one of ___ soups I've ever eaten!
a most filling b the more filling c the most filling

7 Açaí berries became popular ___ than anyone expected.
a quickly b quicker c more quickly

8 I've noticed that the more I eat at lunch, the ___ I want to work in the afternoon!
a little b less c least

PRONUNCIATION

Vowel + *w*

A Circle the word, a or b, which has the same vowel sound as the word in bold.

1 She **knew** her grandma would make her favorite recipe!
a now b you

2 Tell me again **how** you made your famous apple pie.
a about b go

3 Don't **throw** that potato peel in the trash can – we can use it in the garden.
a toe b wow

4 I ate too much for dinner – now I feel **awful**.
a owe b for

5 Are we **allowed** to bring drinks into the museum?
a throw b now

6 You can't smoke in here – it's against the **law**.
a view b draw

7 It didn't rain much this spring, so the plants **grew** very slowly.
a flew b so

8 How much do I **owe** you for this sandwich?
a flower b go

7.2 **B Listen and check your answers. Then practice saying the sentences in Exercise A.**

VOCABULARY
Waste

A Circle the correct option to complete the sentences.

1 If we ***recycled / reduced*** more, we wouldn't have to produce more plastic or glass.

2 I can't believe you ***threw / wasted*** so much money on that silly diet that didn't even work!

3 Once these glass bottles are empty, we can ***reduce / reuse*** them for storing water.

4 There's so much ***trash can / garbage*** in the streets, and it really looks awful!

5 We're trying to ***get rid / reduce*** expenses, so we're buying cheap brands of products.

6 You should ***use up / throw away*** all of the sauce in that jar – don't waste it!

B Complete the conversation with the words in the box.

away can down of garbage up

Gregory: What do you do about recycling in your house, Sasha?

Sasha: Well, my mom had this great idea. She put a small recycling bin next to every trash 1__________ in the house.

Gregory: That sounds handy.

Sasha: It works very well in the bathroom. Instead of throwing 2__________ the packaging of a tube of toothpaste, for example, it gets recycled.

Gregory: I see what you mean. In my house, we only have one place to get rid 3__________ our plastic, paper and glass. And that container fills up really quickly!

Sasha: That's right. I have to say, my mom's system works well. It really cuts 4__________ on the amount of 5__________ we throw away every week. The only disadvantage is that we use 6__________ a lot of plastic garbage bags.

C Complete the crossword using the clues.

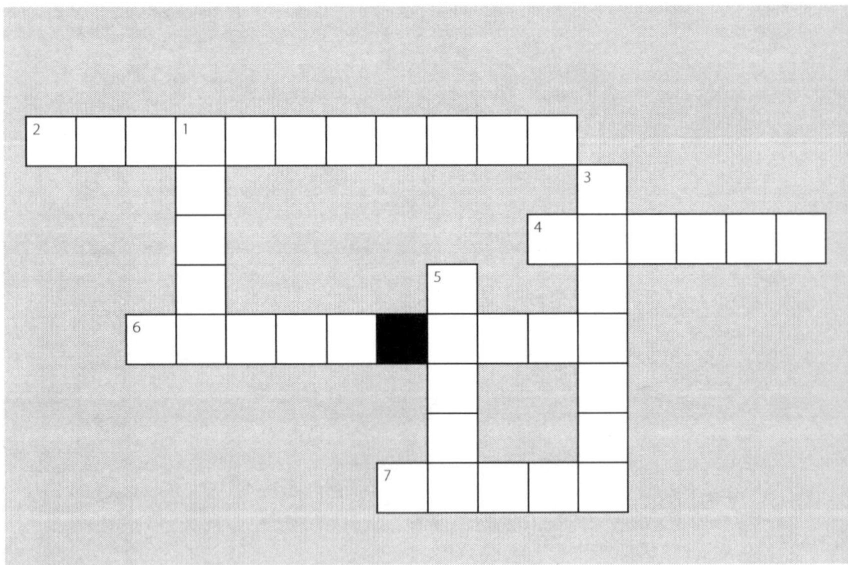

Across

2 a container for putting garbage in

4 to make something smaller or less in size, amount, importance etc

6 to get rid of something that you no longer want, for example by putting it in a trash can

7 to use something again, sometimes for a different purpose

Down

1 things that are no longer useful, such as old food, paper or plastic used for wrapping things, and empty containers

3 to change waste materials such as newspapers and bottles so that they can be used again

5 the failure to use something valuable in an effective way

Angela: Recipe tester

I love cooking and I buy a lot of cooking magazines. One week, I saw an ad: 'Wanted: Recipe Tester – must love cooking.' Well I *do* love cooking and all my free time was spent in the kitchen anyway, so I applied and … that's what I do now. I test recipes for popular food magazines and publishers. There are also jobs available for big manufacturers like Kraft or Nestle but personally, I prefer to work for a smaller company. When you buy a fancy new cookbook, it's me, or someone like me, who has practiced every recipe in that book – once, twice, maybe even three or four times. Some recipe testers have a background in food science or nutrition and some, like me, have taught themselves instead. I've worked on recipes for all kinds of people, even celebrity chefs – it's my job to translate the chef's ideas into practical instructions which are suitable for a home kitchen. I don't earn much but to be honest, I don't mind – I'm just happy doing a job I love!

Jason: Food stylist

I started out in catering. I used to work as a chef and then I moved into writing for magazines and cookbooks. Apart from anything else, I now earn a lot more! Then, for one of my books, I had to create the recipes *and* photograph the dishes. That's when I learned that it's really an art to make food *look* as good as it tastes. Some people in the profession have graduated from a catering school but I'm self-taught. And you can't just show up and take some pretty pictures – you have to make all the dishes yourself, so you have to be a good cook as well as a good photographer! My friends ask me how they can make their Insta pictures look good – well, probably the most important thing is lighting. Use white or light-colored plates to serve the food – it will show off the colors of the food better. If a food is brown-colored, use green herbs or brightly colored vegetables to brighten it up.

Yoko: Food taster

In ancient times, powerful kings and emperors were frequently murdered with poison. That's the origin of a food taster's job – powerful men and women hired servants to taste their food and drink. Not so good for the food taster if it *was* poisoned! But don't worry, the modern-day job doesn't involve getting poisoned! No, my job is to taste new products created by a large international food manufacturer. I have to assess how the food looks and smells, as well as how it tastes. The product must always be exactly the same – customers don't want a product which looks or tastes different every time they buy it. I graduated from college with a degree in nutrition and a lot of my day is spent in the food laboratory where we test products for their nutritional content. I'm well-paid for what I do – in fact, I earn more than most of my friends. The worst thing about my job? I have to watch my weight and I regularly go without lunch or dinner.

READING

A PREDICT What do you think each of these jobs involves?

B READ FOR SPECIFIC INFORMATION Read again. Which person or people …

1. don't have any formal qualifications? ___ ___
2. mentions a negative aspect of his/her work? ___ ___
3. doesn't get a lot of money for the job? ___
4. are concerned with the appearance of food? ___ ___
5. works for a big company? ___
6. has a job which does not include cooking? ___
7. has to understand other people's ideas? ___
8. offers tips on how to do what he/she does? ___

Glossary

assess (v) look at something or test it carefully
manufacturer (n) a company which makes a product

C REFLECT Think about the answers to these questions.

1. In your opinion, which of the three jobs sounds the most interesting?
2. Which job would you like to do? Why?

LISTENING

A In your opinion, which of these are food fads and which are sensible guidelines for a healthy diet?

1 Only eat one kind of food for a week.
2 Eat a balanced diet from all the food groups (proteins, dairy, etc).
3 Eat the same food as prehistoric people.
4 Never cook your food – eat everything raw.
5 Eat five portions of fruits and vegetables a day.

B IDENTIFYING OPINIONS Read these sentences. Are the people describing a fact or expressing an opinion? Write F (fact) or O (opinion).

1 It sounds crazy. ___
2 They only eat food which has been found in the wild. ___
3 Fresh ingredients have more nutrients than processed food. ___
4 They're interesting ways of exploring new ideas. ___
5 I feel more energetic and less tired. ___
6 Olive oil is better for you than butter. ___
7 It prevents heart disease. ___
8 I don't think that's such a big deal. ___

7.3 **C LISTEN FOR SPECIFIC INFORMATION** You will hear three people talking about food fads. Listen and match the sentences (1–6) to the speakers.

1 A varied diet of different foods can prevent serious illness.
2 These foods can't be bought in a grocery store.
3 This diet has been in existence for a very long time.
4 It's OK if you don't stick strictly to a healthy eating plan.
5 Food fads can help people to be more aware of what they eat.
6 This food fad makes me feel sick.

César ___ ___

Olivia ___ ___

Wing Shan ___ ___

Glossary

forage (v) search for food out in the country

D REFLECT Think about the answers to these questions.

1 Have you ever heard of any of these food fads and diets?
2 Would you like to try any of the ideas from the listening exercise? Why/Why not?

FUNCTIONAL LANGUAGE

Complete the conversation with one word in each space.

Ellie: [1] ___ up, Jude?
Jude: I haven't been feeling very well. I'm always tired and I usually feel sick after I've eaten.
Ellie: [2] ___ you tried talking to your doctor?
Jude: No, I haven't.
Ellie: What [3] ___ changing your diet?
Jude: What do you mean?
Ellie: Well, maybe you're eating the wrong foods. If I [4] ___ you, I would go and see a nutritionist. It could be a real help.
Jude: That wouldn't be a good [5] ___. I don't think it would help.
Ellie: It's worth a [6] ___ though, isn't it? [7] ___ don't we go together?
Jude: That's a good [8] ___. OK.

WRITING

A Think about the answers to these questions.

1 How often do you eat out?
2 Would you go to a restaurant because of a friend's recommendation?
3 Have you ever recommended a restaurant to a friend? Why?

B RECOMMENDING Read the forum post and the three replies. Which person (or people) make(s) these mistakes? Write *Gourmand*, *SloppyJoe* or *Sylvya*. Then say whose recommendation you think Betty should follow and why.

1 Doesn't start with a clear recommendation. ______
2 Says the decision '… depends …'. ______
3 Only talks about his/her personal preferences. ______
4 Doesn't mention the wishes of the friend. ______
5 Doesn't end with a clear recommendation. ______

C COMPARING AND RECOMMENDING Read again and circle the correct option to complete the posts.

Message from Betty

Hi everyone. Has anyone been to *Bamu* yet, the new restaurant in town? I've heard good things about it from people at work, but the review in the paper wasn't so good. Says it isn't as good as *Yukio's* if you want authentic Japanese – which I do. I'm thinking of taking a friend there for a birthday treat – she's never tried sushi before. What do you recommend?

Reply from Gourmand:

Are you asking us to choose between the two? I've been to both and I prefer *Bamu*. For a start it's [1]***more quieter / quieter***. OK, *Yukio's* is one of [2]***popular / the most popular*** restaurants in town, but, in my opinion the reviewer got it wrong; *Bamu* is just as authentic. It depends on what you and your friend want. *Yukio's* is [3]***most casual / more casual*** – at *Bamu* I always feel that I have to dress and behave kind of formally, but the food's tastier. [4]***I'd recommend / I like*** Yukio's if you want a fun time and *Bamu* if you want a dining out 'experience'.

Reply from SloppyJoe:

You do realize there's a perfectly good sushi bar in the mall, don't you? Just kidding. Remember, *Bamu* is new and fancy, as my friend calls it – and much more expensive [5]***than / as*** Yukio's. Is your heart set on Japanese food? It may be a small town, but there are other and, in my opinion, [6]***more nice / nicer*** restaurants around here. You can go somewhere just as nice as those two, but cheaper, and then go to a show afterward.

Reply from Sylvya:

I recommend that you put your friend first. What's important is how she feels and what she wants, not which is the best restaurant. [7]***I think you / You should*** try to find out if your friend wants to go to a Japanese restaurant on her birthday. Maybe she'd prefer to eat somewhere else, or even do something else. Not easy to do without spoiling the surprise, I know. [8]***Why don't you / It's better if you*** ask her family and other friends what she'd really like to do?

WRITING PRACTICE

A PREPARE You are going to write a reply to a forum post. Read the forum post below. Think about the answers to these questions and write notes.

1 What are the two options?
2 Can you think of some points for and against each option?
3 Whose wishes should you focus on?

I want to invite some friends who are coming down from New York for dinner. My first thought was that we could have a barbecue in the backyard. I'm really good at grilling food, and barbecues are such fun. But the weather forecast for the weekend is bad. The alternative is to reserve a table at a nice restaurant – less fun, I think, but possibly the safer option. What do you recommend?

B WRITE Write your reply to the forum post in approximately 100 words.

- Use your notes and ideas from Exercise A.
- Remember to start and end with a clear recommendation, giving reasons.
- Don't forget to use comparatives to show why your recommendation is better.

VOCABULARY
Word families

A Complete the text with the correct form of the words given in capital letters.

WHAT WILL YOU DISCOVER?

Is your ambition to become a [1] ____________ and make the next	**SCIENCE**
great discovery? Or maybe you would like to go into the field of [2] ____________ and	**ENGINEER**
help build the machines of the future? Whatever your dreams are, to [3] ____________ in	**SUCCESS**
these fields you need more than just knowledge and a college degree. What will make the difference is your ability to be [4] ____________ and to come	**INNOVATE**
up with original ideas. For instance, creating a [5] ____________ that can be turned	**DESIGNER**
into a [6] ____________ that everyone	**PRODUCE**
needs and wants. The more [7] ____________ you are, the better your chances of becoming the next Steve Jobs!	**INVENT**

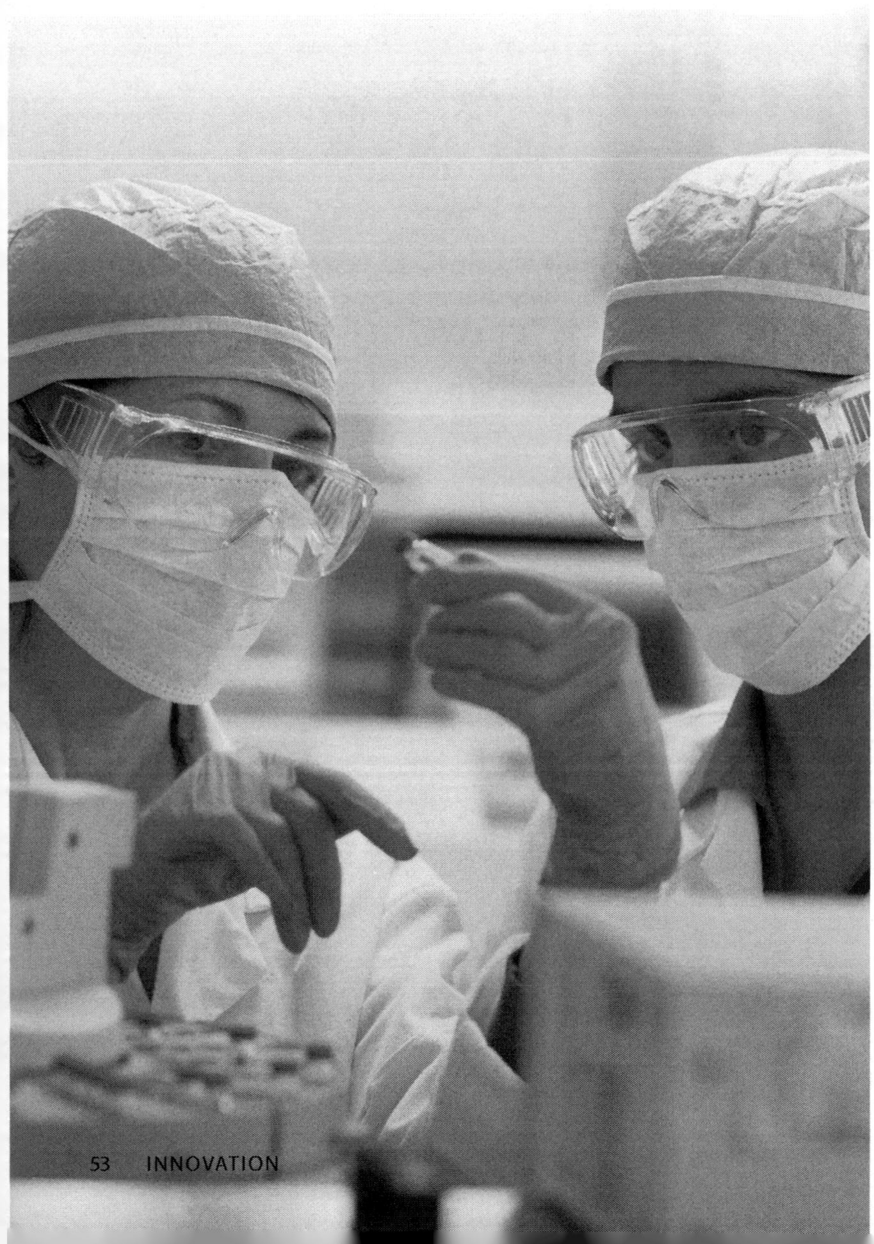

'Creative thinking' phrases

B Circle the correct answer, a, b or c.

1 I need new ideas for the spring fashion show, but my mind's gone ____.
a empty
b blank
c out

2 At today's meeting, we want to come up ____ fresh ideas for the advertising campaign.
a with
b to
c for

3 Try ____ unplug completely for a couple of hours – you'll feel less stressed.
a to
b on
c out

4 A good way to generate new ideas is to ____ your mind wander freely.
a give
b go
c let

5 They say that eating certain kinds of food can ____ your creativity.
a grow
b boost
c switch

6 One characteristic of brilliant inventors is that they can think outside the ____.
a block
b square
c box

7 A lack of confidence can ____ your creativity.
a close
b shut
c block

8 ____ your imagination to picture life in the future.
a Use
b Try
c Feel

9 Yoga and other forms of gentle exercise can help you to ____ new ideas.
a design
b generate
c engineer

10 Why don't you try looking at the problem from the ____?
a outside
b upside
c inside

PRONUNCIATION
Adjective clauses

Listen and check (✓) the sentences
.1 that contain non-essential adjective clauses.

1 ☐ 4 ☐

2 ☐ 5 ☐

3 ☐ 6 ☐

GRAMMAR
Adjective clauses

A Circle the correct option to complete the sentences.

1 It was Afua ***who*** / ***whose*** came up with the idea.

2 The college, ***that*** / ***which*** was established in 1840, is famous for its science department.

3 The invention ***who*** / ***that*** made him famous was the clockwork radio.

4 She visited the Science Museum ***where*** / ***when*** she was in New York last year.

5 I don't know ***which*** / ***whose*** idea it was to use a laser beam.

6 The town ***which*** / ***where*** her parents live is on the northern coast of the island.

7 Cyrus, ***which*** / ***who*** is wearing a black jacket, is an astronomer.

8 It was a decade ago, ***when*** / ***where*** I was still a teenager, that I first became interested in computers.

B Complete the short biography with the words in the box.

when where which which who whose

The amazing Ms. Jackson

Shirley Ann Jackson is a scientist [1] ______________ achievements and research have helped the development of modern communications technology.

Shirley Ann, [2] ______________ was the first African-American woman to get a PhD in Physics in the United States, started her studies in the mid-1960s.

The college [3] ______________ she studied, the Massachusetts Institute of Technology (MIT), [4] ______________ is near the city of Boston, is one of the most famous colleges in the country.

After graduating from college, she worked for the communications company AT&T Bell Laboratories. The 1970s was a time [5] ______________ there were a great many developments in communications technology.

The research for [6] ______________ she is most famous contributed to the development of *call waiting*, portable fax machines and fiber optic cables.

VOCABULARY
Positive adjectives

A Unscramble the words in parentheses to complete the sentences.

1 Nobody is the same as anyone else – we are all ________________. (*quinue*)

2 I think you will look ________________ in that jacket – try it on. (*soorgeug*)

3 We spent a ________________ afternoon at the museum. (*gnifacsniat*)

4 I don't think it's very ________________ to spend all your money on gadgets. (*blessien*)

5 Meeting and talking to an inventor was an ________________ experience. (*blettanforgeu*)

6 My laptop is old and it isn't really ________________ for what I need to do on it. (*blesatui*)

7 His ability to find solutions to problems is very ________________. (*vemispresi*)

8 Those shoes look very nice but they're not very ________________ for walking long distances. (*lactiparc*)

9 The picture on my new TV is ________________ – I can see so much more detail than on the old one. (*bledcreini*)

10 The electrical gadgets in my home are very ________________ and I can control them using my cell phone. (*catphosistied*)

B Complete the text with the missing positive adjectives from Exercise A. The beginning of each word has been given to help you.

Are gadgets a good thing?

Electronic gadgets are getting more and more [1]**s**________________, and we can do an amazing number of [2]**p**________________ things using them – a lot of the work is now done by machines. In home entertainment, technology used to have one [3]**u**________________ job, like playing music or showing videos. Now, the emphasis is on doing many different tasks from a central control point. How much more [4]**im**________________ will our gadgets become? We don't know, but the future promises to be [5]**in**________________.

However, many people worry about the effect that all this technology will have on us. Will we become lazy, or will we be [6]**s**________________ and limit our use of technology so that we can enjoy nature and get healthy exercise? For example, will we still choose to sit and admire a [7]**g**________________ sunset or enjoy the [8]**un**________________ experience of climbing to the top of a mountain? Or will we lose all our creativity because we get all our experiences digitally?

GRAMMAR
Zero and first conditional

A Complete the sentences with the correct form of the verbs in parentheses.

1 The computer gets really slow if you ________ (*keep*) too much on the desktop.
2 I'll buy some new batteries if you ________ (*tell*) me what size you need.
3 Unless we can fix this problem, we ________ (*have to*) change the design.
4 The phone can last about 24 hours if you ________ (*not charge*) it.
5 I ________ (*not buy*) this product again – it's awful!
6 He'll help you tomorrow if it still ________ (*not work*).

B Find and correct the mistakes in four of the sentences.

1 If you'll listen to next week's podcast, you'll hear about some more amazing gadgets.
____
2 Are you angry if I cancel our plans for tonight?
____
3 If the puzzles are too difficult, I usually get bored.
____
4 I won't go out tomorrow unless the weather will be good.
____
5 It's easy to share photos on social media if you want to.
____
6 What happens if you press this button?
____
7 I never buy gadgets unless I don't really need them.
____
8 Will you buy a new tablet if the price is right?
____

Conditionals with modals and imperatives

C Complete the sentences with the words and phrases in the box.

can always borrow	can go	can wait	come and see
don't try	might help	must be prepared	should we still

1 The price will go down if you ________ for a few months.
2 If you stop using electronic gadgets in the evening, it ________ you sleep at night.
3 You can't succeed if you ________.
4 If it rains, ________ go to the beach?
5 If you're free tonight, ________ my band playing live.
6 You ________ to work hard if you decide to take this exam.
7 If you need a laptop, you ________ mine for a day or two.
8 Many restaurants seem to have the attitude: if you don't like it here, you ________ somewhere else.

PRONUNCIATION
'll and *won't*

A 8.2 **Listen to the conversation and underline the phrases you hear the speakers say.**

1 *if you want to / if you won't*
2 *you'll really like it / you really like it*
3 *I want to go / I won't go*
4 *I lend / I'll lend*
5 *I'll enjoy / I enjoy*
6 *we'll have a nice time / we have a nice time*
7 *I won't miss it / I want to miss it*
8 *I call them / I'll call them*

B Practice saying the pairs of phrases in Exercise A.

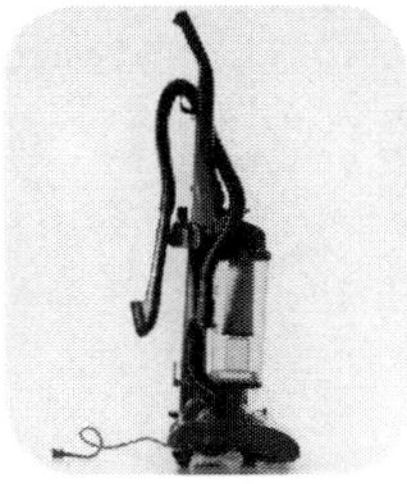

READING

A How long do you spend every day doing the following household tasks? Make a list of the electrical appliances you use to do them.

- washing the dishes
- cooking food
- doing the laundry

B TOPIC SENTENCES Read the article about household gadgets in the Victorian kitchen. Match the topic sentences (A–D) with the main paragraphs (1–4).

A The task of washing, ironing and folding clothes may seem never-ending, but that's nothing compared to how tiring and time-consuming it was in Victorian times.

B The Industrial Revolution was marked by the invention of steam power and the use of mass production, but was this technological progress also reflected in the home?

C Maybe the most important task in any household, old or modern, is cooking, which today we do on a gas or electric stove.

D Another modern invention which we take for granted is the fridge-freezer.

C READ FOR GIST In which main paragraph (1–4) would you expect to read about the following items?

a soap
b food
c different kitchen gadgets
d coal

D READ FOR DETAIL Read again. Are the sentences true (T) or false (F)? Correct the false sentences.

1. According to the writer, people today appreciate the household appliances which they use every day. ___
2. Only the rich benefited from advances in technology in the Victorian era. ___
3. Some of the Victorians' appliances were similar to those we use today. ___
4. Servants had to take coal out of the kitchen range to keep it burning. ___
5. It was possible to preserve food by covering it with salt. ___
6. Rich Victorians could only keep their food cold in the winter. ___
7. Water was available in every Victorian household. ___
8. The 'dolly' was a kind of simple washing machine. ___

E REFLECT Think about the answers to these questions.

1. Which modern household appliance could you *not* live without? Why?
2. Do you think we still spend too long doing housework?

Must-have gadgets – Victorian style!

For most of us, an ordinary day will probably include starting the coffee maker for a cup of coffee, preparing a meal on the stove or in the microwave (using fresh ingredients from the fridge) and maybe loading the washing machine with the family's dirty clothes. These are all household gadgets that we take for granted and wouldn't dream of doing without. But how did people manage in the not-so-distant past?

1 ___ For poor families, the answer is 'no', but for the aristocracy and for well-off middle-class homes, then the answer is a definite 'yes'. Although the gadgets which were used in the Victorian kitchen relied on hand power rather than electricity, they were sophisticated machines which could accomplish many of the jobs that we do today with modern appliances. They had food processors to chop food, machines to slice bread and even a gadget to make ice cream!

2 ___ The Victorian kitchen used an iron *range* which consisted of a kind of iron box with a coal fire – this heated the oven and the hotplates and also boiled water. Although this style of kitchen stove was efficient, it certainly wasn't convenient. Coal had to be carried in regularly and ashes removed throughout the day. A servant would have to light the stove in the early hours of the morning and keep it burning all day.

3 ___ But without electricity, how did the Victorians keep things cold? Traditionally, both rich and poor used other food preservation techniques, such as keeping food in salt or vinegar, or smoking it, in order to make it last longer. However, the very rich had ice houses. The ice house was built underground, near a water source such as a lake, so that during the winter, ice could be taken from it into the ice house. The ice blocks, packed together underground, stayed frozen, even during the warm summer months. Here, the Victorians were able to keep food throughout the year.

4 ___ Since there was no running water, it usually had to be carried some distance, before being boiled in a huge pot over a wood or coal fire. And then just add soap? No, because the soap had to be made by hand, using a mixture of fat and ashes! In wealthier households, the clothes would be put into a *dolly*, a kind of bucket with a long wooden pole which was used to hit and move the clothes around. The whole process would take an entire day!

So, next time you take a carton of cold milk out of the fridge, press a button on your electric oven or complain about having to load the washing machine, spare a thought for the women of the Victorian era, who spent most of their lives doing what electricity and modern gadgets do for us in a few minutes!

Glossary

accomplish (v) to succeed in doing something
dolly (n) a kind of bucket with a long wooden pole
preservation (n) the process of stopping food from going bad
time-consuming (adj) taking a long time

LISTENING

A What advice could you offer a friend in each of these situations?

1 'I have to go to work every day and take care of my children, too.'

2 'There's so much housework that I don't know where to start.'

3 'My teenage children never help around the house.'

.3 **B LISTEN FOR GIST** **Listen to a conversation between two friends, Adam and Lucy. Check (✓) the problems which Adam mentions.**

1 pressure at work ☐
2 studying for his exams ☐
3 preparing for a business trip ☐
4 juggling work and family ☐
5 ironing the clothes ☐
6 not having enough time ☐

.3 **C LISTEN FOR DETAIL** **Listen again and circle the correct answer, a, b or c.**

1 Adam is worried because …
a his wife has to work.
b he can't cope with doing so many things.
c his children are badly behaved.

2 Lucy thinks that it's important to …
a dress your children in clean clothes.
b have a family and a career.
c accept that you can't be perfect.

3 Lucy advises Adam to …
a achieve the most important tasks.
b forget about cooking meals.
c focus only on one goal.

4 Adam will have fewer jobs to do if he …
a sets a better example to his children.
b makes his own sandwiches.
c asks his children to help.

5 What should Adam do to avoid heaps of dirty clothes or dishes?
a Always do jobs right away.
b Do everything at the end of the week.
c Make the children do the dishes.

6 The best kind of checklist includes …
a a list of the day's meals.
b who will do a task and when.
c only a few items.

Glossary

chore (n) a difficult or boring household job
delegate (v) give part of your work or responsibilities to somebody else
juggle (v) try to do several important things at the same time
prioritize (v) decide which order to do a number of different tasks

D REFLECT **Think about the answers to these questions.**

1 Do you agree with Lucy's advice to Adam?

2 Should men and women share the household chores and childcare? Why/Why not?

FUNCTIONAL LANGUAGE

Circle the correct option to complete the conversation between a woman and her granddaughter.

Rhoda: Amber – your mother bought me this new gadget. It's called a tablet, but I don't know how to use it.
Amber: Well, the [1]***first / start*** thing to do is press this little button here – to turn it on.
Rhoda: This one?
Amber: Yes, that's right. [2]***When / As*** you've done that, the screen comes on. See? Now, let's say you want to google something …
Rhoda: Sorry, can you [3]***tell / say*** that again?
Amber: Yes, 'google' something. Google is a search engine. It helps you to find information. So, you touch this little icon – the picture – with the letter *g*. Here – [4]***leave / let*** me show you.
Rhoda: Is this [5]***what / how*** you do it?
Amber: Yes, that's it. Well done, Grandma! [6]***After / Later*** that, you'll see a long white box. Use the letter keys to write what you want to know.
Rhoda: I'm not sure what you [7]***mean / say***.
Amber: Look – can you see the letters of the alphabet? Tap each letter that you want with your finger. [8]***Do / Make*** sure you don't press too hard.
Rhoda: Like this?
Amber: Yes, Grandma. That's it. Finally, you tap this key, and you'll see a list of all the different websites with the information you want.
Rhoda: That's wonderful. Thank you, Amber.

WRITING

A Read the short biography of Ada Lovelace and answer the questions.

1 Who was Ada Lovelace?
2 What was the turning point in her life?
3 What important contribution did she make to the field of computing?

B ORGANIZATION Read the biography again. Match the headings (a–e) with the paragraphs (1–5).

a Her early life. ____
b Introduction. ____
c Conclusion. ____
d A turning point. ____
e Her most important work. ____

C USING LINKING WORDS TO SHOW CONTRAST Complete the sentences with the linking words in bold from the text.

1 ______ she didn't have a college degree, she was treated as an equal by fellow scientists.
2 The design looked good on paper. ______, it proved impossible to build.
3 He managed to complete the project, ______ not having financial support.

Glossary

insist on (phr v) to say that you must have something
pioneer (n) one of the first people to do something important that is later continued and developed by other people

WRITING PRACTICE

A PREPARE You are going to write a short biography of an innovative person. It can be someone famous or someone you know personally. Think about the answers to these questions and write notes.

1 Which person are you going to write about?
2 What do you know about his/her early life?
3 Was there a turning point in his/her life? What was it?
4 How did he/she make an impact?
5 What can we learn from his/her life?

B WRITE Write your biography in 150–200 words.

- Use your notes and ideas from Exercise A.
- Divide your writing into five clear paragraphs.
- Remember to use linking words and phrases to show contrast.

C REVIEW Check and edit your biography.

BIOGRAPHY

Ada Lovelace: the first computer programmer?

1 Ada Lovelace is known as one of the pioneers of computer science. Her methods led her to see the possibilities of what were, at the time, simply *calculating* machines. She realized they could do much more than just calculate.

2 Born in 1815, her father, the poet Lord Byron, abandoned her as a baby, and her mother, Annabella Milbanke, left her to be brought up by her grandmother. **However**, she did insist on Ada getting a good education, especially in science and mathematics.

3 **Despite** her difficult childhood, she proved to be a good student. **Although** women could not enter college in those days, she was educated to a high level by private tutors. One of them introduced her to Charles Babbage, a professor of mathematics at Cambridge University – a meeting that changed her life.

4 Babbage wanted to build a machine that could do calculations and Ada asked to see his plans. She wrote and published notes on the machine including how to give it instructions. That is why she is often called the world's first computer programmer.

5 Ideas matter, and she realized that anything could be operated by computer programs. Her work changed the way the world worked.

VOCABULARY
The arts

A Complete the sentences with the words in the box.

choir concert exhibit instrument musician orchestra performed rehearsed stage studio

1 Maya had never sung better and she left the recording __________ with a big smile on her face.

2 She was the only __________ in her family; her father was an actor and her mother a dancer.

3 Most singers will tell you that it's a great joy to sing at a live __________.

4 They __________ the play every afternoon until the day of the performance.

5 The __________ consisted of violinists, trumpeters and drummers from Eastern Europe.

6 He was really nervous because he had never __________ live before in front of such a large audience.

7 Jose spent hours setting up an __________ of his latest work at the famous art gallery.

8 At what age did you first learn how to play a musical __________?

9 Thirty people sing in our __________ and we perform at festivals all over the country.

10 She stepped out onto the __________ and froze – she couldn't remember her lines!

Verbal idioms

B Circle the correct option to complete the sentences.

1 I'm going to be taking ***note of* / *part in*** a community theater project this summer.

2 The audience didn't find the play funny – all the jokes ***fell* / *dropped*** flat.

3 Can you ***make* / *tell*** the difference between a 3D-printed sculpture and a hand-carved one?

4 Don't do the work for free; your employer might take ***place* / *advantage*** of you later on.

5 Isaac made ***fun of* / *friends with*** the other members of the cast during rehearsals; they still like him to this day.

6 Even famous artists who are wealthy have to ***keep* / *make*** track of their finances like everyone else.

7 When she got the lead role in the movie, she felt as if her wildest dreams had ***come* / *gone*** true.

8 If you want to be a famous director like your uncle, you should ***draw* / *pay*** attention to his advice.

9 The director wants us to ***take* / *make*** use of the whole stage – not just the front part.

10 We're ready for the live concert – the choir is ready and the sound system is working. I hope nothing goes ***wrong* / *off***!

GRAMMAR
Second conditional

A Circle the correct answer, a, b or c.

1 Yiannis would study art in another country if he ___ enough money.
 a has
 b had
 c would have

2 If we all ___ Katrina's work, she'd make a lot of money.
 a would buy
 b will buy
 c bought

3 The actors ___ more if they had time.
 a would rehearse
 b rehearsed
 c can rehearse

4 Do you think more people would visit the museum if they ___ charge an entrance fee?
 a doesn't
 b didn't
 c wouldn't

5 If I ___ you, I'd try to sell my art on the street.
 a were
 b am
 c be

6 He'd give away his art for free if he ___ afford to do so.
 a will
 b would
 c could

7 Would you perform at the Grand Theater even if the job ___ well?
 a won't pay
 b didn't pay
 c doesn't pay

8 If you ___ a gallery, what type of art would you display?
 a would own
 b owned
 c own

B Complete the second conditional sentences with the correct form of the verbs in parentheses.

1 Tony is a talented artist, but he's also lazy! If he __________ (*work*) harder, he __________ (*become*) really successful.

2 If I __________ (*have*) more time, I __________ (*learn*) to play a musical instrument.

3 I __________ (*go*) to the exhibit if it __________ (*be*) free, but I'm not going to pay $20 for a ticket!

4 I love dancing. If I __________ (*cannot*) dance, my life __________ (*be*) so empty!

5 You have a good voice, but you need to practice more. If I __________ (*be*) you, I __________ (*take*) singing lessons.

6 They __________ (*have*) a lot more money if they __________ (*not spend*) it all on paintings!

PRONUNCIATION
/ʧ/, /ʃ/ and /k/

A Read the sentences and underline the *ch* words. Then match the sequence of three phonemes to the order of the *ch* sounds as they appear in each sentence.

1 Her character on the TV show is a young, talented chef from China.
 a /ʃ/, /k/, /ʧ/ ☐
 b /k/, /ʃ/, /ʧ/ ☑

2 Malek is doing research for his role as a chemist, and he's learning a lot about science and technology.
 a /ʧ/, /k/, /k/ ☐
 b /ʃ/, /ʧ/, /k/ ☐

3 When Danny was a child, he wanted to become a mechanic, just like his dad, Charley.
 a /ʧ/, /k/, /ʃ/ ☐
 b /ʧ/, /k/, /ʧ/ ☐

4 She had two choices; she could sing in a choir or play in an orchestra.
 a /ʧ/, /k/, /ʃ/ ☐
 b /ʧ/, /k/, /k/ ☐

5 It's a challenge to learn new singing techniques; in some ways, your voice is like a machine.
 a /ʃ/, /k/, /ʃ/ ☐
 b /ʧ/, /k/, /ʃ/ ☐

6 Standing outside the church, Matthew noticed a strange chemical smell.
 a /ʧ/, /ʧ/, /k/ ☐
 b /ʧ/, /k/, /k/ ☐

9.1 **B** Listen and check your answers. Then practice saying the sentences in Exercise A.

GRAMMAR
Reported speech

A Complete the second sentence so that it has a similar meaning to the first sentence, using the word given. Write between two and five words.

1 'What time are you leaving?'
She asked ______ leaving. (*him*)

2 'We've never read any of J.K. Rowling's books.'
They said ______ any of J.K. Rowling's books. (*read*)

3 'I'm sorry I made a mistake.'
She said she was sorry ______ a mistake. (*she*)

4 'I can't understand why you changed your mind.'
She said she ______ I had changed my mind. (*why*)

5 'Where is the manager?'
They wanted to know ______. (*where*)

6 'Do you want to go to the movie theater?'
They asked me ______ to the movie theater. (*go*)

7 'I won't come tomorrow.'
Susan said that she ______ day. (*come*)

8 'Is Aisha here yet?'
I asked ______ yet. (*there*)

B Complete the dialogue with one to three words in each space. Use the reported conversation to find the information you need.

Dialogue

George: I'm reading a great book right now. It's called *Saturday* and it's by a writer named Ian McEwan. 1 ______ a few of his books. Have you heard of him?

Caroline: No, I haven't. What's it about?

George: I don't want to tell you because I will spoil it for you. I'll probably finish it tomorrow. You 2 ______ it if you want.

Caroline: Thanks. Let me know when you finish it. I 3 ______ a report I'm writing this week so I don't have a lot of time for reading. I read a book on vacation – that was the last time I read a novel.

George: What was it called?

Caroline: *The Rosie Project.*

George: I've heard of that. 4 ______?

Caroline: Yes, 5 ______. Do you want to borrow it?

George: Yeah sure. We can swap!

C Now complete the reported conversation using the information from the dialogue.

Reported conversation

George said that he was reading a great book called *Saturday* by Ian McEwan. He said he'd read a few books by the same writer. Caroline, however, said she hadn't heard of him and she asked what the book 6 ______. George said he didn't want to tell Caroline because he 7 ______ it for her, but he said she could borrow it if she wanted. He said he would probably finish it the 8 ______ day. Caroline told him to let her know when he had finished it but she said that she had to finish a report she was writing that week so she didn't have much time for reading. She said the last time she 9 ______ a novel was on vacation and that it was called *The Rosie Project*. George asked her if it was good. Caroline said it was and she asked George 10 ______ to borrow it.

VOCABULARY
Reporting verbs

A Circle the correct answer, a, b or c.

1 Smith ___ that he had taken the money.
   a told b admitted c wondered
2 The woman ___ that she had been in front of me in the line.
   a reminded b refused c argued
3 Penelope ___ Tom to fix the garden gate.
   a explained b persuaded c replied
4 Giles ___ me he was tired.
   a told b insisted c mentioned
5 I ___ that the store was closed and she would have to come back the following day.
   a explained b asked c told
6 David ___ that he was right, even though it was obvious he had made a mistake.
   a persuaded b insisted c advised
7 Why are you ___? Is the baby asleep?
   a repeating b yelling c whispering
8 Did Farid ___ his sickness during your conversation?
   a mention b advise c remind

B Circle the correct option to complete the sentences.

1 Julia said she was tired and *added that* / *added me that* she had a headache.
2 They warned *us* / *to us* that the test would be hard.
3 I wondered *where* / *that* Rosemary was and why she was so late.
4 Harriet agreed *to come* / *come* with me to the doctor's.
5 He asked *me to go* / *that I go* to the movie theater with him.
6 My boss advised *to me* / *me* to say nothing about our conversation.
7 Frank predicted *to snow* / *that it would snow* the next day and he was right!
8 We reminded *them to leave* / *that they leave* home early.
9 The children refused *them to go* / *to go* outside in the rain.
10 I finally persuaded the police *that* / *to* take action.

PRONUNCIATION
Using your voice to make a story more interesting

A Read the extract aloud.

'Don't worry, my friend,' said the voice, 'I'm not going to hurt you,' the voice died to a whisper. 'But I might kill you! Ha, ha, ha!' 'You'll never get away with it,' Jim warned. 'The police will be here any minute.' Jim was, in fact, just keeping him talking because, unknown to his captor, Jim had almost untied the rope. Suddenly, without a word of warning, Jim leaped free, and using the rope that had held him firmly tied to the chair, he grabbed the man around the neck. 'Don't worry,' whispered Jim as he tightened the rope, 'I might wait for the police ... but I might not.'

9.2 **B** Look at the extract, this time with instructions in brackets. Listen to someone reading the extract while following the instructions. Does it sound different from when you read the extract in Exercise A?

[**spoken in an evil way, like a bad guy from a James Bond movie**] 'Don't worry, my friend,' said the voice. [**said in a sarcastic tone**] 'I'm not going to hurt you,' the voice died to a whisper. [**with more enthusiasm, as if the speaker finds it amusing, followed by an evil laugh**] 'But I might kill you! Ha, ha, ha!' [**frightened but trying to sound brave**] 'You'll never get away with it,' Jim warned. [**hopeful more than realistic**] 'The police will be here any minute.' Jim was, in fact, just keeping him talking because, unknown to his captor, Jim had almost untied the rope. [**dramatically on the word *Suddenly*, speaking fast**] Suddenly, without a word of warning, Jim leaped free, and using the rope that had held him firmly tied to the chair, he [**stress *grabbed* and *neck***] grabbed the man around the neck. [**mimicking the earlier comment from the other man, this time sarcastically**] 'Don't worry,' whispered Jim as he tightened the rope, 'I [**stress *might***] might wait for the police [**dramatic pause; evil, threatening**] but I might not.'

Glossary

mimic (v) to copy someone's voice or behavior, especially in order to make people laugh or to make someone feel annoyed

C Now practice reading the text while following the instructions.

READING

A Look at the pictures and answer the questions.

1 What do the two events have in common?
2 What is different about the two events?
3 How do you think the people at each event feel?

B READ FOR GIST Read *Europe's most unusual (and less well-known) music festivals*. Match the headings (a–e) with the paragraphs (1–5).

a New styles and genres
b More than just music
c Taking part
d See the world
e Unusual venues

C UNDERSTANDING THE WRITER'S OPINION Read again. Check (✓) the statements you think the writer would agree with.

1 I love being with thousands of other people. ☐
2 Things are too expensive at big festivals. ☐
3 I like places which are far away. ☐
4 The most popular styles of music are the best. ☐
5 Music is just one of my interests. ☐

D READ FOR DETAIL Are the sentences true (T) or false (F)? Correct the false sentences.

1 The writer enjoys the feeling of being in a big crowd. ____
2 The Saristra venue was once inhabited by local people. ____
3 Both Saristra and Gottwood Festivals take place in remote locations. ____
4 The writer finds rock and pop music uninteresting. ____
5 You can hear a single style of brass band music in Guca. ____
6 Traveling is a more important experience than music. ____
7 The writer recommends taking part in music contests. ____
8 Some events include large groups of musicians. ____

Europe's most unusual (and less well-known) music festivals

There won't be many readers who haven't heard of the Glastonbury Festival in the UK, Rock in Roma in Italy's capital or Coachella in the US. However, while thousands of festival-goers descend on these venues every year, there are some music-lovers who feel that these mega-events have gotten a little out of control: the huge crowds, the miserable cold and mud (in the UK at least!), not to mention the overpriced food, drinks and accommodations.

1 ____

More and more young people want a festival experience which is less mainstream and more unusual. Sometimes the venue itself is part of the experience. A good example is the Saristra Festival in Greece which takes place in an abandoned village on the island of Kefalonia. The half-ruined houses form a spectacular background to the music events and art installations which are staged there. Similarly, the Gottwood Festival takes place in the depths of a forest in the Welsh countryside and is an absolutely unforgettable experience.

2 ____

In the same way that some festival-goers want to go to more unusual venues, they may also want to listen to a different kind of music. Pop and rock music have dominated the festival scene for decades now, but isn't it time that we started exploring some different styles? It can get so dull listening to the same style of music year after year. And it's for this reason that a lot of young people are seeking out new genres. For example, a festival which has been going on for 50 years, but which has become increasingly popular in recent years, is Guca in central Serbia. And what kind of music can you listen to here? Brass band music! Musicians from all over the Balkans bring their own magical touch to brass instruments with gypsy music, funk and jazz.

3 ____

You will have understood by now that another very important element of this new wave of festivals is travel. Why stay in your home country which you probably know really well already? Where's the fun in that? People are ready and willing to travel all over Europe, to experience something new. It means that they can combine a once-in-a-lifetime vacation to a little-known European country, with a whole new world of music. Traveling by train or by bus to these remote locations gives an added excitement to the whole experience.

4 ____

And it's not just a love of travel and music which motivates these festival-goers. If you travel to a different country to listen to music, then of course you're going to experience a different culture, too. If the nighttime is for partying, then the daytime is for visiting incredible archaeological sites, listening to the words of a new language or sampling delicious local specialities.

5 ____

Maybe the most exciting music experience of all is actually performing yourself! More and more venues are setting up platforms for young people to showcase their talents in a friendly, noncompetitive atmosphere. Like-minded instrumentalists and vocalists come together to share their knowledge and their skills. Sometimes a whole choir or orchestra travels far from home to share their passion for music with others.

So what's stopping you? Pack your bags and leave the crowds behind. A whole new world of musical and cultural experiences is out there waiting for you!

Glossary

abandoned (adj) which is no longer used or lived in
mainstream (adj) considered ordinary or normal and accepted or used by most people
seek out (v) look for
vocalist (n) singer

E REFLECT Think about the answers to these questions.

1 Have you ever been to a music festival? If not, would you like to?
2 Would you prefer to go to a big, well-known event or a smaller, less popular event? Why?

LISTENING

A **Look at the picture and answer the questions.**

1 Do you think it's a good idea to study art? Why/Why not?
2 Do you enjoy painting and drawing?
3 What other kinds of art do you think you can study at art college?

9.3 **B** **LISTEN FOR GIST** **Listen to a conversation between Agata and Ethan about studying art. Answer the questions.**

1 Have Agata and Ethan seen each other recently?
2 Did she enjoy the course?
3 Did Agata study one or many areas of art?
4 What is her view of the project called *Pathways*?
5 Is she enjoying her current course of study?

9.3 **C** **LISTEN FOR DEFINITIONS OF NEW WORDS** **Listen again and complete the definitions with the words in the box.**

attractive bridge examples idea pressing subject wool

1 art foundation course: course of study in art and design which is a ________ between school and college
2 portfolio: a collection of artwork which you use as ________ of your work
3 discipline: a ________ that people study, especially at a college or university
4 conceptual art: kind of art where the ________ the artist wishes to express is more important than the end product
5 fleece: the ________ on a sheep
6 printmaking: the process of making images by ________ paper against a surface
7 illustration: a picture in a book used for explaining something or to look ________

9.3 **D** **LISTEN FOR DETAIL** **Complete the sentences with one or two words in each space.**

1 Agata explains her year-long course was a ________ between high school and college.
2 A good portfolio should demonstrate a ________ of different styles.
3 Agata enjoyed learning about ________ kinds of art.
4 Conceptual art first appeared during ________ ________.
5 The project which Agata's fellow student did involved dressing up as ________.
6 She made ________ of her experience using 14 cameras.
7 Agata thinks that the word '________' does not describe the other student's project well.
8 According to Agata, you can use wood, ________ or ________ to create a print.
9 Agata is now learning how to create ________ for books.

E **REFLECT** **Think about the answers to these questions.**

1 Which of these disciplines on Agata's foundation course would you be most interested in: drawing, painting, fashion and textiles, printmaking or 3D design? Why?
2 What do you think about the idea of 'conceptual art'? Can you think of any examples of conceptual artworks?

FUNCTIONAL LANGUAGE

Complete the conversation with the words and phrases in the box.

actor ending follow like scene tearjerker worth

Kate: I watched an excellent movie on TV last night. It was called *Message in a Bottle*. I cried so much at the end!
Eleni: Oh, I love movies that make me cry!
Kate: Well, if you [1] ________ sad movies, then this is the movie for you. It's about this woman who finds a tragic love letter in a bottle on the beach and she tries to find the person who wrote it.
Eleni: And of course she finds him and he's incredibly good-looking and they fall in love!
Kate: Exactly! It has Kevin Costner in it, and he's a wonderful [2] ________. And then at the end, …
Eleni: No – don't tell me!
Kate: Well, just let me say that there's a sad [3] ________ – a real [4] ________.
Eleni: It sounds like it's really [5] ________ watching.
Kate: It is. The plot was a little difficult to [6] ________ but I loved the [7] ________ where he writes the letter to his dead wife.
Eleni: OK. Don't say anymore because I'm definitely going to watch it!

WRITING

A Think about the answers to these questions.

1. What is the purpose of a book review?
2. Where would you find a book review?
3. Have you ever been influenced by a review to buy a book?
4. What other art forms can you read reviews of?

B Read the book review and answer the questions.

1. Is the review mainly positive or negative?
2. Is the book a novel or a collection of short stories?
3. Are the nine sections of the book related in any way?
4. What negative point does the reviewer make about the book?

David Szalay: *All That Man Is*

1 I greatly enjoyed David Szalay's first novel, *London and the South-East*, a darkly comic novel about a young man dissatisfied with life in London. This new book, *All That Man Is*, his fourth, is similar in its themes but has several protagonists and explores new territory.

2 For a start, is it a novel? It is made up of nine sections each about a different male character: they range from the 17-year-old Simon to 73-year-old Mr. Parson. So, there is no plot, although the sections are thematically linked: let's call them short stories.

3 These men are trying to make sense of life and are mostly disappointed by it. They are lonely and their main concerns seem to be love and money. If this makes it sound depressing, it isn't: Szalay's prose is lively throughout. And while he exposes their faults, he does so sympathetically and without mocking them.

4 If there is a fault – remember it is a book about men – it is the lack of any fully rounded female characters. But, that aside, I urge you to read him because his is a rare talent and he is one of the most interesting fiction writers we have.

C **ORGANIZATION** Read again. Match the topics (a–d) with the paragraphs (1–4).

- **a** plot and characters ___
- **b** title, themes, main characters ___
- **c** overall assessment, reasons for recommendation ___
- **d** more detailed analysis, writing style ___

D Find three colons in the review. Note how they are used to introduce explanations. Then match the beginnings of the sentences (1–3) with the endings (a–c).

1 I stopped reading after 20 pages:	___	**a** there are some disturbing scenes.
2 There's a lesson to be learned from this:	___	**b** don't believe everything the reviewers say.
3 You need a strong stomach to read this:	___	**c** the writing was awful and the plot unbelievable.

WRITING PRACTICE

A **PREPARE** You are going to write a review of a book which you have read recently and particularly enjoyed. Write notes about each of the points below.

- Write down the title, genre, theme and main characters.
- Think about the main points of the plot.
- Think about the writing style. Write down one or two adjectives.
- Take note of anything you didn't like about the book.
- Think about your overall impression of the book and why somebody else should read it.

B **WRITE** Write your review in 150–200 words.

- Use your notes and ideas from Exercise A.
- Divide your writing into clear paragraphs.
- Remember to use colons to introduce explanations.

VOCABULARY
Psychology verbs

A Complete the sentences with the words in the box. The first two sentences have two possible answers.

affects	assume	attract	avoid	encourage
influences	persuade	regret	tempted	tricking

1 Store owners want to ________ / ________ you to spend as much money as possible.

2 The thing that most ________ / ________ my decision to buy something is the price.

3 I was ________ by that flat screen TV, but I thought I'd wait until the prices fall a little.

4 Reducing the prices of things is just a way of ________ you into buying something you don't need.

5 I ________ spending so much money on a computer – it was a big mistake.

6 A store window is designed to ________ customers as they pass by.

7 If you buy something second-hand, you shouldn't ________ that it's in good condition.

8 Try to ________ buying things on impulse (in other words, don't buy anything without thinking it through beforehand).

Expressions with *mind*

B Complete the sentences with one word in each space.

1 I've ________ up my mind – I'm getting that new car!

2 If you're tempted to buy more than you can afford, just walk away – it's all ________ the mind.

3 I lost some data on my computer, but ________ mind – I had backed it up.

4 I'd love to see you next week. Just ________ in mind that I will be away on Wednesday.

5 I was of ________ minds about whether to buy this tablet, but I bought it anyway.

6 If you ________ your mind to it, I'm sure you'll make the right decision.

7 Paul used to hate smartphones, but he's ________ his mind now!

8 ________ you mind if I copied some music from you sometime?

PRONUNCIATION
Third conditional

10.1 **A Listen to two speakers saying the same sentence. Check (✓) the speaker who pronounces the sentence correctly.**

1 If I'd had all the information, I'd have made a better decision.

Speaker A: ☐ Speaker B: ☐

2 You'd have done better if you'd bought it online.

Speaker A: ☐ Speaker B: ☐

3 If I'd been of two minds, I would never have bought anything!

Speaker A: ☐ Speaker B: ☐

4 What would you have done if I'd been late?

Speaker A: ☐ Speaker B: ☐

5 I wouldn't have minded if you'd decided to cancel.

Speaker A: ☐ Speaker B: ☐

6 I could have made other arrangements if they'd told me sooner.

Speaker A: ☐ Speaker B: ☐

B Practice saying the sentences in Exercise A with the correct pronunciation.

GRAMMAR

Third conditional

A **Complete the third conditional sentences with the correct form of the verbs in parentheses. Use short forms where possible.**

1. You ______________ (*get*) better from your sickness much sooner if you ______________ (*not go*) away for the weekend.
2. If I ______________ (*know*) the watch was made of plastic, I ______________ (*not pay*) so much for it!
3. If the teacher ______________ (*tell*) us about the test a little earlier, we ______________ (*can / spend*) more time preparing for it.
4. I ______________ (*not choose*) that language school if I ______________ (*think*) about the number of students who failed the exam.
5. If you ______________ (*not assume*) the saleswoman was trying to help you, you ______________ (*might / make*) a better decision.
6. Sam ______________ (*might / not / be / tempted*) to spend all that money if he ______________ (*not go*) shopping.
7. The poor man ______________ (*can / avoid*) a lot of trouble if he ______________ (*read*) the details on the contract.
8. If I ______________ (*realize*) how much the ink costs, I ______________ (*not buy*) this make of printer.

should have + past participle

B **Read the conversation and rewrite the underlined sections with *should/shouldn't have* + past participle.**

Margarita: I wouldn't have bought this laptop if I'd realized I'd have to pay for all these extras.

Angela: Oh dear. And I knew that. [1]<u>I wish you'd asked me</u> before you made up your mind to buy it.

Margarita: Then I found exactly the same laptop for 50 dollars cheaper in the store closest to my house!

Angela: Sometimes the bigger stores are more expensive, not less. [2]<u>It would've been better if you'd checked</u> the prices.

Margarita: I was in too much of a hurry to buy it. [3]<u>It would've been better if I'd waited</u>.

Angela: Yes – [4]<u>it was a mistake to buy</u> it at the first store you went to.

Margarita: Do you know what [5]<u>it would've been better to do?</u>

Angela: What's that?

Margarita: [6]<u>It would've been better to take</u> you with me!

Angela: Next time!

1 ______________
2 ______________
3 ______________
4 ______________
5 ______________
6 ______________

VOCABULARY
Reflexive verbs

A Complete the sentences with the correct reflexive pronouns.

1 Even though it wasn't our fault, we couldn't help but blame ________.

2 There's ham and cheese in the fridge and bread on the counter; if you want a sandwich, you can make it ________.

3 That silly dog of mine; he's always getting ________ into trouble.

4 Children! If you can't control ________, we're going home right now!

5 Do you mind if I help ________ to one of these snacks?

6 After she got the promotion, Lucy treated ________ to an expensive meal in a fancy restaurant.

7 What goals have you set ________ for the next six months?

8 The team decided to reward ________ for doing a great job on the project and turning it in on time.

Staying organized

B Circle the correct option to complete the sentences.

1 After I finish ***cleaning / sorting*** up my desk, I'm going to write a long to-do list.

2 If you ***focus / keep*** a record of your finances, you'll improve your spending habits.

3 Her life was a mess, so she ***sorted / scheduled*** an appointment with a lifestyle guru.

4 Martin got so involved in the details that he completely forgot the main ***action point / objective***.

5 Where can we ***store / sort*** all these old files and papers?

6 So we've done the first task; what's the next ***objective / action point*** on the list?

7 Once you have your plans ***sorted / tidied***, let me know what you're doing.

8 I have a simple ***task / objective*** for you – fold the invitations and put them into the envelopes.

PRONUNCIATION
Emphasis and reflexive pronouns

A Read the sentences, paying particular attention to the reflexive verbs. Underline either the main verb or the reflexive pronoun which should be stressed in each sentence.

1 Mary brought a cake into work and I helped myself to a slice at lunchtime.

2 You're good at praising others when they do well, but how do you reward yourself?

3 You'll have to prepare John's lunch today, because he can't make it himself.

4 When something goes wrong, my Aunt Tilda tends to blame herself.

5 I believe that it's a good idea to set yourself goals in life.

6 They treated themselves to pizza after winning the game.

10.2 **B Listen and check your answers. Practice saying the sentences in Exercise A.**

GRAMMAR
Hopes and wishes

A Circle the correct answer, a, b or c.

1 I hope you ___ Leon to change his mind about leaving.
  a would persuade
  b persuade
  c persuaded
2 He wishes he ___ keep his desk neat.
  a had
  b can
  c could
3 Good luck! I hope your mom ___ yell at you for being late!
  a couldn't
  b doesn't
  c didn't
4 Tomas wishes he ___ his mind to passing the exam; he regrets not studying.
  a puts
  b had put
  c put
5 Look at these beautiful gold earrings – I wish I ___ rich enough to afford them!
  a am
  b would be
  c were
6 It sounds like you had fun on your trip. I wish I ___ with you!
  a could have come
  b can come
  c could come
7 I can't remember what we decided at the meeting – I wish I ___ a record of what we said.
  a kept
  b have kept
  c had kept
8 Dylan is responsible for the project for the next month; I hope he ___ the action points.
  a wouldn't forget
  b didn't forget
  c doesn't forget

B Circle the correct option. Then complete the short conversation with the correct form of the verbs in parentheses.

1 **Natalie:** I (hope) / *wish* we ___are___ (*be*) able to cover all the material before the exam.
Devin: Me, too. I ***hope*** / ***wish*** we ______ (*plan*) it better. We could have finished already!

2 **Isaiah:** Beth wants me to pick up some things we need for moving to a new house. I ***wish*** / ***hope*** I ______ (*can / remember*) everything she told me!
Ben: Moving is difficult. I ***wish*** / ***hope*** it ______ (*go*) well for you.

3 **Rosana:** My sister has a terrible social anxiety; she always tells me that she ***hopes*** / ***wishes*** she ______ (*no be*) so shy.
Pravat: I know the feeling. I ***hope*** / ***wish*** everyone ______ (*can / have*) confidence, but for some, it takes a lot of effort.

4 **Josey:** I talked to Margie the other day. She ***wishes*** / ***hopes*** you and she ______ (*can / meet*) soon.
Ivan: Oh, how nice! I think next Friday could be good. I asked my boss for that day off. I ***wish*** / ***hope*** he ______ (*give*) it to me.

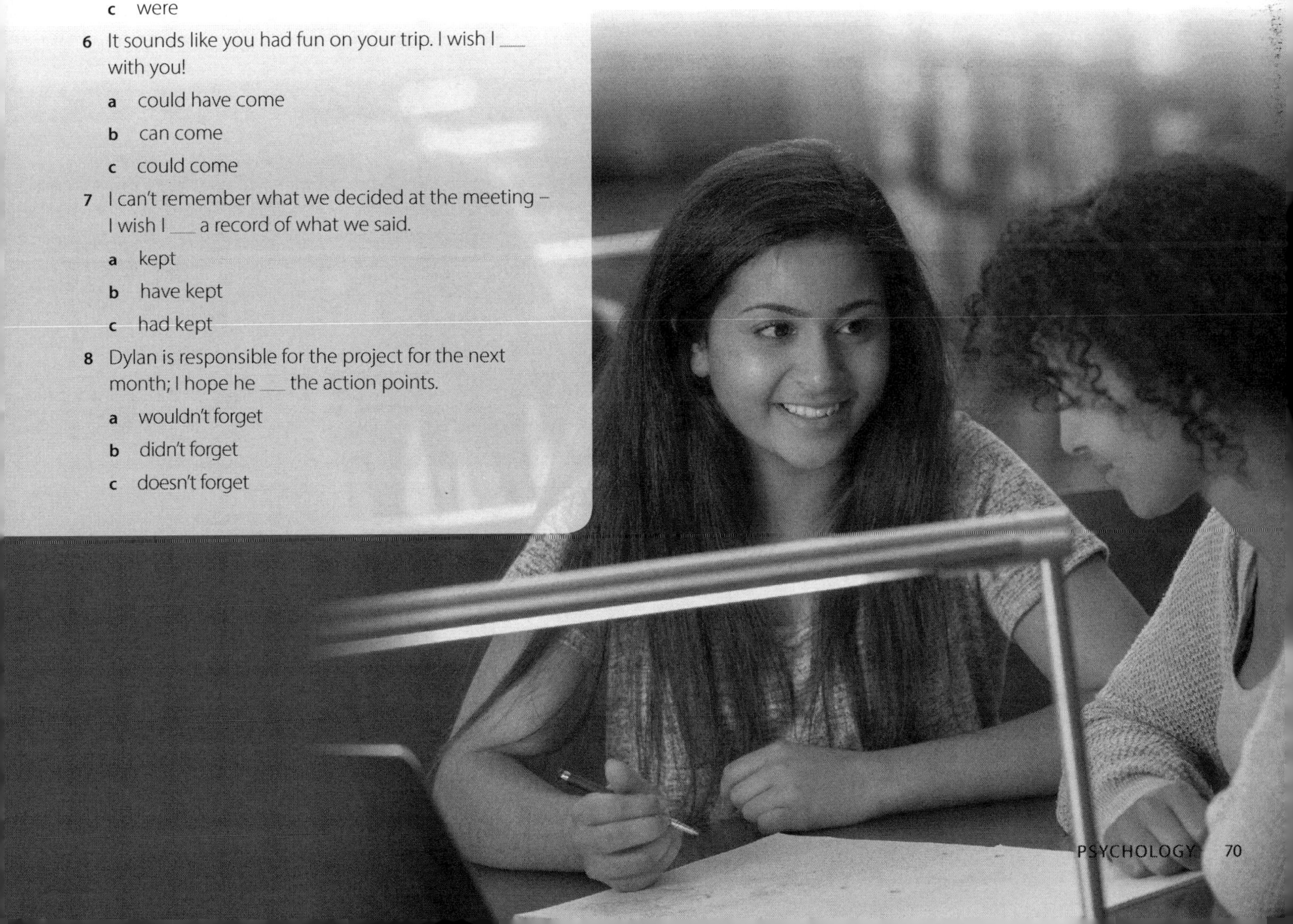

READING

A Read the statements. Do they surprise you? Why/Why not?

1 Most adults will suffer from anxiety and depression at some point in their lives.

2 Millions of people suffer from anxiety or depression worldwide.

B READ FOR GIST Read the article about anxiety. According to the article, are these statements true (T) or false (F)?

1 Anxiety has both psychological and physical symptoms. ____

2 People who suffer from anxiety usually face serious work, family or health issues. ____

3 The origins of anxiety as a human problem are very old. ____

4 It's a good idea for sufferers to avoid situations which upset them. ____

5 Sufferers can be helped by using a variety of different treatments. ____

6 Calming activities and exercises can help sufferers to cope better. ____

Glossary

dread (n) fear of what might happen in the future
overcompensate (v) do more than is necessary in order to correct a problem

C READ FOR KEY INFORMATION Read again and look carefully at the underlined parts. Complete the article with the missing sentences (1–5).

1 A longer-term and more effective strategy is to use a combination of psychotherapy, behavioral therapy and, in extreme cases, medication.

2 Implementing a stress management plan could include keeping an eye on deadlines, creating lists to organize different aspects of work and home life and allocating time off from school or work.

3 Back then, humans had an internal alarm system which was there to protect them from the very real dangers which they had to face in the wild.

4 Fear of such ordinary people and places may lead the sufferer to avoid seeing certain people or going to certain places.

5 Psychologists believe that this primitive alert system, in a world where we are no longer in danger from wild animals or aggressive attackers, is what prompts the feelings which we know today as *anxiety*.

D REFLECT Think about the answers to these questions.

1 What common social or work situations could cause anxiety?

2 How could family members help somebody who is suffering from anxiety?

Anxiety:
what it is and what can be done about it

We frequently hear people talking about *anxiety* but what is it exactly? Anxiety is a normal but unpleasant part of our everyday lives which can affect different people in different ways. Sufferers describe it as a feeling of unease, nervousness or dread. It may produce symptoms such as nausea, trembling or increased heart rate. Anxiety isn't necessarily triggered by a situation which is genuinely dangerous or difficult – it can be an everyday event, such as going into the grocery store or having to talk with colleagues, which brings on symptoms.

a____ They might start shopping in a different grocery store, or pretending to be overworked in the office so that they don't have to interact with colleagues. Some people start working late because they are anxious about completing tasks, or waking up in the middle of the night to check their to-do lists in case they have forgotten something.

Anxiety can make a person believe that things in their life are worse than they really are. Some people even reach the stage of thinking they are losing their sanity or *going crazy*. However, what is important to remember is that anxiety is normal and exists due to physical reactions that have existed since prehistoric times.

b____ It caused individuals to be on the alert for possible attack and produced a boost of adrenaline that increased the heart rate and the amount of oxygen in the blood. This response is commonly known as the *fight or flight* reaction.

c____ However, instead of our system reacting to a real danger, it is overcompensating by reacting to perfectly normal problems and difficulties which everybody faces in their everyday lives.

So what can sufferers do to reduce the symptoms of anxiety and cope better with their lives? What they usually do is to simply avoid the anxiety-provoking situation, as we saw earlier. However, although such a strategy does provide short-term relief, it does not solve the overall problem. There will no doubt be another situation to replace the one you've managed to avoid.

d____ Many people successfully treat their anxiety by implementing a number of self-help techniques, without resorting to a medical practitioner. These may include any or all of the following: stress management, relaxation techniques and physical exercise.

e____ Relaxation techniques vary from person to person but could include breathing exercises, a long bath or yoga and meditation sessions. Physical exercise is also known to increase serotonin levels which in turn trigger positive emotions.

LISTENING

A Which of these statements do you agree with? Why?

1. If you have a mental health disorder, it's better not to say anything about it.
2. Most people think that mental health problems are related to violence.
3. People shouldn't feel embarrassed to talk about mental health problems.

10.3 **B** **LISTEN FOR KEY PHRASES** Listen to an extract from a radio show about mental health. Check (✓) the phrases you hear.

1. According to research ☐
2. … statistics … have shown that … ☐
3. But surely … ☐
4. As you can imagine, … ☐
5. For example, … ☐
6. Obviously, … ☐
7. In fact, … ☐

Glossary

bipolar disorder (n) a serious mental illness where people experience extreme mood changes
discrimination (n) unfair treatment because of race, religion, illness, etc
stigma (n) a feeling that something is wrong or embarrassing

10.4 **C** **LISTEN FOR DETAIL** Now listen to the complete recording and underline the correct option to complete the sentences.

1. According to Doctor Patel, over 615 million people suffer from anxiety or depression *in the UK / all over the world*.
2. In the UK, *a quarter of the population / one or two people* suffer from mental health problems.
3. Doctor Patel has shown that a majority of people with mental health problems have to deal with *discrimination / aggression*.
4. People with mental health problems are *more likely / less likely* to be able to find work.
5. Most patients are *violent / not violent* or aggressive.
6. Publicity campaigns organized by *charities / research groups* have a positive effect.
7. Employers are *not allowed / allowed* to refuse somebody a job because of their mental health problems.

D **REFLECT** Think about the answers to these questions.

1. Do you think that there is a stigma attached to mental illness in your country?
2. What could be done to improve the situation?

FUNCTIONAL LANGUAGE

Complete two short conversations with one word in each space.

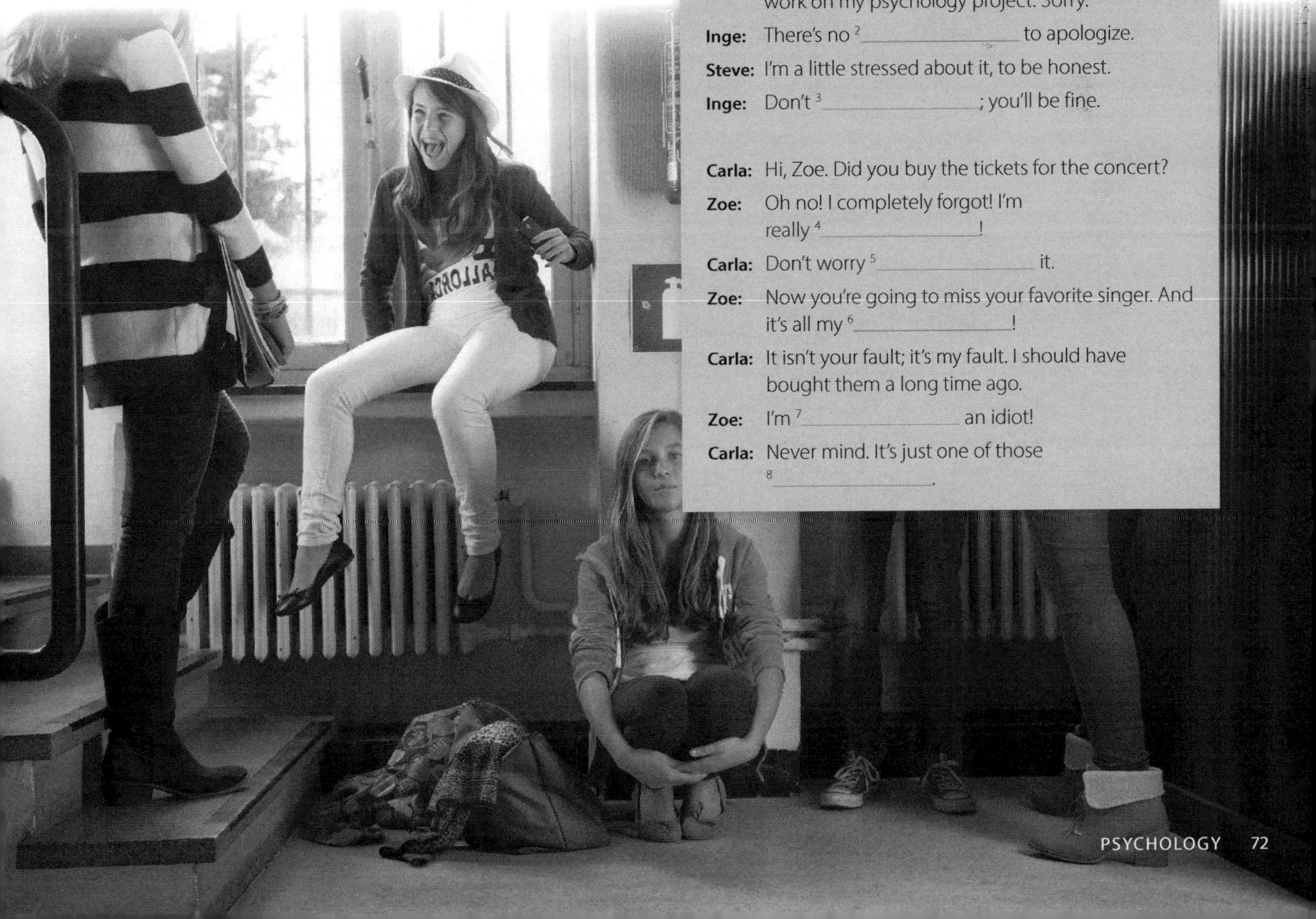

Steve: It's [1] __________ for me to go. I have to work on my psychology project. Sorry.
Inge: There's no [2] __________ to apologize.
Steve: I'm a little stressed about it, to be honest.
Inge: Don't [3] __________; you'll be fine.

Carla: Hi, Zoe. Did you buy the tickets for the concert?
Zoe: Oh no! I completely forgot! I'm really [4] __________!
Carla: Don't worry [5] __________ it.
Zoe: Now you're going to miss your favorite singer. And it's all my [6] __________!
Carla: It isn't your fault; it's my fault. I should have bought them a long time ago.
Zoe: I'm [7] __________ an idiot!
Carla: Never mind. It's just one of those [8] __________.

WRITING

A Read *Report on Downey Town Fair* and answer the questions.

1. What is the main purpose of the report?
2. To what extent was the fair a success?
3. What was/were the main problem(s)?
4. What measures do you think they will adopt next year?

B **ORGANIZATION** Read the report again. Match the headings (a–f) with the paragraphs (1–6) in the report.

- **a** Poor planning
- **b** Summary
- **c** Analysis
- **d** Wrong predictions
- **e** Recommendations
- **f** Background

Report on Downey Town Fair

1 ___

On June 14th, we held our Town Fair to raise money for local projects. Although we met our financial targets, we received complaints about poor organization. This report explores what we did wrong.

2 ___

The fair has become increasingly popular, attracting visitors from all over the country. This year more people came than we had planned for, and lack of parking areas caused chaos both in town and in the surrounding area.

3 ___

I believe we should have foreseen the larger number of visitors because this has been increasing annually. In fact, the matter was raised at one meeting, and the offer by Mr. Orton, a farmer, of one of his fields for parking was refused.

4 ___

Lack of parking spaces led to traffic jams extending five to ten miles out of town, and at the end of the day, it took hours for the traffic to return to normal.

5 ___

Obviously, we need more parking spaces and better signs and directions. In the future, we should take up the offers of landowners such as Mr. Orton.

6 ___

We should have more people employed to direct cars to available parking spaces and, if possible, get the police involved in regulating traffic in and out of town.

WRITING PRACTICE

A **PREPARE** You are going to write a short report about an event you helped to organize where there were some problems. Think about the answers to these questions and write notes.

1. Which event are you going to write about? When did it take place?
2. What happened? What was/were the problem(s)?
3. What was the cause of the problem(s)?
4. What are your recommendations for future events?

B **WRITE** Write your report in 150–200 words.

- Use your notes and ideas from Exercise A.
- Divide your writing into clear sections.
- Remember to use headings, bullet points and numbered lists.
- Include some facts and figures and examples of the problems.

Irregular Verbs

Base form	Simple past	Past participle
be	was/were	been
become	became	become
begin	began	begun
break	broke	broken
bring	brought	brought
build	built	built
buy	bought	bought
can	could	been able to
catch	caught	caught
choose	chose	chosen
come	came	come
cost	cost	cost
cut	cut	cut
drink	drank	drunk
eat	ate	eaten
fall	fell	fallen
feel	felt	felt
find	found	found
forget	forgot	forgotten
get	got	got
give	gave	given
go	went	gone/been
grow	grew	grown
have	had	had
hear	heard	heard
hit	hit	hit
hold	held	held
hurt	hurt	hurt
keep	kept	kept
know	knew	known
leave	left	left
lend	lent	lent
let	let	let

Base form	Simple past	Past participle
lose	lost	lost
make	made	made
mean	meant	meant
meet	met	met
must	had to	had to
pay	paid	paid
put	put	put
read	read	read
ride	rode	ridden
run	ran	run
say	said	said
see	saw	seen
sell	sold	sold
send	sent	sent
set	set	set
shut	shut	shut
sing	sang	sung
sit	sat	sat
sleep	slept	slept
speak	spoke	spoken
spell	spelled	spelled
spend	spent	spent
stand	stood	stood
steal	stole	stolen
take	took	taken
teach	taught	taught
tell	told	told
think	thought	thought
throw	threw	thrown
understand	understood	understood
wear	wore	worn
win	won	won
write	wrote	written

PHONETIC SYMBOLS

Single vowels			Diphthongs			Consonants					
/ɪ/	fish	/fɪʃ/	/uw/	news	/nuw/	/p/	pen	/pen/	/s/	snake	/sneɪk/
/iː/	bean	/biːn/	/eɪ/	face	/feɪs/	/b/	bag	/bæg/	/z/	zoo	/zuː/
/ʊ/	foot	/fʊt/	/ɔɪ/	boy	/bɔɪ/	/t/	tea	/tiː/	/ʃ/	shop	/ʃɒp/
/uː/	shoe	/ʃuː/	/oʊ/	nose	/noʊz/	/d/	dog	/dɒg/	/ʒ/	television	/'telɪvɪʒən/
/e/	egg	/eg/	/ju/	use	/juz/	/ʧ/	chip	/ʧɪp/	/m/	map	/mæp/
/ə/	mother	/'mʌðər/	/aɪ/	eye	/aɪ/	/ʤ/	jazz	/ʤæz/	/n/	name	/neɪm/
/ɜː/	word	/wɜːrd/	/aʊ/	mouth	/maʊθ/	/k/	cake	/keɪk/	/ŋ/	ring	/rɪŋ/
/ɔː/	talk	/tɔːk/				/g/	girl	/gɜːrl/	/h/	house	/haʊs/
/æ/	back	/bæk/				/f/	film	/fɪlm/	/l/	leg	/leg/
/ʌ/	bus	/bʌs/				/v/	verb	/vɜːrb/	/r/	road	/roʊd/
/ɑː/	arm	/ɑːrm/				/θ/	thing	/θɪŋ/	/w/	want	/wɒnt/
/ɒ/	top	/tɒp/				/ð/	these	/ðiːz/	/j/	yes	/jes/

Audio scripts

UNIT 6

Lesson 6.4, Listening, Exercise B

7.3 Good morning and thank you for coming. Today's presentation is called *Passion into Profit* and it's all about how you can achieve the dream of turning what you love into a profitable business. No doubt everybody in this room has a hobby which they're passionate about – whether it's baking beautiful cupcakes, making jewelry or collecting vintage cars. Now, many people think that their hobbies are just that – something to do in your free time. But what if you could make a living from something you actually like doing instead of earning money in a boring or unsatisfying job?

Turning your hobby into a successful business can seem like a scary idea, but you must not let that discourage you. Many people are afraid to take action and leave their job or career because they are afraid they might fail. Well, I'm here to tell you that an amazing 37% of entrepreneurs have created their businesses from what was originally a hobby! And the results of a recent survey show that 86% of people who started a hobby-based business said they were happier now than before they gave up their traditional nine-to-five jobs.

My first piece of advice is focus on your goal. Like everyone starting a business for the first time, you will have your ups and downs, but the important thing is to set a target and stick to it. Make a plan of what exactly you want to achieve and by when; a detailed week-by-week schedule of actions and results will help to keep you on target.

That brings me to the subject of flexibility; you may need to do more than one thing in order to actually make money from your hobby. For example, if you make jewelry, you might sell your jewelry online, but you could also teach other people to make jewelry, or have a stand at a flea market and sell jewelry-making supplies.

The next point I would like to explore is marketing. You may create beautiful objects or be extremely skilled, but if nobody knows it, then you'll never get any customers. Use social media to advertise your product or service and develop your sales. Some online platforms allow you to list your products for free. Join online forums and chat groups so you can attract customers who have the same interests as you.

Finally, learn to think like a businessperson – after all, this isn't just a hobby anymore. Learn how to manage your finances by balancing your income and your expenses. Set up a bank account and don't be afraid to ask for advice from the experts – your bank manager or a professional accountant will be able to advise you on the best way to keep your new business financially healthy!

So, the next question is when do I …

UNIT 7

Lesson 7.4, Listening, Exercise C

6.3 **M = Mark C = César O = Olivia W = Wing Shan**

M: On today's edition of *Food for Thought*, we're here in the center of Birmingham to find out what people think about the latest food fads. Here we go …. excuse me … good morning …

C: Um … hi …

M: Hi, I'm Mark from *Food for Thought* on Radio 7. What's your name? Can we talk to you?

C: Yes, sure. I'm César.

M: OK. Thanks for talking to us, César. So … I'd like to ask you a question. What do you think about food fads? Do you believe they're a good thing or do you think they're just nonsense?

C: Food fads? Well, um … some food fads are good, like, you know, the five-a-day thing. It's a really good idea to encourage people to eat plenty of fruits and vegetables, you know, but … some others … like oh yes … foraging. I've read about that and it sounds crazy. It's this new fad where they only eat food which has been found in the wild. Stuff like mushrooms, green leaves, wild garlic, nuts. I mean, like I said, I think it's a good idea to eat fresh ingredients. There are more nutrients than in processed foods, but I mean, come on! I heard of one restaurant where they put these special ants – yes, the insects – into their salads. Makes the salad taste lemony or something. I think it sounds disgusting.

M: OK. Thanks César. Good to talk to you. Excuse me. Can we ask you a question? What do you think about food fads?

O: Hiya. I'm Olivia. Oh, I think any kind of food fad can help people to eat more healthily. Whatever it is, it gets you thinking about what you eat, doesn't it? To be honest, I wouldn't really call them fads. I think they're interesting ways of exploring new ideas. For example, I've been on the Paleo Diet for six months and I feel great – more energetic, less tired. It's a kind of eating plan where you only eat foods that existed millions of years ago – from Paleolithic times … paleo – get it? So that means lots of seeds and nuts, heaps of fruits and vegetables and, of course, no sugar, wheat or dairy. It's like if a caveman – or cavewoman – didn't eat it, then neither do I.

M: I see. Well thanks, Olivia. That's fascinating. And, this lady, … um … excuse me. Hi … what's your name? Can I ask you a question?

W: My name's Wing Shan. Sure, go ahead.

M: What do you think about food fads?

W: I don't really believe that food fads can help us. I think that what's important is to stick to a balanced diet. I just think that if you eat a little of everything then it's the best way. Having said that, I do believe that the Mediterranean diet is a good way of eating. But that's not really a fad, is it? It just means cooking and eating plenty of fresh food – a lot of fish, of course, and not so much meat. Lots of olive oil – it's much better for you than butter or animal fat. A lot of fresh fruits and vegetables. They say that it helps to prevent heart disease and cancer. Keeps your blood pressure down, too. I'll be brutally honest, though – I do sometimes have a burger. But honestly, if you eat … fast food … unhealthy food … now and then, I don't think that's such a big deal, do you?

M: And that was Wing Shan with her view on food fads. So, back to studio where we're going to discuss the latest trends with Doctor …

UNIT 8

Lesson 8.1, Pronunciation

8.1

1 The internet, which is a relatively new invention, is now a vital part of people's lives across the world.

2 It was Edison who first used publicity to promote a new invention.

3 The Cloud is where many people store photos and other files.

4 In the 1980s, when I was in school, no one had a cell phone.

5 Coco Chanel, who invented the little black dress, was a very influential fashion designer.

6 The physicist whose theories have influenced generations of scientists is Einstein.

Lesson 8.2, Pronunciation, Exercise A

8.2 **W = Woman M = Man**

W: You know … I've been thinking … if you want to go to the theater on Saturday night, it's OK with me.

M: To be honest, I was surprised you weren't more interested. I think you'll really like it.

W: I know. I'm sorry. I want to go – it's just that I don't have a lot of money.

M: I'll lend you the money if you want. Or we can do something cheaper.

W: That's very sweet of you! No, it's OK. I enjoy the theater. I'm sure we'll have a nice time.

M: Great. I'm really happy that I won't miss it. I think they still have some seats left. I'll call them now.

Lesson 8.4, Listening, Exercise B

8.3 **L = Lucy A = Adam**

L: What's the matter, Adam? You look a little stressed.

A: Yes, I am a little. It's exam time at school, and I have to grade all my students' exam papers and be at school to help with the organization of the exams. The thing is that my wife's away on a work trip right now. I mean, we normally share all the household chores, and childcare of course, but this week, I have to manage the house, the kids and work, … well … it's a lot of pressure.

L: My kids are grown-up now, but I have a lot of experience juggling a family and a job. I can give you plenty of tips. And my first piece of advice is – don't be such a perfectionist! I mean, did your children have breakfast and get to school on time?

A: Well, yes of course they did. But their school shirts were wrinkled because I hadn't had time to iron them.

L: Now, you see. That's exactly what I mean. Don't be so hard on yourself. I mean, we all want our lives to be reasonably organized, but sometimes it's just not possible. Well, I'm here to tell you that it isn't the end of the world, you know? Have you achieved what you wanted, but not as well as normal? Well, that's OK.

A: Yes, I suppose you're right. So what else do you suggest?

L: When you have a lot of different tasks to achieve and not enough time, you have to prioritize. Think about what is absolutely essential, what you have to do, and focus only on that. It sounds to me as if you're doing that already. I mean, the important thing is that your children are at school and that they had a good breakfast before they left.

A: Yes, but I forgot to make sandwiches for them – you know, to have at lunchtime.

L: OK, well that's the next thing. You simply must delegate.

A: Delegate? Can you give me an example?

L: Your example is right there! Your children aren't so little anymore. I mean, your daughter's fifteen, isn't she? Well, delegate the task of making sandwiches to her. She's old enough. She can make her own sandwiches and her little brother's. That's one less thing for you to worry about – and it will teach them to be more responsible.

A: Yes, you're right. That's a really good idea. But what about the rest of the housework? There's just more and more – heaps of dirty dishes, dirty laundry, recyclables …

L: It's true that if you don't keep on top of the housework, it can get out of control. So – my advice? Clean as you go. Do the dishes right after dinner. Same with the dirty clothes. Put them straight into the washing machine. And get the kids to do the same. That way, you won't end up with a huge pile of dirty laundry or dishes at the end of the week.

A: Sounds good. To be honest, I sometimes forget what I need to do. There are so many things to remember that my mind just goes blank.

L: Then make a list. Write down those essential tasks that we talked about, but make a note of when you're going to do them and, of course, who is going to do them. For example, 'sandwiches – Josie, early morning.' You'll find that it really focuses your mind.

A: Lucy – I feel better already. Thanks. You've been a big help.

L: You're welcome. Let me know how it goes.

UNIT 9

Lesson 9.4, Listening, Exercise B
9.3 **E = Ethan A = Agata**

E: Hi Agata. I haven't seen you in a long time. How are you? What have you been doing since we left high school?

A: Hello, Ethan. Good to see you. Well, I took a year-long art foundation course.

E: What's that exactly?

A: Well, it's supposed to be a transition period between high school and the study of specialist art and design courses in college.

E: Oh, right. So where did you go to do that?

A: At Kingston College of Art and Design. The course is designed to help you … unlock your creative abilities. That's the idea anyway! And of course, it gives you the
10.3 chance to build your portfolio. That's a collection of all your work – drawings, paintings, sketches. It should be fairly … um … diverse. So people can see that you have a range of styles and ideas. Anyway, it was really fun because I tried all kinds of different disciplines as well as straightforward drawing and painting – fashion and textiles, printmaking, 3D design.

E: But …?

A: Yes, there was a but! A lot of the projects we did were conceptual art and that was, well, it just isn't me.

E: You've lost me.

A: It's very popular at most art schools, and galleries and so on. It was a movement which emerged in the 60s, and the theory is that the concept behind the art is more important than the finished artwork itself. To give you an example, one of my fellow students did a project entitled *Pathways*. She did this thing where she wore a fleece.

E: Sorry, I didn't catch that.

A: A fleece – a … like a sheepskin … a big woolly sheepskin that you wear like a coat …

10.4 E: OK …

A: Anyway, she wore this sheep … coat and she attached fourteen little cameras all over her and crawled along the paths on a mountain. I mean, can you believe it? The idea was that she would experience and understand the mountain, the life of the sheep, the landscape … or something. And the video was displayed at a gallery afterwards.

E: Well, that sounds interesting.

A: Interesting? Anyway, that's the kind of thing that we were expected to do, well not that exactly, but something similar. Well … to be brutally honest, I just find it all … let's just say, it's not my kind of thing.

E: So, what are you doing now?

A: Well, after I finished the course … I specialized in printmaking, by the way. That's where you create an image on a block of wood or metal, could be a stone, too – you carve the image into the material – and then you cover the block in ink and press paper onto it. The image is transferred to the paper. Well, that's a very simplistic explanation, but that's basically it. So, anyway, I got my diploma and now I'm at a different college studying illustration.

E: Illustration? You mean like for books?

A: Yes, basically. An illustration is any drawing that accompanies a written text – it might help to explain what's in the text, or maybe it's just there for decoration. For instance, children's books are full of illustrations because children are more responsive to visual images than to the written word. Anyway, that's what I'm studying now, and guess what? I love it!

E: Well, that's good news!

A: But enough about me, what about you. Did you go traveling like you told me …

UNIT 10

Lesson 10.4, Listening, Exercise B
D = Dr. Patel J = John Ingrams

D: Well, we're talking about a huge variety of conditions, ranging from social anxiety and mild depression to very serious illnesses such as bipolar disorder. In fact, statistics from the World Health Organization have shown that more than 615 million people suffer from anxiety or depression on a worldwide scale. And in the UK, for example, one in four people will suffer from some kind of mental health problem at some point in their lives. So we're not talking about just one or two people.

J: Those are pretty scary numbers, Doctor Patel. But surely that must mean that there's more understanding in society about these conditions?

D: Well John, there certainly should be. But even though so many people suffer from mental health problems, there is still a stigma attached to them. According to research carried out by my team at the college, nearly nine out of ten people with mental health problems say that they've experienced discrimination.

Lesson 10.4, Listening, Exercise C
J = John Ingrams D = Dr. Patel

J: Good morning and welcome to *Mind Matters* with me, John Ingrams. Today, I'm going to be talking to Doctor Patel about mental illness and the stigma of mental illness. So tell me, Doctor Patel, is it really possible that in the 21st century there is still a certain amount of … well, let's say shame related to mental illness?

D: Unfortunately, yes. That's very much the case.

J: First of all, what do we mean by mental illness?

D: Well, we're talking about a huge variety of conditions, ranging from social anxiety and mild depression to very serious illnesses such as bipolar disorder. In fact, statistics from the World Health Organization have shown that more than 615 million people suffer from anxiety or depression on a worldwide scale. And in the UK, for example, one in four people will suffer from some kind of mental health problem at some point in their lives. So we're not talking about just one or two people.

J: Those are pretty scary numbers, Doctor Patel. But surely that must mean that there's more understanding in society about these conditions?

D: Well John, there certainly should be. But even though so many people suffer from mental health problems, there is still a stigma attached to them. According to research carried out by my team at the college, nearly nine out of ten people with mental health problems say that they've experienced discrimination.

J: So what does that mean for them in practical terms?

D: Well, it can affect many aspects of their lives. For instance, they are more likely to be unemployed. This comes about because many employers believe that people with mental illness are violent or dangerous, but that just isn't true. A tiny percentage of patients display aggressive or antisocial behavior. As you can imagine, this has a negative impact on a person's feelings of self-worth and confidence.

J: Clearly something has to be done to overcome these kinds of negative impressions, but what?

D: Well, John, a lot of good work is being done by mental health charities which run publicity campaigns and workshops. Research has shown that those kinds of actions are really helpful in changing the negative views which are associated with mental health conditions.

J: What are the authorities trying to do about this problem?

D: A lot has been done already. Actually, here in the UK, the 2010 Equality Act makes it illegal to discriminate against somebody in the workplace because they have a mental health disorder, and that has helped a great deal. In addition, official organizations, such as our college, for example, are creating blogs, newsletters and so on, where we raise awareness of the problem. And to tell you the truth John …

Answer key

6.1 Take part!

GRAMMAR

A

1 b
2 a
3 b
4 c
5 b
6 a

B

1 shouldn't
2 don't need to
3 must not
4 must
5 shouldn't
6 don't have to
7 don't need to
8 don't have to

VOCABULARY

A

1 competitive
2 massive
3 aggressive
4 effective
5 creative
6 impressive

B

1 stadium
2 champion
3 players
4 final
5 trophy
6 fan
7 medal
8 league
9 tournament
10 spectator

C

1 coach
2 trophy
3 league
4 stadium
5 tournament
6 fans
7 champion
8 players
9 spectator
10 final

PRONUNCIATION

A

Stay tuned, (/) folks. (/) We have an exciting show for you today. (/) Later on in the show, (/) Lionel Messi (//) – world famous athlete, (/) considered by some to be the greatest soccer player of all time – (/) will be joining us to talk about his life and career. (/) We'll speak about the challenges he's faced, (//) both on and off the field, (/) and how he overcame them to be who he is today.

6.2 Hobbies

VOCABULARY

A

1 escape
2 relaxing
3 get
4 collecting
5 close
6 are

B

1 society
2 hobby
3 thing
4 member
5 active
6 fan

GRAMMAR

A

1 have/'ve never known
2 has/'s been playing
3 have you been taking part
4 has/'s been training
5 has/'s completed
6 have not / haven't achieved
7 has/'s just come in
8 has/'s been working out

B

1 's/has been living here for
2 's/has been playing tennis since
3 have not been going
4 've/have been training for a

C

1 I didn't need to buy a yoga mat because my sister lent me hers.
2 We **had** ~~have~~ to have lessons before we could jump out of the plane for the first time.
3 Julio need**ed** to practice a lot before he became good at fly fishing.
4 Kayleigh **didn't have** ~~hadn't~~ to watch the ukulele teacher because she already knew how to play the song.
5 She didn't **have** ~~had~~ to do anything yesterday so she spent the day relaxing at home.
6 I had **to** spend a lot of money to buy this stamp, but I'm pleased that I did.
7 The coach said we needed **to** practice more, so we did.
8 I had **to** use my friend's Ping-Pong paddle last week because I broke mine.

PRONUNCIATION

A

1 I've never been to <u>India</u>.
2 Tanya's been playing tennis <u>for hours</u>.
3 He's been <u>very quiet</u> all day.
4 How long have you been <u>captain</u> of the <u>club</u>?
5 We've been training since <u>last year</u>.
6 Have you been <u>surfing</u> before?

6.3 Reading

READING

A

brass bands

B

1 b 2 a 3 c

C

1 b
2 c
3 a
4 c
5 b
6 a

6.4 Listening; Functional Language

LISTENING

B

a 3
b 5
c 1
d 6
e 2
f 4

C

1 c
2 b
3 b
4 a
5 a
6 c

FUNCTIONAL LANGUAGE

1 for instance
2 another example
3 If you
4 my opinion
5 don't think
6 brutally honest
7 probably right

6.5 Write an article for a magazine

WRITING

B

a 2 b 3 c 1 d 5 e 4

C

1 f
2 c
3 a
4 d
5 b
6 e

WRITING PRACTICE

B

Model answer

Fishing may not sound exciting, but I can tell you that there's nothing like the thrill you get when you feel the pull on your line as a fish takes the bait.

One of the great things about fishing is that you spend time outdoors – either in the peace and quiet of the country or by the ocean. You can relax and think and leave the worries of everyday life behind.

Another thing I like about fishing is how it helps the environment. One good thing about our hobby is that we keep rivers and waterways clean and trash-free. As for the fish, most of us usually throw them back into the water. Although, and this is another great thing about it, you may go home with a delicious fish for supper!

Another good reason to take up fishing is that you don't need any expensive gear to enjoy it, just a simple rod and some bait and a little stool to sit on.

Everyone wants to escape from the stress of their busy lives, and fishing is an inexpensive and peaceful way to do it. I'm hooked – and I think you will be, too, once you try it!

7.1 Eating out

PRONUNCIATION

A

1 could be
2 can't be
3 must be
4 might be/could be
5 might not be
6 can't be
7 must be
8 might take/could take

B

1 d 2 b 3 g 4 c 5 a 6 f 7 e

VOCABULARY

A

1 try out
2 giving up
3 shows up
4 serve up
5 took off
6 started off
7 set up

B

1 disgusting
2 raw
3 watery
4 salty/savory
5 filling
6 tasty
7 rich
8 cheesy
9 fruity
10 spicy

C

Positive	Neutral	Negative
rich	cheesy	disgusting
tasty	fruity	raw
	raw	rich
	salty/savory	salty
	spicy	watery

GRAMMAR

A

1 That **can't** ~~must not~~ be our bill – we only had a snack!
2 We should call and make a reservation – there might **not** ~~don't~~ be a table.
3 You must ~~to~~ think I'm very rude eating with my fingers!
4 You **may/might/could** ~~maybe~~ be right about this food – it doesn't taste good.
5 Let's try this new restaurant – it **may/might/could** ~~could maybe~~ **be** good.
6 This place might **not** have ~~not~~ the best food, but it's good enough and very cheap.

B

2 may/might/could contain
3 can't (possibly) want
4 might not taste
5 can't/couldn't be; must be
6 must/may/might think

7.2 Food fads

GRAMMAR

A

1 the least salt
2 cooks better than
3 the spicier the
4 tastes fruitier than
5 more / the most calories
6 worse than me

B

1 c **2** b **3** a **4** c **5** a **6** c **7** c **8** b

PRONUNCIATION

A

1 b **2** a **3** a **4** b **5** b **6** b **7** a **8** b

VOCABULARY

A

1 recycled
2 wasted
3 reuse
4 garbage
5 reduce
6 use up

B

1 can
2 away
3 of
4 down
5 garbage
6 up

C

Across: 2 wastebasket **4** reduce **6** throw away **7** reuse
Down: 1 trash **3** recycle **5** waste

7.3 Reading

READING

B

1 Angela, Jason
2 Yoko, Angela
3 Angela
4 Jason, Yoko
5 Yoko
6 Yoko
7 Angela
8 Jason

7.4 Listening; Functional Language

LISTENING

B

1 O **2** F **3** F **4** O **5** F **6** F **7** F **8** O

C

César 2, 6 Olivia 3, 5 Wing Shan 1, 4

FUNCTIONAL LANGUAGE

1 What's
2 Have
3 about
4 were
5 plan/idea
6 try/shot
7 Why
8 suggestion/idea

7.5 Write a reply in an online discussion forum

WRITING

B

1 SloppyJoe
2 Gourmand
3 Gourmand
4 SloppyJoe
5 SloppyJoe, Sylvya

C

1 quieter
2 the most popular
3 more casual
4 I'd recommend
5 than
6 nicer
7 You should
8 Why don't you

WRITING PRACTICE

B

Model answer

I think you should go for the restaurant option. So many things can go wrong with a barbecue – not just the weather. Your guests might be tired after a long trip, and it's more comfortable and relaxing to be seated at a table and waited on than it is to stand around trying to balance a paper plate in one hand and a drink in the other. Besides, in my experience it's just as expensive and time-consuming to have a barbecue as it is to dress up and go out to a restaurant. You can relax and talk rather than attend to the cooking. So, I'd recommend going to a nice restaurant. Better to be safe than sorry!

8.1 Making a difference

VOCABULARY

A

1 scientist
2 engineering
3 succeed
4 innovative
5 design
6 product
7 inventive

B

1 b 2 a 3 a 4 c 5 b 6 c 7 c 8 a 9 b 10 a

PRONUNCIATION

1 ✓ 2 – 3 – 4 ✓ 5 ✓ 6 –

GRAMMAR

A

1 who
2 which
3 that
4 when
5 whose
6 where
7 who
8 when

B

1 whose
2 who
3 where
4 which
5 when
6 which

8.2 Must-have gadgets

VOCABULARY

A

1 unique
2 gorgeous
3 fascinating
4 sensible
5 unforgettable
6 suitable
7 impressive
8 practical
9 incredible
10 sophisticated

B

1 sophisticated
2 practical
3 unique
4 impressive
5 incredible
6 sensible
7 gorgeous
8 unforgettable

GRAMMAR

A

1 keep
2 tell
3 will have to
4 don't charge
5 won't buy
6 doesn't work/isn't working

B

1 If you~~'ll~~ listen to next week's podcast, you'll hear about some more amazing gadgets.
2 **Will** ~~Are~~ you **be** angry if I cancel our plans for tonight?
3 correct
4 I won't go out tomorrow unless the weather **is** ~~will~~ good.
5 correct
6 correct
7 I never buy gadgets unless I ~~don't~~ really need them.
8 correct

C

1 can wait
2 might help
3 don't try
4 should we still
5 come and see
6 must be prepared
7 can always borrow
8 can go

PRONUNCIATION

A

1 if you want to
2 you'll really like it
3 I want to go
4 I'll lend
5 I enjoy
6 we'll have a nice time
7 I won't miss it
8 I'll call them

8.3 Reading

READING

B

1 B **2** C **3** D **4** A

C

Suggested answers

a 4 **b** 3 **c** 1 **d** 2

D

1 F (We take them for granted today.)
2 T
3 T
4 F (They had to take out the ashes, not the coal.)
5 T
6 F (The ice blocks stayed frozen, even in the summer.)
7 F (There was no running water. / They had to carry the water some distance.)
8 T

8.4 Listening; Functional Language

LISTENING

B

1, 4, 5 and 6.

C

1 b **2** c **3** a **4** c **5** a **6** b

FUNCTIONAL LANGUAGE

1 first
2 When
3 say
4 let
5 how
6 After
7 mean
8 Make

8.5 Write a short biography

WRITING

A

1 A pioneer in the field of computer science.
2 Meeting Charles Babbage.
3 She wrote and published notes about the first calculating machine (computer) including how to give it instructions. It was the first-ever computer program.

B

a 2 **b** 1 **c** 5 **d** 3 **e** 4

C

1 Although
2 However
3 despite

WRITING PRACTICE

B

Model answer

Trevor Baylis

Trevor Baylis is best known for his invention of the wind-up radio, which brought information, education and entertainment to millions of poor people around the world.

He was born in 1937 and raised in London. From a very young age, Baylis enjoyed making things. However, his education was disrupted by the Second World War, and he failed his school exams. Despite this setback, he was able to study mechanical and structural engineering at the local technical college.

The idea for his most famous invention came to him in a flash when he was watching a TV show about the poor in Africa. He realized that communication and education would help them enormously. Radio was the answer – but in many parts of Africa, there was no electricity. So, he decided to invent a wind-up radio.

His invention has brought information, communication and education to millions of people around the world who most needed them.

He once said, 'Anyone can have a good idea and turn it into something that works. If you find yourself trying to solve a problem, you are halfway to inventing something'. That's something for us to think about.

9.1 Art for everybody

VOCABULARY

A

1 studio
2 musician
3 concert
4 rehearsed
5 orchestra
6 performed
7 exhibit
8 instrument
9 choir
10 stage

B

1 part in
2 fell
3 tell
4 advantage
5 friends with
6 keep
7 come
8 pay
9 make
10 wrong

GRAMMAR

A

1 b **2** c **3** a **4** b **5** a **6** c **7** b **8** b

B

1 worked, would/'d become
2 had, would/'d learn
3 would/'d go, were/was
4 couldn't, would be
5 were, would/'d take
6 would/'d have, didn't spend

PRONUNCIATION

A

2 research, chemist, technology; a
3 child, mechanic, Charley; b
4 choices, choir, orchestra; b
5 challenge, techniques, machine; b
6 church, chemical; a

9.2 Tell me a story

GRAMMAR

A

1 him what time he was
2 they had never read / they had not read / they hadn't read / they hadn't ever read
3 (that) she had/'d made
4 couldn't understand why
5 where the manager was
6 if / whether I wanted to go
7 wouldn't come the next/following
8 if / whether Aisha was there

B

1 I have/'ve read
2 can borrow
3 have to finish
4 Is it good
5 it is

C

6 was about
7 would spoil
8 following/next
9 had read
10 if / whether he wanted

VOCABULARY

A

1 b 2 c 3 b 4 a 5 a 6 b 7 c 8 a

B

1 added that
2 us
3 where
4 to come
5 me to go
6 me
7 that it would snow
8 them to leave
9 to go
10 to

9.3 Reading

READING

B

1 e 2 a 3 d 4 b 5 c

C

Students check 2, 3 and 5.

D

1 F (The writer says that mega-events have gotten out of control, especially the huge crowds.)
2 T
3 T
4 T
5 F (There's gypsy music, funk and jazz.)
6 F (The writer believes that the two experiences complement each other.)
7 F (These events are friendly and noncompetitive.)
8 T

9.4 Listening; Functional Language

LISTENING

B

1 No, they haven't seen each other *in a long time*.
2 Not really. She liked learning about different kinds of art, but didn't enjoy doing *conceptual art*.
3 She studied many.
4 She thought it was silly.
5 Yes, she is.

C

1 bridge
2 examples
3 subject
4 idea
5 wool
6 pressing
7 attractive

D

1 transition period
2 range
3 different
4 the 60s (1960s)
5 a sheep
6 a video
7 interesting
8 metal, stone
9 drawings/illustrations

FUNCTIONAL LANGUAGE

1 like
2 actor
3 ending
4 tearjerker
5 worth
6 follow
7 scene

9.5 Write a short review

WRITING

A

Suggested answers

1 To describe a book for others in order to persuade them to read it, or possibly to discourage them from reading it.
2 In a newspaper, a magazine or a website about books.
3 Students' own answers.
4 Movies, plays, concerts, exhibits, etc.

B

1 Mainly positive.
2 The reviewer thinks it's like a collection of short stories.
3 They have a similar theme.
4 There are no fully rounded female characters.

C

a 2 **b** 1 **c** 4 **d** 3

D

1 c **2** b **3** a

WRITING PRACTICE

B

Model answer

Val McDermid's new psychological thriller, *Insidious Intent*, will be a big hit with fans of crime-busting duo, DCI Carol Jordan and profiler Tony Hill. Once again, they are on the hunt for a bright and terrifying criminal.

It all starts on a quiet country road with a car engulfed in flames and a body in the driver's seat. They realize that this is no ordinary accident and discover a series of similar cases. More lives are at risk, and Tony and Carol must go to extreme lengths to catch the evil genius behind the crimes. They are forced to question the very idea of justice.

As you would expect from this writer, the plot is complex and intriguing and will grip you from start to finish. But it's not all about plot with Val McDermid – her books are as character-driven as many so-called literary novels. The difficult relationship between Tony and Carol is beautifully done, and her writing displays her descriptive powers and psychological insight.

I needed no persuading: this is a first-class thriller by a master of the genre. If you haven't read her yet, go out and buy this book: you're in for a treat.

10.1 Making up your mind

VOCABULARY

A

1 encourage/persuade
2 affects/influences
3 tempted
4 tricking
5 regret
6 attract
7 assume
8 avoid

B

1 made
2 in
3 never
4 bear
5 two
6 put
7 changed
8 Would

PRONUNCIATION

A

1 Speaker A
2 Speaker B
3 Speaker B
4 Speaker B
5 Speaker A
6 Speaker A

GRAMMAR

A

1 'd have gotten, hadn't gone
2 'd known, wouldn't have paid
3 had told, could have/'ve spent
4 wouldn't have chosen, 'd thought
5 hadn't assumed, might have/'ve made
6 might not have been tempted, hadn't gone
7 could have/'ve avoided, 'd read
8 'd realized, wouldn't have bought

B

1 You should have/'ve asked me
2 You should have/'ve checked
3 I should have/'ve waited
4 you shouldn't have bought
5 I should have/'ve done
6 I should have taken

10.2 Wish lists

VOCABULARY

A

1 ourselves
2 yourself
3 himself
4 yourselves
5 myself
6 herself
7 yourself
8 themselves

B

1 cleaning
2 keep
3 scheduled
4 objective
5 store
6 action point
7 sorted
8 task

PRONUNCIATION

A

Students underline

1 helped
2 yourself
3 himself
4 herself
5 set
6 treated

GRAMMAR

A

1 b 2 c 3 b 4 b 5 c 6 a 7 c 8 c

B

1 wish, had planned
2 hope, can remember; hope, goes
3 wishes, weren't/wasn't; wish, could have
4 hopes, can meet; hope, gives

10.3 Reading

READING

B

1 T
2 F (Anxiety can be triggered by everyday events.)
3 T
4 F (This strategy does not solve the overall problem.)
5 T
6 T

C

1 d 2 e 3 b 4 a 5 c

10.4 Listening; Functional Language

LISTENING

B

1, 2, 3, 5 and 7.

C

1 all over the world
2 a quarter of the population
3 discrimination
4 less likely
5 not violent
6 charities
7 not allowed

FUNCTIONAL LANGUAGE

1 time
2 need
3 worry
4 sorry
5 about
6 fault
7 such
8 things

10.5 Write a report

WRITING

A

1 To discuss problems which occurred at Downey Town Fair.
2 It was financially a success, but not in terms of organization.
3 Not enough parking space and problems with traffic on the roads.
4 Larger number of parking spaces, more areas (e.g. fields) allocated for parking, volunteers to direct traffic and parking.

B

1 b 2 f 3 c 4 d 5 a 6 e

WRITING PRACTICE

B

Model answer

Report on The Huffington and District Mobile Library

Summary

The mobile library was set up to satisfy a demand to provide books to rural areas in the county. It is a subscription service, yet despite the initial demand, we can barely afford to pay running costs. This report explores the problem.

Background

We provide a library service to areas where there is no easy access to books, magazines, DVDs and music CDs. A survey suggested that the service was much needed, yet the actual number of subscribers is far short of what we expected.

Analysis

1 **Lack of information:** Not enough people are paying the subscription, usually because they did not realize that they had to. Also, many did not know that such a service existed.
2 **Reading habits:** Some have complained about the limited choice of reading matter available. While it is difficult to please everybody, we should stock a wider variety of books and magazines.

Recommendations

- An advertising campaign to publicize the service. Send out flyers through the mail and hold a town hall meeting to explain.
- Conduct a survey in the area to establish reading habits and tastes to provide a better service.

Notes

Notes